WITHDRAWN

REBECCA JOHNSON is an international peace and justice campaigner and author, with a PhD on multilateral diplomacy from the University of London School of Economics (LSE). Her recent book on civil society and government strategies to achieve the Comprehensive Test Ban Treaty (CTBT), entitled *Unfinished Business*, was published by the United Nations in 2009.

ANGIE ZELTER is a peace, human rights and environmental campaigner and the author or editor of several books on campaigning and the law, including *Trident on Trial* and *Faslane 365*, both of which were published by Luath Press.

Trident and International Law

Scotland's Obligations

EDITED BY REBECCA JOHNSON AND ANGIE ZELTER

Luath Press Limited

EDINBURGH

www.luath.co.uk

First published 2011

ISBN: 978-1-906817-24-4

The paper used in this book is recyclable. It is made from low chlorine pulps
produced in a low energy, low emissions manner from renewable forests.

Printed and bound by
Bell & Bain Ltd., Glasgow

Typeset in 11pt Sabon by
3btype.com

Contents

Preface and Acknowledgements

THIS BOOK IS BASED on the proceedings of the international conference on 'Trident and International Law: Scotland's Obligations' held at Dynamic Earth in Edinburgh on 3 February 2009. It is published as part of collaborative work on Nuclear Weapons and International Law, carried out through 2006–2009 by the Acronym Institute for Disarmament Diplomacy, the Edinburgh Peace and Justice Centre and Trident Ploughshares. Due to unusually heavy snowfalls that caused flight cancellations and travel disruptions, a number of the featured speakers were prevented from attending the Conference at the last minute. Where possible, these participants contributed their papers for publication, which also includes documents of legal advice and opinion provided by lawyers for various non-governmental organisations on issues relevant to Britain's nuclear policy and treaty obligations, including consideration of the legality of the replacement and modernisation of the Trident nuclear weapon system.

We are very grateful to the following for their generous contributions to the Edinburgh Conference and publication of this book: Nuclear Education Trust; Polden-Puckham Charitable Foundation; Ploughshares Fund; Lord Murray; Iain Banks; Luath Press and a number of anonymous supporters. Thanks also to Luath Press for making it possible for this book to be published and distributed.

All the authors and contributors deserve our utmost appreciation for participating in this project and kindly waiving any fees and agreeing to their work being published in this book. Greenpeace and Public Interest Lawyers are also acknowledged and thanked for commissioning two of the papers and agreeing to our publication of them.

Janet Fenton, Rebecca Johnson and Angie Zelter

Acronym Institute for Disarmament Diplomacy
24 Colvestone Crescent
London E8 2LH
website: www.acronym.org.uk
email: info@acronym.org.uk

Edinburgh Peace and Justice Centre
St John's Church
Princes Street
Edinburgh EH2 4BJ
website: www.peaceandjustice.org.uk
email: contact@peaceandjustice.org.uk

Trident Ploughshares
42–46 Bethel St
Norwich NR2 1NR
website: www.tridentploughshares.org
email: tp2000@gn.apc.org

Introduction

DR REBECCA JOHNSON

THE GENESIS FOR THE 2009 Edinburgh Conference and this book lay in four related developments:

- the decision by the British government to renew the Trident nuclear weapons system, despite acceding to legal obligations to pursue disarmament as enshrined in the Treaty on the Non-Proliferation of Nuclear Weapons (NPT) and reinforced by the International Court of Justice in 1996;

- majority support in the Scottish Parliament for removing all nuclear weapons from Scotland, thereby contributing towards building security in a world free of nuclear weapons, as evidenced by the overwhelming Scottish Parliament vote against Trident renewal on 14 June 2007, which led to the creating of the Scottish Government Working Group on Scotland without Nuclear Weapons, chaired by the Minister for Parliamentary Business;

- growing international concerns about the implications of doctrines of nuclear deterrence, increasingly viewed as deeply flawed and dangerous in terms of security, legality, military logic, behavioural analysis, and the role of nuclear deterrence policies in justifying perpetual nuclear possession and proliferation; and

- developments in legal understanding that recognise that any use of nuclear weapons would constitute a crime against humanity and contravene international and humanitarian law applicable in times of both war and peace.

On 14 March 2007, the House of Commons in Westminster passed the following motion: 'this House supports the Government's decision as set out in the white paper The Future of the United Kingdom's Nuclear Deterrent (CM6994) to take the steps necessary to maintain the UK minimum strategic nuclear deterrent beyond the life of the existing system and to take further steps towards meeting the UK's disarmament responsibilities under Article VI of the Non-proliferation treaty'.

Since both the Labour and Conservative Parties imposed three-line whips, the motion was carried by 409 votes to 161. This apparently overwhelming support does not convey the true extent of the actual opposition to the decision to procure a further generation of Trident nuclear weapons. Of particular relevance, a majority of MPs from all parties representing Scottish constituencies voted against renewing Trident. Several Scottish junior ministers and ministerial aides, including the deputy leader of the House of Commons, Nigel Griffiths, chose to resign government jobs rather than go along with the whip. This Scottish revolt is significant because the UK's entire nuclear weapons system is based in Scotland, on the Clyde, some 35 miles northwest of Glasgow – over 200 warheads (of which 160 are deemed 'operationally viable') are stored at the Royal Naval Armaments Depot (RNAD), Coulport, and the four Vanguard class nuclear submarines that carry the US-made Trident missiles are home-ported at Faslane, near Helensburgh.

Two months later, on 3 May, in regional elections for Scotland's own parliament, re-established under the devolution settlement codified by the 1998 Scotland Act, the Scottish National Party (SNP) replaced Labour as the majority party in Scotland. As noted in the opening address to the Edinburgh Conference by Angus Robertson MP, Spokesperson for the SNP on Foreign Affairs and Defence in the UK (Westminster) Parliament, 'the SNP was elected on 3 May 2007 on a pledge that they would work towards removing nuclear weapons from Scotland'. On 14 June 2007, the Scottish Parliament debated a Green Party motion calling on the UK Government to reconsider the decision to renew the Trident nuclear weapons system. The motion was overwhelmingly passed by 71 votes to 16 with 39 abstentions. Those voting in favour were a mixture of SNP, Liberal Democrat, Labour and Green Members of the Scottish Parliament (MSP). The Conservatives voted against, and the rest of the Labour MSPs abstained.

Following from this clear opposition to Trident renewal, the Scottish Government held the first ever Summit for a Nuclear Free Scotland on 22 October 2007, three weeks after the end of Faslane 365's year of grass-roots mobilising and nonviolent blockading actions at the Trident deployment base at Faslane. The Summit was held in Glasgow and involved Scottish Members of Parliament from both Westminster and Holyrood, Church and Faith leaders, Councillors, trades unionists, prominent lawyers, journalists and peace activists, including several members of the Faslane 365 Steering Group. Opening the Summit, Deputy First Minister of the Scottish Government, Nicola Sturgeon MSP, paid direct tribute to Faslane 365 for mobilising public opinion and providing impetus and arguments for Scotland to reject Trident.[1]

The Government subsequently established a Working Group on 'Scotland Without Nuclear Weapons', an awkward title designed to get round its lawyers' concerns that for the government to discuss how to make Scotland nuclear free could be construed as violating the separation of powers and responsibilities set out in the 1998 Scotland Act that established the limits of Scottish devolution. I was invited to serve on this Working Group, together with representatives from the Scottish Churches and Islamic Communities, Trades Unions, Industry, environmental and peace organisations, academics and a local councillor from Argyll and Bute Council, which includes the Faslane nuclear base. The Working Group was chaired by Bruce Crawford MSP, Minister for Parliamentary Business.

The Working Group was charged, among other things, with exploring 'the various international opinions that exist on the legality of nuclear weapons so far as relevant to matters within the devolved competence of the Scottish Government'.[2] To feed into the Working Group discussions, the Acronym Institute for Disarmament Diplomacy, the Edinburgh Peace and Justice Centre and Trident Ploughshares jointly organised an international conference on 'Trident and International Law: Scotland's Obligations', which was held in Edinburgh on 3 February, 2009, with participation by Members of the Scottish Parliament, eminent Scottish and international legal scholars and practitioners, and representatives of Scottish civic and political society.

In my capacity as a Working Group member, I circulated the presentations from the Edinburgh Conference, and arranged for Judge Weeramantry to speak directly to the Working Group, present his arguments and respond to members' questions. Though some of the key arguments discussed at the Conference were incorporated into the Working Group report, particularly the introduction and chapter 2 (political and legal issues), the process of negotiations among government officials, lawyers and members of the Working Group resulted in equivocal recommendations. It appeared that a major reason for watering down the conclusions and recommendations was to avoid giving any grounds for political opponents or London officials to claim that the Working Group (and by extension, the Government) had stepped beyond the confines of the devolution settlement in the 1998 Scotland Act.

The report contained four chapters, covering economic and social issues, political and legal issues, regulatory issues and promoting peace and disarmament.[3] Three of the conclusions in particular are relevant for this book:

i   The deployment and storage of the UK's nuclear arsenal in Faslane and Coulport places Scotland in a special position and means that the Scottish Government has a particular and legitimate interest in, and contribution to, issues relating to strengthening the Non-Proliferation Treaty (NPT) which States Parties will discuss at the Treaty's eighth Review Conference at the United Nations in May 2010;

ii The Working Group encourages the UK Government to be bolder in carrying through its commitments and to consult with the Scottish Government and others in preparation for ending the deployment of British nuclear weapons;

iii Opinions on the legality of nuclear weapons and the responsibilities of States and administrations within States are divided. Consideration should be given to understanding the implications of all the relevant legal opinions, especially for the assistance given by the Scottish Government and agencies to the deployment and operation of the Trident system.

The Working Group Report was made public in November 2009, together with an eight page response from the Scottish Government.[4]

In its public response, the Scottish Government agreed with many of the findings of the Working Group, 'including the irrelevance of nuclear weapons in today's society and the case for removal of nuclear weapons at an early date'. Noting the 'moral, economic and strategic arguments against the renewal of Trident', the Scottish Government clearly stated its opposition to,

> the use, threat of use and possession of nuclear weapons and to the UK Government's commitment to replace the current Trident system at an estimated cost of up to £100 billion (total cost of replacement and operation over 50 years) and strain on public spending.

The Government accepted that 'Scotland has a special position as a nation within a State, opposed to the presence of nuclear weapons on its territory and the implications for its devolved responsibilities'. On the legal issues raised by the Working Group, however, the Government took a very cautious view. While acknowledging the usefulness of examining 'a range of competing arguments around the legality of nuclear weapons' it decided

> that the legality of the presence of Trident in Scotland remains governed in law by the binding decision of the High Court of Justiciary in the leading Scottish authority on the issue, *Lord Advocate's Reference No. 1 of 2000.*

It is right and understandable that the Scottish Government should consider itself 'legally and constitutionally bound to abide by the law'. The issue – discussed by eminent judges and lawyers in this book – is which laws take precedence. The Government was advised that the Lord Advocate's Reference (LAR) No. 1 of 2000 is the pre-eminent and binding law on nuclear weapons in Scotland. Incorporating a range of analyses on the current application of international and humanitarian law to the use and deployment of nuclear weapons, this book demonstrates where the High Court of Justiciary in its Lord Advocate's Reference No.1 of 2000 went wrong in its interpretation of international law and the 1996 Advisory Opinion of the International Court of Justice (ICJ) on the use and threat of use of nuclear weapons. Since the Lord Advocate's Reference was misdirected in law, it should no longer be relied upon by the Scottish Government.

As set out in their detailed and compelling arguments, several of the judges and lawyers participating in the Edinburgh Conference advised that neither the LAR nor the 1998 Scotland Act could take precedence over the legal obligations of Scottish citizens, courts and responsible government officials to comply with international law, including the principles and obligations of international humanitarian law.

This LAR was the outcome of the decision of a Scottish Sheriff Court to acquit three Trident Ploughshares activists (Angie Zelter, Ulla Roder and Ellen Moxley) charged with 'malicious damage' after tipping into Loch Goil various computers and other equipment involved in facilitating the transport and deployment of Trident nuclear missiles. The three women argued that they had been justified in causing such damage because they were seeking to prevent the Trident nuclear weapons system from being used. They successfully made the case before the Sheriff that the deployment of Trident was in breach of customary international law, and therefore in breach of Scots law, and that their actions as 'citizen interveners' were intended to enforce the law. That was the basis on which they were acquitted. Although there could be no appeal of such an acquittal, certain points of law raised in this decision could be presented by the Lord Advocate for the opinion of the High Court. Afraid that the Sheriff's acquittal could set a precedent that would encourage other courts to acquit anti-nuclear protesters, the Lord Advocate referred the legal points to the High Court in 2000. The LAR Opinion on these points of law has been the subject of controversy ever since.

In this book eminent judges and lawyers, including a former President and a Vice President of the International Court of Justice, several law professors and Queen's Counsels, provide a range of arguments, analyses and insights concerning the relationship between international and domestic law and the current state of international law with regard to the use, threat of use, deployment, renewal and modernisation of nuclear weapons. From these deep, scholarly analyses, five basic conclusions emerge:

- The launching of a nuclear-armed Trident missile would be unlawful in any conceivable circumstance.

- The deployment, renewal and modernisation of nuclear weapons and the application of deterrence doctrines based on the use or threat of use of nuclear weapons, including the Trident nuclear weapons system, violate existing international law.

- Scotland's obligations and responsibilities under international law are not nullified by the 1998 devolution settlement.

- Citizens have a lawful right to protest the deployment of nuclear weapons and breaches of international law by governments and State authorities.

- In addition to national obligations to cease deploying, developing and renewing nuclear weapons, there is an international law obligation to conclude multilateral negotiations to achieve the total abolition of nuclear weapons, encompassing prohibitions on the acquisition, deployment and use of nuclear armaments and the progressive elimination of all existing arsenals.

These conclusions suggest that the LAR and the advice received by the Scottish government were overly cautious and may, in their errors, owe more to political expedience than to the legal obligations and facts pertaining to nuclear weapons in general and the Trident nuclear weapons system in particular.

The fundamental question that confronts us is what we do about this now.

Under both international and domestic law, individuals and governments have obligations to prevent crimes, especially criminal actions that harm and threaten innocent, vulnerable people. International law makes it particularly clear that civilians and non-combatants should not be military targets. Domestic law provides for lawful excuse when it is necessary to damage property or restrain an aggressor in order to save lives or prevent serious crime. Judge Christopher Weeramantry explicitly addressed these challenges, arguing that

> anti-nuclear civil resistance is the right of every citizen of this planet, for the prevention of such an international crime is basic to human dignity.

Intended as a resource for legal practitioners, politicians and responsible citizens, this book is made even more necessary because of what Judge Mohammed Bedjaoui called the 'regrettable legal vagueness' surrounding nuclear weapons. The Working Group's equivocation and the Scottish Government's regrettable timidity on this issue underscore yet again the need to develop further effective campaigns to clarify and give unequivocal legal force to the widely accepted understanding that the use, threatened use and therefore deployment of nuclear weapons are contrary to our humanity. We need domestic and global civil society and governments to campaign in partnership against nuclear possession, deployment and doctrines of nuclear deterrence, and so transform the current, partial, divided non-proliferation regime into a global security architecture. As recognised in the consensus final document of the 2010 NPT Review Conference, some form of universally applicable, multilaterally negotiated nuclear weapons convention will be needed – a framework or treaty covering all aspects of nuclear weapons abolition, including specific prohibitions and a timetable for verified elimination. This is the tried and tested approach taken when the international community decided to ban other weapons systems, including biological and chemical weapons, land mines and cluster munitions.[5]

To lay the groundwork for such negotiations will take time, however. As nuclear arsenals are reduced, the tipping point for abolition will come when nuclear-armed governments and militaries recognise that there is no legitimate or useful role for nuclear weapons in their doctrines and security policies. An important step, therefore, could be to engage the International Criminal Court, the UN Security Council or other appropriate bodies in developing clearer legal recognition that any use of nuclear weapons would be contrary to international law and should be treated as a war crime and crime against humanity. Whichever approach was pursued, the aim would be to clarify once and for all that nuclear weapons cannot legally be used by anyone for any purpose. Such legal clarification would reinforce the non-proliferation regime, firmly embed the taboo against nuclear use that has developed since 1945, and pave the way for negotiations on a universal nuclear weapons convention.[6]

One of the most important lessons learned from recent efforts to prohibit land-mines and cluster munitions and ban nuclear testing, as well as on campaigns to reduce poverty, environmental destruction and climate chaos, is that for transformational progress to occur, civil society must rise up and push governments to go beyond the powerful but narrow interests of the military and industrial establishments that continue to manufacture and profit from the tools and technologies that bring us destruction and insecurity. Unless people in the streets are motivated to demand nuclear abolition, governments will remain too timid and constrained to face up to the challenges of disarmament.

The perception that there is a 'grey area' in the application of domestic and international law to nuclear weapons has been exploited by the nuclear-weapon states who have been complicit in deploying, retaining, up-grading, renewing and continuing to proliferate nuclear weapons for far too long. Though the range of legal arguments in this book demonstrate beyond doubt that the use, threat of use, deployment and renewal of the Trident nuclear weapons system already contravene existing international laws and binding agreements, it is likely that until additional political action brings about further treaties, resolutions and rulings, timid politicians, lawyers and governments will continue to be complicit in allowing international and humanitarian law to be flouted or wrongly sidelined by domestic courts, legislation and political interests. Concerted civil society and international action must therefore pursue further non-violent actions and legal and political initiatives to rule out all nuclear uses, prevent unilateral proliferation such as the replacement of Trident, and promote a multilateral nuclear weapons convention that will provide an unequivocal, legally-binding prohibition on the use and deployment of nuclear weapons for all.[7]

Key Points from the Edinburgh Conference

1   **The launching of a nuclear-armed Trident missile would be unlawful in any conceivable circumstance.**

H.E. Mohammed Bedjaoui, President of the International Court of Justice from 1994 to 1997, during which time the Court adopted its historic 1996 Advisory Opinion on the Use and Threat of Use of Nuclear Weapons (see Appendix), summarised the Court's view, including:

> The International Court of Justice highlighted two cardinal principles that it declared to be 'intransgressible principles of international customary law': first, that states must never target civilians, nor use arms that are incapable of distinguishing between civilian and military targets; and second, that it is not permitted to cause superfluous harm to combatants, i.e. states do not have an unlimited right as to the arms they may utilise. The Court also referred to the 'Martens clause', according to which civilians and combatants remain under the protection and rule of the principles of the law of nations, as they result from established customs, from the laws of humanity, and from the dictates of the public conscience.

Noting that the ICJ had been asked to consider only a general case, Judge Bedjaoui applied its findings to the specific facts concerning the UK's Trident nuclear weapons system and concluded:

> In accordance with evidence heard by the Court, it is clear that an explosion caused by the detonation of just one 100 kt warhead would release powerful and prolonged ionising radiation, which could not be contained in space or time, and which would harmfully affect civilians as well as combatants, neutral as well as belligerent states, and future generations as well as people targeted in the present time. In view of these extraordinarily powerful characteristics and effects, any use of such a warhead would contravene international and humanitarian laws and precepts. In other words,

even in an extreme circumstance of self-defence, in which the very survival of a State would be at stake, the use of a 100 kt nuclear warhead—regardless of whether it was targeted to land accurately on or above a military target—would always fail the tests of controllability, discrimination, civilian immunity, and neutral rights and would thus be unlawful.

Accordingly,

the use of even a single [Trident] warhead in *any* circumstance, whether a first or second use and whether intended to be targeted against civilian populations or military objectives, would inevitably violate the prohibitions on the infliction of unnecessary suffering and indiscriminate harm as well as the rule of proportionality including with respect to the environment. In my opinion, such a system deployed and ready for action would be unlawful.

Philippe Sands QC and Helen Law, of Matrix Chambers, argued that

The use, or threat of use, of nuclear weapons in self-defence will be unlawful under the *jus ad bellum* where it fails to meet the requirements of necessity and proportionality. Where their use is contemplated in response to a threatened rather than actual attack, the additional requirement of imminence must be fulfilled. The use of nuclear weapons to protect such interests ['vital interests' as described in the 1998 Strategic Defence Review] is likely to be disproportionate and therefore unlawful under Article 2(4) of the UN Charter.

Sands and Law also noted:

It is difficult to conceive of any circumstances in which the use of nuclear weapons in self-defence to deter future chemical or biological attacks on UK forces overseas could be proportionate and therefore lawful.

Moreover,

It is hard to envisage any scenario in which the use of Trident, as currently constituted, could be consistent with the [International Humanitarian Law] IHL prohibitions on indiscriminate attacks and unnecessary suffering. Further, such use would be highly likely to result in a violation of the principle of neutrality.

2 The deployment, renewal and modernisation of nuclear weapons and the application of deterrence doctrines based on the use or threat of use of nuclear weapons, including the Trident nuclear weapons system, violate existing international law.

Dr John Burroughs, law professor at Rutgers University, noted,

> The fact that the use of nuclear weapons would be unlawful under the law of armed conflict necessarily means that any specific threat to use nuclear weapons would be unlawful. This arises from the established rule of the law of armed conflict that it is unlawful for a state to threaten to use force that it would be unlawful in fact to use.

Burroughs argued:

> While declining to make a formal pronouncement on the policy of 'deterrence', the International Court of Justice concluded that the policy would be unlawful under the United Nations Charter if use of nuclear weapons in self-defence pursuant to the policy would violate the principles of necessity and proportionality.

HE Judge Christopher Weeramantry, member of the International Court of Justice from 1991 to 2000, stated:

> Deterrence is not an act of deception but a demonstrated intent to use. Hence, a real intent of use in certain circumstances underlies the activity of preparation and the concept of deterrence.

Judge Weeramantry concluded,

> In relation to the positive obligation imposed by the unanimous opinion of the International Court of Justice, the continuing work on Trident and its replacement with a further nuclear weapon system constitutes a violation of Article VI of the NPT.

Judge Bedjaoui stated:

> Article VI, which lays out the obligation to negotiate nuclear disarmament in good faith, was clearly conceived as the necessary counterpart to the commitment by the non-nuclear states not to manufacture or acquire nuclear weapons; it is without a doubt one of the essential elements of the 'acceptable equilibrium of mutual responsibilities and obligations between nuclear powers and non-nuclear powers' which, according to the [United Nations] General Assembly, was to be established by the Nuclear Non-Proliferation

Treaty which it called for in 1965. In 1995, at the time of the fifth Conference of Parties, which decided the extension of the NPT for an indefinite duration, the reciprocal nature of the said obligations was vigorously reaffirmed. Article VI should for this reason be considered an *essential provision* of the NPT, the breach of which could be considered 'material' in terms of Article 60 of the Vienna Convention on the Law of Treaties and could entail the legal consequences thereto attached.

Hence,

The modernisation, updating or renewal of such a nuclear weapon system would also be a material breach of NPT obligations, particularly the unequivocal undertaking by the nuclear-weapon states to 'accomplish the total elimination of their nuclear arsenals leading to nuclear disarmament' and the fundamental Article VI obligation to negotiate in good faith on cessation of the arms race and on nuclear disarmament, with the understanding that these negotiations must be pursued in good faith and brought to conclusion in a timely manner.

In view of this, Judge Bedjaoui advised,

any state that aids and abets another country in the deployment and maintenance of nuclear warheads of 100 kt or comparable explosive power would also be acting unlawfully.

Burroughs argued,

Article VI and the commitments made in 1995 and 2000 enjoin reduction and elimination of nuclear arsenals. They are wholly incompatible with planning and implementation of maintenance and modernization of nuclear forces for decades to come.

With specific reference to UK nuclear policies, Sands and Law argued:

A broadening of the deterrence policy to incorporate prevention of non-nuclear attacks so as to justify replacing or upgrading Trident would appear to be inconsistent with Article VI [of the NPT]; attempts to justify Trident upgrade or replacement as an insurance against unascertainable future threats would appear to be inconsistent with Article VI; enhancing the targeting capability or yield flexibility of the Trident system is likely to be inconsistent with Article VI; renewal or replacement of Trident at the same capability is likely to be inconsistent with Article VI; and in each case such inconsistency could give rise to a material breach of the NPT.

Rabinder Singh QC and Professor Christine Chinkin argued that

the use of the Trident system would breach customary international law, in particular because it would infringe the 'intransgressible' requirement that a distinction must be drawn between combatants and non-combatants.

Singh and Chinkin further advised,

The replacement of Trident is likely to constitute a breach of Article VI of the NPT. Such a breach would be a material breach of that treaty.

Professor Nick Grief QC stated,

Law must play a decisive role as the embodiment of normative values. The rule of law is a fundamental principle of civilised society and respect for the rule of law is an essential prerequisite of international order... Either we have the rule of law or we do not. As Judge Shi declared in the *Nuclear Weapons Case*, the policy of nuclear deterrence should be an object of regulation by law, not vice versa. International law is not simply whatever those with 'the say' (in practice, the nuclear weapon states) say it is.

3 Scotland's obligations and responsibilities under international law are not nullified by the 1998 devolution settlement

Scottish solicitor and Member of the Scottish Parliament, Roseanna Cunningham MSP, stated,

Although the Scottish Parliament does not have power over nuclear weapons or nuclear power stations, it does have environmental, planning and transport powers which may turn out to be more effective... practising lawyers need to be more imaginative in looking at ways in which some of these issues can be dealt with, how we can block or put obstacles in the way of nuclear weapons using the common or garden variety of laws and by-laws that may already be in existence. This is an interesting and very important debate for Scotland because it is a way in which we could express the view of the Scottish people.

Aidan O'Neill QC, noted,

> Section 58 [of the 1998 Scotland Act] provides the basis for an enforceable legitimate expectation to the effect that the actions of the Scottish devolved institutions will be compatible with the UK's international obligations. On this basis it might be said that the Scotland Act effectively binds the Lord Advocate (and the other Scottish Ministers) to respect the whole range of international treaty obligations which have been ratified by the Crown, even where they have not been incorporated into the domestic law of the United Kingdom.

O'Neill stated,

> the United Kingdom Parliament arguably also effectively introduced Nuremberg derived principles regarding the justifiability of conduct under national and international law directly into domestic law... there can properly be no conflict between the requirements of the (domestic) 'law of the land' and any 'moral imperative' – at least as derived from international legal principles – since both domestic law and international humanitarian and human rights law would now appear to operate in principle within the same normative framework.

In discussing the judgement of the LAR (2000), O'Neill noted,

> customary international law was recognised by the [High Court of Justiciary] automatically to form part of municipal Scots law without need for any formal treaty incorporation. It would appear that the Court implicitly accepted, too, that customary international law could be relied upon by individuals in determining the lawfulness of their actions – and the lawfulness of the actions of the State.

O'Neill quoted the Special Rapporteur of the International Law Commission charged by the United Nations in 1950 with the task of re-formulating the Principles applied by the Nuremberg Tribunal, who stated that,

> international law may impose duties on the individual without any interpretation of domestic law directly... That international law imposes duties and liabilities upon individuals as well as upon States... has long been recognised.

Highlighting the meaning of various Nuremberg Principles, O'Neill emphasized

> Nuremberg Principle VII provides that 'complicity in the commission of a crime against peace, a war crime, or a crime against humanity as set forth in Principle VI is a crime under international law.'

Judge Weeramantry wrote,

> All nations are required to comply with international law. It is elementary that there cannot be one law for some and another law for others... The principles of international and humanitarian law exist and are active, not only in times of war but also in times of peace. The fallacy that humanitarian law is silent in times of peace is parallel to the fallacy that international law is silent in times of war.

With regard to Scotland, Judge Weeramantry held that,

> Although the 1998 Scotland Act provides that the conduct of international relations is a matter reserved for the UK Parliament and the UK Government, paragraph 7(2) (a) provides *inter alia* that implementing and observing international obligations are not so reserved. This gives strength to the view that gross violations of international obligations are not excluded from the purview of the Scottish Parliament.

Moreover,

> Even if foreign policy and defence are the prerogative of the UK government, the health and safety of the population of Scotland, the welfare of future generations and the protection of the environment and adjacent seas are concerns for Scotland's people and their government.

4   **Citizens have a lawful right to protest the deployment of nuclear weapons and breaches of international law by governments and State authorities.**

Janet Fenton, Coordinator of the Edinburgh Peace and Justice Centre, recalled:

> The UK Ministry of Defence recognises that it is possible that an accident on public roads involving the convoys carrying fully armed nuclear warheads could result in a nuclear explosion. At

the very least, any major accident would be likely to cause the dispersal of plutonium and other radioactive substances over a wide area. A nuclear accident would involve police and other services in the protection of the public, as well as requiring actions across the range of responsibilities devolved to the Scottish government, notably health, agriculture and fishing.

Recognising that 'Civil defence is devolved', Fenton noted,

In the event of a nuclear attack as an act of war or terrorism, targets could include Faslane or Coulport, with immediate and devastating effect in Scotland. Other targets might include waterways where nuclear submarines might be located, or roads where warheads might be being transported.

Judge Weeramantry advised,

The people of Scotland have a right to demonstrate their concern with their safety, their health, their environment, their food chains, their future generations and their cultural inheritance. If it is a basic human right to be free of threat or violence, if the right to life is a basic human right, and if the protection of children and future generations is a basic human duty, anti-nuclear civil resistance is the right of every citizen of this planet, for the prevention of such an international crime is basic to human dignity.

Noting that 'Deterrence means the threat of use', Judge Weeramantry argued:

Use attracts retaliation, with a likely target being the geographical area where the weapons are based. The decision to use Trident will be a decision taken by the UK Government. International law cannot stand aside when human rights are violated and negated by doctrines of state sovereignty.

O'Neill suggested testing the current law in Scotland, proposing an approach that would

bring before the domestic court the current state of international criminal law on matters of war and peace. This would be to request the State prosecution authorities to initiate criminal investigations and the prosecution of persons within the jurisdiction against whom a case might colourably be made of their complicity in recognised international crimes—in particular the crime of international aggression, or other crimes against peace.

Arguing that

> it would appear to be at least competent for the prosecution authorities in Scotland, if so advised, to raise prosecution in Scotland in respect of the international crime of aggression,' O'Neill stated, 'Insofar as the Scottish prosecution authorities fail or refuse to do so where there are otherwise reasonable grounds for so proceeding, it would seem in principally that such a decision might itself be the subject of challenge before the courts by way of judicial review.

Noting, however,

> that the judges in Scotland are, if anything temperamentally, culturally and institutionally even more conservative than their English counterparts,

O'Neill conceded that

> the likelihood of any such challenge having any immediate success, at least before the judges in Scotland, would not be great. However, given that judicial review is a matter of civil law in Scotland, there would remain the possibility of taking the case, as a matter of constitutional right without the need for leave of any court, on appeal to the House of Lords, or as from October 2009, its replacement the UK Supreme Court.

5 **In addition to national obligations to cease deploying, developing and renewing nuclear weapons, there is an international law obligation to conclude multilateral negotiations to achieve the total abolition of nuclear weapons, encompassing future prohibitions on the acquisition, deployment and use of nuclear armaments and the progressive elimination of all existing arsenals.**

Judge Bedjaoui underlined,

> The International Court of Justice unanimously recalled to all the states party their good-faith duty to negotiate nuclear disarmament in accordance with Article VI of the 1968 Treaty on the Non Proliferation of Nuclear Weapons (NPT), which they ratified, and also went on to task them with a second, vigorous obligation – to 'bring to a conclusion' these negotiations – which is nothing more nor less than actually to bring about concrete nuclear disarmament.

Noting 'the impossibility of limiting nuclear weapons' effects to military objectives necessarily places them in contradiction with the principles and rules of the law of armed conflict and of humanitarian law' Judge Bedjaoui concluded that this

> cannot therefore do otherwise than make it a weapon prohibited under international law. Hence, though the Court concluded that conventional and customary law did not directly prohibit nuclear weapons as such, it recognised that the whole body of the law of armed conflict, and especially humanitarian law, indirectly prohibits this highly lethal weapon. Though not explicitly and specifically forbidden by international law, nuclear weapons are... weapons whose effects are clearly contrary to certain prescriptions of that *corpus juris* of certain rules of humanitarian law.

Acknowledging that 'the direct prohibition of the use of nuclear weapons as such lies in a kind of legal grey area,' Judge Bedjaoui concluded,

> It is therefore necessary to put an end to this regrettable legal vagueness, and the complete nuclear disarmament so long promised seems the best way to achieve this result.

> The obligation [in Article VI of the NPT] to negotiate nuclear disarmament in good faith is an obligation to adopt a certain conduct to achieve a certain result. This is an obligation of conduct that requires parties to that Treaty to give meaning to the negotiations on nuclear disarmament; to reach a mutually satisfactory compromise, not insisting on their own position without envisaging any modification of it; to make serious efforts with the goal of reaching an agreement.

Scotland's Opportunity – Opening Speech of the Conference

ANGUS ROBERTSON MP

MOST OF YOU FROM Scotland are well aware that the Scottish Parliament debated the issue of nuclear weapons in June 2007 and gave clear support for the Scottish Government's view that nuclear weapons have no place in a modern forward looking society. Parliament passed a motion by a margin of 71 votes to 16 with 39 abstentions that said they congratulated the majority of Scottish MPs for voting on 14 March 2007 to reject the replacement of Trident and called on the UK Government not to go ahead at this time with the proposal in the White Paper that calls for the renewal of the Trident nuclear weapons system. Opinion poll after opinion poll in Scotland have shown that the majority of people in this country are opposed to the UK Government spending £25 billion, which will probably be considerably more than that, on a new missile system to replace Trident. The majority of Scots would rather see the money spent on improving public services such as local schools, hospitals and police, and if not nuclear weapons then conventional equipment that might help in our peace keeping responsibilities. Recent demonstrations marking the end of the Faslane 365 anti-nuclear protests and all the demonstrations that have taken place at Faslane over the past 20 years or so are a reflection of the growing public opinion that exists here which is of course against nuclear weapons. There is now widespread support for the view that spending vast sums of money on renewing weapons of mass destruction is unjustifiable and the majority of Scottish people want no part in it.

The Scottish National Party was elected to government on a pledge that we would work towards removing nuclear weapons from Scotland's soil and there are many people (of all political persuasions and none) who share that view. But you should be under no illusions – it is likely to be a long road. Nuclear weapons will not disappear overnight. The difference now is that not only do we have the support of the majority of the Scottish people, but you also have the support of the Scottish Parliament, moreover the backing of the Scottish Government. In our first few months in office the First Minister wrote to the permanent representatives based in the UK, which are parties to the Non Proliferation Treaty, informing them of the debate in the Scottish Parliament and of the position of the Scottish Government. That is a powerful combination of forces and one that has strength and purpose. The people of Scotland have spoken and now is the time for governments in the UK and beyond to listen, to take heed of what the majority of this country's population actually want.

The Trident nuclear weapons system based at Faslane in Scotland violates the law of all the jurisdictions of the UK, including Scotland, in so far as we all recognise the relevant aspects of international law. The deployment of Trident can be seen as preparation for a war crime, namely for the unrestricted use of a weapon which is inhumane in its indiscriminate use and causes massive pollution. We know from Article 2, paragraph 4, of the UN Charter, as interpreted by the International Court of Justice, that if a particular use of force is unlawful the threat to use such force must also be unlawful. It might be argued that the possession of nuclear weapons does not constitute a threat to use them. However, the UK does not merely possess nuclear weapons; it deploys Trident submarines on permanent patrol and has repeatedly stated that in certain circumstances it would use those weapons.

There have been recent indications by both the Russian and US Governments that both countries want improved relations and are prepared to consider their nuclear posture. In contrast the UK Government has sadly continued its previous position which is more aligned with the neo-conservatives of the outgoing Bush administration.

But we are beginning to hear strong persuasive voices in the UK too, perhaps from some surprising directions, arguing for a new course. In a letter to the *Times* newspaper on 15 January, Field Marshall Lord Bramall, former head of the Armed Forces, backed by General Lord Ramsbotham and General Sir Hugh Beach, denounced Trident and described it as irrelevant and completely useless, and referred to its influence and effectiveness as a deterrent as a fallacy. Lord Bramall queried how the UK could exert any credible leadership or influence on the issue of nuclear disarmament if the government insisted on a costly successor to Trident which would continue the UK's nuclear power status well into the second half of the

21st century and as he put it, might also actively encourage others to believe that nuclear weapons were still somehow vital for the secure defence of self respecting nations. Furthermore, Lord Bramall and his colleagues queried Trident's value for money, saying that the sums of money being spent on replacing submarines which carry Trident missiles could be better used on conventional weapons, which in their view, were badly needed by the armed forces. They expressed the view that, *'nuclear weapons have shown themselves to be completely useless as a deterrent to the threats and scale of violence we currently, or are likely to face – particularly international terrorism; and the more you analyse them the more unusable they appear.'* On BBC2's Newsnight programme, Field Marshall Lord Bramall also said he thought the UK Government's decision to renew Trident was driven more by political considerations than by the requirements of national defence.

What is happening here in Scotland is very important. Having attended conferences elsewhere I know other people in other parts of the world are actually looking to Scotland as the great hope. I think we should grasp that opportunity with both hands. I see a vision of Scotland as having an ethical foreign policy and playing a positive role in international affairs and this conference is a large part in making that vision come to fruition.

Trident and International Law: Scotland's Obligations

H.E. JUDGE CHRISTOPHER WEERAMANTRY

TRIDENT-RELATED ACTIVITY is replete with issues concerning the long-term future of humanity. It cannot be considered in isolation as an episode in itself, but needs to be viewed against a long-term historical background of the uneasy compromise that has existed throughout the centuries between humanity's higher instincts and its use of weapons of destruction.

Historical flashback

When Genghis Khan was engaged on his blood-drenched career of world conquest, he is said to have proclaimed a policy that any cities which defied him would be razed to the ground with not a hut standing and not a whimper of life remaining. Not even a dog or mouse would survive; let alone the humans who would be exterminated with no exceptions.

The powerful nations, even in the early 20th century liked to describe themselves in international documents as 'civilized nations'. Yet the successors of these nations are prepared, even in the 21st century, to manufacture, stockpile and undertake research on weapons which can in fact outdo such primitive brutality. Indeed they claim the right to use a weapon that can exterminate all life in the target city down to the last microbe. Its use would automatically pollute the environment not only of the victim state but of all surrounding neutral states and cause damage that lasts for over twenty thousand years. Despots like Genghis Khan would dearly have loved to enjoy this power, the brutality of which goes far beyond anything they could envisage. One of the strange contradictions of our contemporary world is that there are nation states pledged to the maintenance of civilised values that at the same time cherish and preserve this power despite the fact that it reeks so heavily of barbarism at its worst.

We must here note another factor that distinguishes the modern use of nuclear weapons from the indiscriminate slaughter perpetrated by the despots of the past. They were limited in their devastation to the city or state which defied them. The modern nuclear state causes inevitable damage to the entire global environment and not merely to the opposing state. In addition it harms future generations, but these circumstances do not seem to deter the nuclear states from asserting their claim to use the weapon.

There is another important feature which we tend to ignore in these discussions. When primitive tyrants ruthlessly built up their empires they were not trampling on international law, for it did not exist. They were not violating a charter of the nations, for that concept was unknown. They were not ignoring human rights, for such a notion still lay in the womb of time. All these have now been established through the sacrifice of millions of lives. To override them all today involves greater culpability than could have been attributed to the most merciless despots of the past. It is pertinent to recall in this context the speech of the Belgian delegate at the Congress of Versailles after World War 1, when he reminded the assembled delegates that the failure to establish a system of international justice would be a betrayal of the sacrifices of the millions of people who had given up their lives to give us a better world.

Yet, despite the existence of a UN Charter, a system of international law and a recognised body of human rights – all achieved through the sacrifice of millions of lives – the nuclear nations assert the right to commit indiscriminate slaughter and devastation of the environment. They cherish this right and defend it against all comers, claiming that they are entitled both morally and legally to use such power.

As the 21st century gets into its stride, we need to reflect very closely on this anomaly if we are to be true to our claim that we are seeking to protect human dignity, human rights and human values. In particular we need to consider the discipline of international law which is the principal weapon of civilization against this weapon of barbarism.

This assumes critical importance at a time when the world is teetering on the brink of the nuclear abyss, with a dozen or more factors in operation, any one of which is capable of exploding at any time and providing the flashpoint for humanity's ultimate catastrophe – the use of the nuclear weapon.

With a new administration now in place in the world's leading nuclear power, the time is now opportune for a reconsideration of these issues, in the light of the higher principles to which democratic governments are committed and the universal values which underlie international law.

Some anomalies in humanitarian law

'Civilized nations' have indeed not been insensitive to their obligations to avoid the use of weapons that cause unnecessary suffering. They have evolved an extensive body of humanitarian law, rooted in religious and ethical principles. In the late 19th Century there was grave concern, for example, about the dum-dum bullet which caused cruel and unnecessary suffering by exploding on its entry into the victim's body. It was resolved in the 1899 Hague Declaration concerning Expanding Bullets that the weapon was too cruel to be used in warfare. We should not therefore be too ready to accuse 'civilized nations' of insensitivity in this regard. The sensitivity has always been there. The legal and institutional response to such sensitivity is what has been lacking. Any means by which this sensitivity can be translated into legal and practical efforts needs to be welcomed.

Even a schoolchild or a notional visitor from outer space could ask, with some surprise, how the dum-dum bullet stands banned for its excessive cruelty while the same nations who are concerned with its cruelty claim the right to use a bomb that exceeds that cruelty a million fold or more. They could well ask also how, when international law is founded upon the higher values taught by all cultures and civilizations, it can permit the existence, the threat and the use of such weapons, which contradict every value that international law upholds.

I base this discussion on the assumption that the indiscriminate slaughter of civilians, the devastation of the environment, the infliction of excruciating suffering on hundreds of thousands, the infliction of genetic damage for generations and the wholesale destruction of a nation's cultural inheritance are all acts which even individually constitute a crime against humanity. In combination it is irrefutable that they fall within this category.

If such a crime is contemplated whether by individuals or by governments there is an inherent duty imposed on those who treasure the basic values of civilization to ensure that these things do not happen.

Linkages between preparation and use

There is of course a gap between the act of using the weapon and the acts of deployment and research. The expenditure of millions of pounds and the heavy scientific and military effort involved are clearly not incurred to keep the weapons for showcase display. These things are clearly done with an intention of use. If one does not really intend to use them one cannot convince others that one will use them if the circumstances occurred for their engagement. The whole purpose of the exercise is to convince others of that intention, thereby using them as a form of deterrence. Others will not be so convinced if the party seeking to induce that belief has a secret intention not to use it. This is dissimulation at its worst, for intention is in the last resort the essence of this activity. Deterrence is not an act of deception but a real intent to use.

Statements are not indeed lacking at the highest governmental levels, Indicating the readiness of nuclear powers to use these weapons. The former British Defence Secretary Geoff Hoon MP said in 2002 that,

> For that to be a deterrent, a British government must be able to express their view that ultimately and in conditions of extreme self defence, nuclear weapons would have to be used.

And:

> It is therefore important to point out that the Government have nuclear weapons available to them, and that – in certain specified conditions to which I have referred – we would be prepared to use them.[1]

We do not however need such specific pronouncements to reach the self evident conclusion that a real intent of use in certain circumstances underlies the activity of preparation and the concept of deterrence.

Humanitarian law is not quiescent in times of peace

This body of principles exists and is active, not only in times of war but also in times of peace. Indeed it cannot be silent in times of peace for it is largely during periods of peace that preparations are made for war. If humanitarian law is silent in times of peace, we are laying the groundwork for its violation in times of war, thereby defeating its very purpose and rationale. This is particularly so in this nuclear age, when long and careful preparation of these weapons of ultimate cruelty takes place in times of peace to achieve readiness for their use in times of war. No nuclear nation waits for the outbreak of war to make these weapons.

Indeed, we would be facilitating the violation of humanitarian law by neglecting the preparations for it at a time when such future violations could be minimized with much less effort. From this point of view it is vitally important that we do not wait till war breaks out but that we activate these principles in times of peace as well.

There was a fallacy once prevalent that laws are silent in times of war 'Silent enim leges inter arma'. The answer to this was the evolution of humanitarian law which stated in no uncertain terms that far from being silent in times of war, it is particularly important that the law be active in times of war. Indeed this was a principle recognised by all religions as well, for the literature of Hinduism, Judaism, Christianity and Islam has numerous specific passages on this.[2] More than two thousand years ago, the Indian classics, the Ramayana and the Mahabharatha, afford evidence that Hinduism specifically prohibited the use of a hyper destructive weapon which could ravage the enemy's countryside and indiscriminately kill its population. Buddhism went even further, condemning war in every shape or form, including the use of even mildly dangerous weapons.

The fallacy that humanitarian law is silent in times of peace is parallel to the fallacy that the law is silent in times of war. Such a belief renders it particularly easy for humanitarian law to be violated in times of war. 'Si vis pacem, para bellum' ran the ancient maxim, 'if you desire peace prepare for war'. Conversely, if you envisage war, you must necessarily prepare for it in time of peace. Those who prepare for war well know that they cannot wait to make their weapons till war breaks out. Making weapons in times of peace is thus a preparation for war, no matter what terminology one may use, whether it be deterrence or any other. The use of nuclear weapons is not possible unless they are prepared and researched in times of peace. Humanitarian law is meaningless unless it can reach this period of preparation and that invariably is the time of peace. Indeed it would make nonsense of humanitarian law if it is powerless to prevent the preparation and the stockpiling of an enormous cache of hyper-destructive weapons, to be let loose as soon as war breaks out. Indeed, even at the present moment more than a thousand nuclear weapons in the arsenals of the world are in a state of readiness to be triggered off in minutes should the occasion arise. Humanitarian law cannot reach them then. If it is to have any meaning, it must reach them now.

Moreover deterrence and threats, themselves illegalities, assume a greatly reinforced strength if such a fallacious view prevails regarding the reach of humanitarian law. When war does break out it would be far too late to bring the principles of humanitarian law into operation. To quote time honoured human wisdom, 'prevention is better than cure' – especially in situations where cure after the damaging event is patently impossible.

Folklore of the nuclear age

Our vision of this problem tends to be blurred – often deliberately – by the folklore of the nuclear age which seeks to obscure many of the salient features of the anti-nuclear debate. It includes such observations as

- See how for sixty years our possession of the nuclear bomb has prevented attack by our cruel adversaries!
- See how Hiroshima and Nagasaki prosper despite attack by nuclear weapons! The nuclear weapon is obviously not the end of all civilization!

There is a whole array of such fallacies which can together be described as the folklore of the nuclear age, calculated by those who propagate it to lull the world's population into attitudes of apathy rather than protest, in a world bristling with nuclear weapons.

The first fallacy ignores the fact that we have been within a hair's breadth, time and again, of a global nuclear confrontation. The erection of the Berlin wall 1948, the Suez canal crisis 1956, the Taiwan Straits crisis 1958 and the Cuban Missile crisis 1962 readily come to mind as a few instances where humanity was on the verge of a nuclear catastrophe. In addition, nuclear accidents have occurred time and again. Launch-on-warning systems have more than once readied themselves to launch a missile and have been held back, providentially, with only seconds to go.

The second fallacy ignores the fact that tomorrow's nuclear war will not be an attack upon a sitting duck type of target with no power of retaliation. The retaliatory bomb will be part of a nuclear exchange which could produce a nuclear winter and all those dreaded consequences which the nuclear powers know so well, but choose to ignore. The nuclear winter could destroy the food chain and wipe out all living things.

The beliefs induced by such fallacies still prevail despite their irrelevance and despite their total unreality.

The growing ascendancy of international law

Another historical consideration relevant to this discussion is the fundamental change that has taken place over the last half century in the standing and reach of international law. From being a specialised subject confined to a small group of experts, it has during this period developed into a discipline producing a very real impact on every branch of domestic law. It has assumed a relevance which has transported it from a largely academic body of knowledge to the level where every citizen needs to know something about it and needs to do what he or she can to protect and preserve it and to ensure its application.

Where once international law was nourished and fertilized by domestic law, international law has developed to such an extent that the traffic today is largely in the reverse direction. International law today fertilizes and enriches every department of domestic law – criminal law, military law, environmental law, health law, human rights law, constitutional law, family law, industrial law, commercial law and every other department of law. Standards and concepts of international law form an integral part of all of them. No longer can international law be placed in a compartment separate and distinct from domestic law. It pervades every section of it and is as much part of the life of every citizen as domestic law.

Consequently international law is no longer a matter for governments only. Today every citizen needs to be involved in it, to understand it, and to be involved in its application. Just as the average citizen was once encouraged to take an active interest in the domestic legal system, at the present day the average citizen needs to be encouraged likewise to take an active interest in the international legal system. While we are all citizens of our respective nations we all need to recognise also that we are citizens of the global community whose common home needs protection from all the assaults that modern technology and modern weaponry are making upon it.

Every individual is encouraged by all legal systems to defend the constitution and the interests of his or her state. The circumstances of our time demand that every individual be encouraged to defend international law and the interests of the global community. This is an imperative of our time. The stakes could not be higher, for they concern the very survival of civilization and of humanity itself.

Another important factor in elevating the authority of international law is that all nations should comply with it. Every citizen knows from ordinary experience that a policeman who seeks to enforce the law must not make a mockery of that law by flagrantly and openly violating the very law he seeks to enforce. Every piece of conduct on the part of the policeman violating the very rule he proposes to enforce provokes others to violate that very rule and extends the ranks of violators. The self appointed nuclear policemen of the world need to realise how their actions totally destroy their credibility. The way to the universal abolition of nuclear weapons is for the nuclear states themselves to provide the example. No amount of policing by them or by the UN can be effective so long as they claim the right to have the weapon. Moreover all the moral authority that should lie behind the rule disappears if it is not universally complied with. It is elementary that there cannot be one law for some and another law for others.

Some incontrovertible legal and factual propositions

I set out a number of incontrovertible legal and factual propositions each of which has a bearing on the Trident operation. The incontrovertibility of the legal propositions follows in my view from the incontrovertibility of the factual propositions set out. To assert otherwise is to undermine the fundamental principles of humanity, justice, good faith and concern for the future on which international law depends.

A Legal Propositions

1   The use of nuclear weapons is illegal in any circumstances whatsoever.
2   The threat of use of nuclear weapons is illegal in any circumstances whatever.
3   The possession of nuclear weapons is illegal, for possession is not for show-case display but for use if required.
4   The further development of nuclear weapons is illegal.
5   The manufacture and testing of nuclear weapons are illegal.

6   The use of nuclear weapons violates every rule of humanitarian law.

7   The use of nuclear weapons violates every principle of human rights, to which all nations are committed.

8   The use of nuclear weapons is a crime against humanity.

9   Nuclear weapons are a weapon of genocide.

10   There is an obligation on all nuclear states to take meaningful steps to reduce and eliminate their stocks.

11   Failure to reduce stocks with a view to their total elimination is a violation of the requirements laid down by the unanimous opinion of the International Court of Justice.

12   The testing and improvement of existing nuclear weapons is a contravention of the obligations of nuclear states under international law and of the unanimous opinion of the International Court of Justice.

13   Every citizen has an obligation to use his or her influence to prevent crimes against humanity.

14   There is an absolute contravention of international law if belligerent states cause irretrievable damage to neighbouring states.

15   It is an absolute contravention of international law to cause irretrievable damage to the environment.

16   It is an absolute contravention of international law to cause irretrievable damage to future generations.

17   Devastation of the enemy's countryside and the mass slaughter of its population go far beyond the purposes of war and are international crimes.

18   There cannot be self appointed enforcers of the rule against nuclear weapons, especially if the self-appointed enforcers are themselves principal violators of this rule.

19   There cannot be one law for some members of the international community of nations and another law for others.

20   Those who take the decision to launch a nuclear weapon are personally guilty of a crime against humanity.

B   Factual Propositions

1   Nuclear weapons constitute a threat to the health of the community.

2   Nuclear weapons cause indiscriminate slaughter of the enemy population.

3   Nuclear weapons are a source of environmental pollution for thousands of years

4   Nuclear weapons cause excruciating suffering which goes far beyond the needs of war.

5   Nuclear weapons are a health hazard for an unforeseeable number of generations.

6   Nuclear weapons produce social disintegration.

7   Nuclear weapons contaminate and destroy the food chain.

8   Nuclear weapons cause genetic defects and deformities transmissible in perpetuity to future generations.

9   Nuclear weapons produce lasting psychological stress and fear syndromes.

10 Nuclear weapons wreak cultural devastation, irretrievably destroying historical monuments, historical documents and works of art, which are the inheritance of centuries.

Neither of these lists is comprehensive and each can be considerably supplemented.

Growing immediacy of the nuclear threat

All this assumes the gravest urgency when a number of volatile disputes in today's international arena could trigger the use of a nuclear weapon, not merely by states but potentially by irresponsible terrorist elements of all sorts.

Here are some of the circumstances that render the international situation so susceptible to the sudden use of a nuclear weapon.

1   The number of states having access to nuclear weapons is ever on the increase. There are states that have nuclear weapons and have not declared them and there are others who seek nuclear weapons but have not declared their intentions.

2   There is a phenomenal increase in the power and spread of terrorist groups. They are often in league with arms manufacturers, drug runners and other elements of society which pay scant regard to humanitarian values.

3   The knowledge necessary to make a nuclear weapon has ceased to

be the preserve of a few experts walled within the security establishments of states. With the proliferation of information technology the know-how necessary to make a nuclear weapon has
spread to the extent that a clever university student or code
buster/hacker could break into the necessary information.

4   The materials necessary for putting together a nuclear weapon,
especially the by-products of nuclear reactors, are available in
increasing quantities, with the proliferation of nuclear reactors
all over the world.

5   Even the International Atomic Energy Agency (IAEA) does not have
a proper check on all records of this material.

6   Some nations have put their defence systems on alert in accordance with what is known as a launch on warning capability
(LOWC). No decision of a head of state is required to trigger
them off. The machine takes the decision, does so within seconds
and can well be in error.

7   Nuclear accident is an ever present possibility. There have been
numerous such accidents in the past, and considering the fact
that there are tens of thousands of these weapons around, the
dangers are grave.

8   The number of occasions when the world was on the verge of
nuclear war in the past sixty years is considerable. In well over a
dozen cases the world was hovering on the brink and it was only
by a series of happy accidents that humanity was saved from
nuclear war.

9   The number of mini wars throughout the world is on the
increase. There is an ever present danger of nuclear powers
becoming embroiled in these conflicts, for the nuclear powers
have an interest in some of these conflicts.

10   There has been a trend in recent years for International Law to
be disregarded as and when it suited those who felt they were
in a position to disregard it. An instance is the invasion mounted
on Iraq by two of the permanent members of the Security
Council in disregard of the several rules that have grown up in
international law forbidding precisely the sort of unilateral
action that was resorted to.

11   Another source of danger is that there is a vast gulf between the

rich world and the poor world and this gulf is constantly widening. There are many nations in a state of desperation, unable to acquire even the basic necessities for their sustenance.

12 Another factor to be borne in mind is that research on the improvement and refinement of nuclear weapons is proceeding across the world.

13 The increasing number of suicide bombers now available for carrying out desperate tasks is a phenomenon of our times.

14 Even outer space has not been free of nuclear weapons and testing and the deployment of weapons in space constitutes a potential future danger.

15 There are a number of scientists once employed in nuclear establishments whose expertise is available at a price to bidders for this knowledge.

Matters of particular concern to Scotland

All of this underlines the importance of citizens being concerned with the proliferation and deployment of a weapon that makes them targets and imperils their children and their children's children, a weapon that endangers their environment, their fishing grounds, their food chain and their cultural heritage. These are all areas which must necessarily be concerns of the Parliament of Scotland even if it is totally devoid of power regarding foreign policy and defence. We may note in this context that although The Scotland Act 1998 provides that the conduct of international relations is a matter reserved for the United Kingdom Parliament and the United Kingdom Government, paragraph 7(2) (a) provides *inter alia* that implementing and observing international obligations are not so reserved. This is a factor which gives strength to the view that gross violations of international obligations are not excluded from the purview of the Scottish Parliament. The absence of power in the former area cannot cancel out its responsibilities in the latter.

The Trident nuclear weapons developed by the UK Government and positioned within the area over which the Scottish Parliament has jurisdiction highlights the issue in a special way and stimulates reflection on the duties and responsibilities of elected assemblies down to provincial and local levels.

Scotland will be a target for retaliation if the Trident missile should ever be used. The people of Scotland will be the sufferers. When the International Court heard the case regarding the use and threat of nuclear weapons, the evidence that was placed before it in regard to the human suffering caused by the nuclear weapon and by nuclear testing was so harrowing that one could be left in no doubt of the need for the abolition of nuclear weapons. Witnesses came to us from distant places like the Marshall Islands giving us the saddest descriptions of the birth deformities and the continuing suffering imposed on the islanders through nuclear testing.

A woman from the Marshall Islands said that Marshallese women after exposure to nuclear weapons testing

> give birth, not to children as we like to think of them, but to things we could only describe as 'octopuses', 'apples', 'turtles' and other things in our experience. We do not have Marshallese words for these kinds of babies because they were never born before the radiation came.

> Women on Rongelap, Likiep, Ailuk and other atolls in the Marshall Islands have given birth to these 'monster babies'... One woman on Likiep gave birth to a child with two heads... There is a young girl on Ailuk today with no knees, three toes on each foot and a missing arm... The most common birth defects on Rongelap and nearby islands have been 'jellyfish' babies. These babies are born with no bones in their bodies and with transparent skin. We can see their brains and hearts beating... many women die from abnormal pregnancies and those who survive give birth to what looks like purple grapes which we quickly hide away and bury...

> My purpose in travelling such a great distance to appear before the court today is to plead with you to do what you can not to allow the suffering that we Marshallese have experienced to be repeated in any other community in the world.[3]

The people of Scotland have every right to protest against the possibility of this experience being repeated in Scotland.

The Vanuatu delegate to the 46th World Health Assembly (1993) spoke of the birth after nine months of 'a substance that breathes but does not have a face or legs or arms'.[4]

The Mayors of Hiroshima and Nagasaki also placed before us one of the most lamentable tales of human suffering ever recorded – facts and records over many of which the nuclear powers had thrown a blanket of secrecy and which they still choose to ignore.

Nobody aware of that evidence could be left in the slightest doubt that every step that can be taken legally towards the abolition of this weapon of brutality needs to be taken and that those steps should be taken not nominally but effectively, not leisurely but urgently, not hesitantly but decisively. Good faith should pervade the whole operation, for good faith is an essential element in every aspect of the application and observance of international law.

True, foreign policy and defence are the prerogative of the national government. Yet the safety of the population of Scotland is the concern of Scotland. The health of the Scottish population is the concern of Scotland. The welfare of future generations of its population is the concern of Scotland. The protection of the environment of Scotland is the concern of Scotland. The purity of the seas and the ocean life around Scotland are the concern of Scotland.

Growing importance of citizen involvement

There is a dilemma here for people of all countries, for many nuclear activities across the world present conflicts of interest between local populations and central governments. It is for international law to resolve these problems by providing the necessary guidelines based upon human dignity, human rights and human welfare.

The Nuremberg principles give effect to the most solemn duties and responsibilities that are carried by states and those in power. The principles of democracy impose a responsibility on citizens to elect their representatives to power and to exercise a continuing vigilance over their exercise of that power. That vigilance is all the more imperative when it concerns the highest powers of state and the gravest crimes that governments can commit. The question we have to ask ourselves is whether that duty of vigilance melts away when the power exercised or misused is the defence power of the nation state. Does the participatory responsibility of the citizens of a democracy disappear in the fields of defence and foreign affairs when what may be an international crime is prepared by a sovereign government? Does the law, whether domestic or international, require a concerned citizenry to remain silent and inactive if their government is taking action that can contravene the Nuremberg principles?

Do the people of Scotland have a right to demonstrate their concern with their safety, their health, their environment, their food chains, their future generations and their cultural inheritance? Modern human rights learning and doctrine would indicate an affirmative answer to these questions.

Moreover, the missile is being perfected for deterrence. Deterrence means the threat of use. Use attracts retaliation. The target for retaliation is the geographical area where the missiles are located. The victims of retaliation will be the people of Scotland. The decision to use the missile will be a decision taken by the UK Government. Is there a conflict here which international law needs to resolve? International law cannot stand aside when human rights are violated and negated by doctrines of state sovereignty.

Indeed anti-nuclear civil resistance is the right of every citizen of this planet, for the nuclear threat, attacking as it does every core concept of human rights, calls for urgent and universal action for its prevention. If it is a basic human right to be free of threat or violence, if the right to life is a basic human right, and if the protection of children and future generations is a basic human duty, international law must unhesitatingly recognise that the right to non-violent resistance activities, for the prevention of such an international crime, is basic to human dignity.

It is clear from the foregoing considerations that there is an increasing need in the modern world, whether in Scotland or elsewhere, for citizens to take a greater interest in international law and in the way their government fulfils its obligation in this regard. This is increasingly a matter for the citizenry of the world and if they do not rise to their obligations in this respect, future generations will pay dearly for this inaction.

Seminal importance of the unanimous Opinion of the International Court of Justice

Reference has been made earlier to the unanimous Opinion of the International Court of Justice on nuclear disarmament. Whatever other differences there might have been amongst the Judges, they all agreed, without exception, that:

> There exists an obligation to pursue in good faith and bring to a conclusion negotiations leading to nuclear disarmament in all its aspects under strict and effective international control.

It cannot be stressed too strongly that there cannot be a more authoritative statement of international law than a unanimous Opinion of the international community's highest judicial tribunal. Moreover this is an age in which, if there is to be a peaceful world, there needs to be respect paid to international law particularly by the most powerful states. International law depends, just as the International Court of Justice does, not on force of arms but on the force of its moral authority. Those who deprive international law of its moral authority are doing a distinct disservice to the community of nations and the future of humanity.

The Opinion in question was probably the most important judicial statement delivered in the history of the Court. The Opinion was sought by a majority of the nation states through a request for an Opinion by the General Assembly of the United Nations. It saw the largest number of nation states recorded as participating in the hearing of any case. It was perhaps the longest judicial hearing. A vast amount of material was placed before the Court including documents with millions of signatures. The record room of the Court could not hold the documentary material submitted, so vast was it in bulk. Every judge of the court wrote a considered opinion.

Such an Opinion of the International Court is also cogent evidence that the principles that it enunciates have entered the field of customary international law, which is a principal source of international law. All states are obliged to recognize such a principle and to act upon it. A treaty embodying such a rule is scarcely necessary when a principle of customary international law is so clear.

To treat such a judicial pronouncement with scant regard is not, in this day and age, responsible conduct on the part of any state.

Violation of the 1968 Treaty on the Non-Proliferation of Nuclear Weapons

In relation to this positive obligation imposed by the unanimous opinion of the International Court of Justice, the continuing work on the Trident missile system and its replacement constitutes a violation of Article VI of the Nuclear Non Proliferation Treaty 1968.

This is a cardinal provision of the treaty and it must be remembered also that a provision as important as this must necessarily attract the principle of good faith in the observance, implementation and interpretation of the Treaty. It can scarcely be said that an interpretation of Article VI which leaves room for the activities in question accords with the fundamental principles of the Vienna Convention on the Law of Treaties, which stresses that the words of a treaty are to be interpreted in the light of its object and purpose. That object and purpose would be entirely defeated by the interpretation in question.

Contrast between preparations to usher in the 20th century and lack of preparations for the 21st century

I close as I began with a historical perspective which will cause us to consider how sadly we have neglected the task of planning for a new century of peace to succeed the bloodiest century in human history. There was much thinking in the air when the 20th century began, regarding what should be done to leave behind a century of war and usher in a century of peace. The thinkers of the world and the governments of the world met together at the greatest peace conference that the world had seen till then. That was the Hague Peace Conference of 1899 which built a bridge between the worlds of philosophy and power. These two worlds had with a few exceptions functioned separately from each other from the dawn of history and the hope was that by bringing them together some sparks of inspiration from the world of philosophy would enter the corridors of power and help in the task of building a better world.

There was a sense of urgency and the 400 peace societies across the world looked on in eager anticipation of some meaningful progress along the road to peace, for this was a time if any for humanity to take a turn towards establishing a peaceful world. Czar Nicholas II of Russia, himself an absolute potentate, saw the need for the planning and assembling of such a conference. He had been influenced by several factors not the least of which was the writings of Tolstoy.

Another major influence, very pertinent to our current topic, was that the Czar had made a study of a monumental six volume work by Jan Bloch, a member of the Russian Council of State on the War of the

Future. The concluding volume asserted that in view of the awesome power of new weapons of war, the war of the future would result in a break up of the entirety of social organization. War as a means of solving disputes had thus become impossible.[5] The next war, said Bloch, would see the elimination of such vast numbers that there would be neither victors nor vanquished but two devastated nations. War had lost its relevance.

If the thinkers and rulers of that age had gone so far, having regard to the weaponry then available, how much further should not today's thinkers and rulers go!

Whatever the other influences which might have acted on him, the Czar was aware of these writings and saw value in convening such a meeting, which was held at The Hague. Despite all the difficulties in the way of an International Court of Justice, at least a Permanent Court of Arbitration emerged, giving effect to the principle that future conflicts should be resolved by peaceful means rather than by war. The first step had been taken towards establishing the institutional structure of a more peaceful world.

Such were the thoughts that were uppermost in the minds of some at least of the powerful nations at the commencement of the 20th century. One wonders whether at the commencement of the 21st century there was a similar analysis in high places of fresh approaches towards world peace so that we could learn from the mistakes of the 20th century and make the 21st century a century of peace.

Sadly, the opening years of the 21st century have been disfigured by war and every effort is needed, from the citizen in the street to the highest echelons of power, to mend this error and to place this new century on the route to peace. The nuclear weapon stands like an enormous road block on this route. All hands are needed to eliminate it and eliminate it we must, if we have any regard for the human future.

The issue is the survival of civilization

At the dawn of the 21st century we did not have a peace conference of such proportions. The world of philosophy and the world of power still functioned in separate compartments though the need was even more urgent to bring them together, for this was the first century to dawn with humanity having the power to destroy itself. For this reason the century before us is our century of last opportunity and we must fervently hope that every avenue will be explored, every factor making for peace will come to the forefront and every obstacle in the way of peace will be removed.

What is at stake? It is nothing less than the survival of civilization and the key factor in this whole scenario is the nuclear weapon. We either destroy it or it will destroy us. Unlike the 20th century which, though bungled, had a 21st century to succeed it, the 21st century if bungled will be our last; for if we fail to put our affairs in order, nuclear weapons will emerge from their closets and civilization will be at an end. We must be conscious that just as the 20th century was a century of lost opportunity this is our century of last opportunity if civilization is to survive.

Philosophers have said more than once that society suffers not for the wrongs of evil doers but for the complacency of good citizens in the face of evil. There can be little complacency about an evil so great as the nuclear weapon.

Since the century that should have been ushered in on a note of peace has been ushered in on a note of war and since we need to treasure and protect the achievements of millennia of human effort, which have taken the sacrifice of millions of lives to achieve, we must all contribute what we can to eliminate the nuclear scourge.

When a crime against humanity is involved every citizen has a duty to contribute what he or she can to prevent it. Every legal system which cherishes human rights would give its citizens every opportunity of peaceful demonstration in support of such causes.

International law gives due recognition to the right of sovereign states to determine matters of foreign policy and defence. This is their undoubted right. Yet it is a right to be exercised within the framework of international law. All ethical standards dictate that it should be exercised on the basis of good faith. International law condemns the threat or use of nuclear weapons. Good faith dictates that the obligation to abolish them must be discharged in good faith.

If the law is truly to be the custodian of the rights and liberties of present and future generations, anti-nuclear civil resistance is the right of every citizen, for the nuclear threat, attacking as it does every core concept of human rights, calls for urgent and universal action for its prevention. If the right to life is a basic human right, and if the protection of children and future generations is a basic human duty, international law must unhesitatingly recognise that non-violent resistance activities for the prevention of such an international crime is basic to human dignity.

The remedy is a more active international law strengthened by citizen participation

We pressingly need more understanding of international law, more respect for international law, more compliance with international law, more support for international law and more good faith in the observance of international law. Whatever can be done to achieve these is activity which can help meaningfully to preserve humanity, civilization and the values we cherish.

We also pressingly need more citizen involvement in all these issues, for international law needs public support if it is to function effectively. Social motivation is essential to its success.

In an age in which the destructive power of weaponry was minuscule compared to its power today, Shakespeare could still see havoc as the inevitable result of war. 'Cry 'havoc' and let slip the dogs of war'[6] describes it all. In an age of nuclear weapons every citizen has a right and duty to protest against any preparations enabling any entity to 'cry 'havoc' and let slip' these bolts of doom.

Good Faith, International Law and Elimination of Nuclear Weapons

H.E. JUDGE MOHAMMED BEDJAOUI

ON JULY 8 1996, the International Court of Justice gave its Advisory Opinion on the request from the General Assembly. In its resolution 49/75K of 15 December 1994, the question posed by the Assembly was as follows, 'Is the threat or use of nuclear weapons permitted in any circumstance under international law?' Resolution 49/75K asked the Court to render its opinion 'urgently.'

The Content of the Advisory Opinion

1   The law applicable to armed conflicts

Finding neither a conventional rule of general application nor a customary rule specifically forbidding the threat or use of nuclear weapons as such, the Court thereupon approached one of the most delicate questions presented to it:

> determining whether recourse to nuclear arms should be... considered illicit in view of the principles and rules of international humanitarian law applicable... in armed conflicts, as well as the law of neutrality.

This body of law consists fundamentally of what is usually called the 'Law of the Hague' and the 'Law of Geneva', those two branches of law applicable to armed conflict having developed such close connections that they are regarded as having gradually built a single complex system, as demonstrated by the Additional Protocols of 1977 to the Geneva Conventions of 12 August 1949. This is to say that the Court now stood at the very heart of one of the most sensitive areas of contemporary international law, as it bears on some of the most essential values of humankind.

A   The cardinal principles of humanitarian law

In proceeding to the examination of international humanitarian law, the Court highlighted two cardinal principles.

The first established the distinction between combatants and non-combatants: states must never target civilians, nor use arms that are incapable of distinguishing between civilian and military targets.

The second principle affirms that it is not permitted to cause super-fluous harm to combatants: thus, states do not have an unlimited right as to the arms they may utilize. The Court also referred to the 'Martens clause', according to which civilians and combatants remain under the protection and rule of the principles of the law of nations, as they result from established customs, from the laws of humanity, and from the dictates of the public conscience.

For me there is no doubt that most of the principles and rules of humanitarian law (and, in any case, the two principles forbidding the use of weapons with indiscriminate effects on the one hand, and on the other, the use of weapons causing superfluous harm) are part of *jus cogens*.

In its opinion, the Court mentioned the point, but declared itself not obliged to rule on it, as the question of *the nature* of humanitarian law applicable to nuclear weapons did not enter into the framework of the General Assembly's request. Nonetheless the Court did expressly consider those fundamental principles (and I quote) as 'intransgressible principles of international customary law'. This was a step forward in accepting them as *jus cogens*.

B   Applicability of these principles to nuclear weapons

Moving to the question of the applicability of the principles and rules of humanitarian law to the possible threat or use of nuclear weapons, the Court stressed that it was not possible to conclude that these principles and rules do not apply to nuclear weapons. According to the Court, such a conclusion would in effect misconstrue,

> the intrinsically humanitarian nature of the judicial principles at issue, which permeate the entire law of armed conflict and apply to all forms of war and to all weapons, those of the past and those of the present and future.

But at the same time the Court did remark that the *consequences* that should be drawn from the applicability of humanitarian law to nuclear weapons are controversial.

In short, this means that the Court was fully aware that 'nuclear weapons' clearly have a double nature: on the one hand, they are *weapons,* and thus justiciable under the general legal system applying to all weapons; and on the other, they are *nuclear,* and thus necessarily subject to a special regime because of this characteristic.

The Court found that, as regards the unique characteristics of nuclear weapons, the use of these weapons seemed scarcely reconcilable with respect for the demands of the law applicable in armed conflict.

2   The Court's uncertainty

Nonetheless, the Court did consider that

> it did not have at its disposal adequate elements to permit concluding with certainty that such a use would necessarily be contrary in all circumstances to the principles and rules of the law applicable in armed conflict.

The Court added that it should not meanwhile lose sight of the fundamental right of survival of all states and thus the right of a state to resort to legitimate self defence when that survival is at stake; and neither could the Court ignore the practice known as the 'policy of deterrence' to which a sizeable segment of the international community has adhered for years. Consequently, in view of the present state of international law considered in its entirety, as examined by the Court, and of the elements of fact at its disposal (in particular what is unknown about the existence of supposedly 'clean' nuclear weapons), the Court had to find that it

> could not reach a definitive conclusion on the legality or illegality of the use of nuclear weapons by a state in an extreme circumstance of legitimate defence in which its very survival would be at stake.

3   The only way out of the uncertainty: the obligation to negotiate in good faith and bring nuclear disarmament to actuality

Having reached this conclusion, the Court insisted on observing that in the end, international law, and with it the stability of the international order it is intended to govern, is bound to suffer from differences of view with regard to the legal status of weapons as deadly as nuclear weapons. Therefore it judged that there was reason to end this state of affairs: the complete nuclear disarmament promised for so long seemed to the Court to be the best means of reaching this outcome.

In these circumstances the Court emphasized the great importance of the consecration, in Article VI of the Treaty on the Non-Proliferation of Nuclear Weapons (NPT), of a good-faith obligation to negotiate nuclear disarmament. And the Court recalled that this double obligation – to negotiate in good faith and to arrive at nuclear disarmament in all its aspects – formally concerns all the states party to the NPT, that is to say the very large majority of the international community, and requires the cooperation of all states.

4   A useful 'caveat'

At the end of its Advisory Opinion, the Court made clear that its response to the question posed by the General Assembly rested upon the full array of the legal grounds set forth, which should be read in relation to one another. In effect the Court's opinion constitutes a totality, from which passages ought not to be extracted, especially not in isolation from their context.

5   The obstacles which the Court had to confront

Such being the legal situation, it was suitable for the Court to present its conclusions. It did so in a particularly cautious manner, to avoid possible misinterpretation. In examining the legal situation, the Court declared itself confronted with questions it could not decide definitively and in utter clarity, in one sense or another, and especially because of the state of international law on the matter. It felt it could not go beyond what the law says, such as it had interpreted the law. It thus made a special effort to avoid two major obstacles in describing the legal situation—to show, depending on the case, that existing international law

1   would permit the threat or use of nuclear weapons; or on the contrary,

2   would prohibit such threat and such use.

Beyond the need for the Court to deal with these obstacles, each of its members was also confronted with a very serious problem of conscience, since none of them failed to recognize the stakes involved—the very survival of humankind. Witness the adoption by a 7-to-7 vote, with the President's deciding vote, on the second clause of paragraph (2)E of the dispositif. This conclusion of the Court, very synthesized and marked by its balanced structure, reads:

> It follows from the above-mentioned requirements that the threat or use of nuclear weapons would generally be contrary to the rules of international law applicable in armed conflict, and in particular the principles and rules of humanitarian law;

> However, in view of the current state of international law, and of the elements of fact at its disposal, the Court cannot conclude definitively whether the threat or use of nuclear weapons would be lawful or unlawful in an extreme circumstance of self-defence, in which the very survival of a State would be at stake.

The Court itself was quite clearly aware right away of the unsatisfactory nature, on first view, of the response it was offering to the General Assembly. It will be seen how much criticism it provoked for having apparently quit in mid-course the task it had been assigned.

In the second clause of point (2) E, the Court indicates that it reached a point in its reasoning beyond which it could only go at the risk of failing before the two obstacles I have cited, that is, adopting a conclusion that would go beyond what it deemed legitimate. This is the Court's position as a judicial body.

A number of judges have taken this position, but probably each of them with his or her own approach and interpretation. It is clear that the distribution of the votes, as many in favour as against point (2) E, followed no geographic or ideological cleavage, which is a sign of the independent thinking of the members of the Court, I am pleased to emphasize.

The Court thus limited itself to an observation, even as it felt unable to go further. We can say that the vote was not easy for certain judges. The first clause of paragraph E declares the illegality of nuclear weapons. It is good to note that two judges from countries belonging to the 'Nuclear Club' did nonetheless vote to confirm it. The idea of the second clause was to accommodate everyone by leaving the door open to both legality and illegality. It was approved by two judges from the Third World and rejected by three others on one hand, and on the other it won the favourable vote of two judges from nuclear nations and negative votes from three others.

So, paragraph E had positive votes from two judges from the Third World, two European judges from countries without nuclear weapons, and two judges from nations that do have such weapons: it is hard to imagine a better spread. Against paragraph E, the vote was three judges from the Third World, two judges from countries that do possess the weapons, and one judge whose country had been a victim of its use. So there too the votes were thoroughly mixed. The distribution of the votes certainly showed the independent thinking of the members of the Court, and demonstrated that its members are not in the least ruled by clan spirit or the concern to accommodate their countries of origin.

6 Pronounce law and risk falling into *non-liquet*?

The Court was sharply reproached, by a segment of the doctrine, for its inability to say whether

> the threat or use of nuclear weapons would be lawful or unlawful in an extreme circumstance of self-defence, in which the very survival of a State would be at stake.

It is true that it is difficult to give a 'non-opinion', or an empty opinion, to the General Assembly of the United Nations which was expecting to be enlightened by the Court on what policy to follow, especially in such a vital domain.

But a few points need to be clarified:

(a) First of all, we should not fear to acknowledge that international law is still relatively little developed and that it has gaps in it. To postulate otherwise would be to leap ahead in time.

It is also the reason why a judge has in principle the power to refuse to rule. This situation is not peculiar to international law. Any juridical system is formed of a multitude of norms and, from this very fact, is by nature discontinuous. To avoid such an 'unstitching,' Paul Reuter tells us to draw on certain principles, like that of *good faith*, which can encompass a broad expression and expansion and which allow the legal system under consideration to adapt more readily to new problems as they arise.

(b) According to certain writers, the incomplete normativity of international law is balanced by a *de facto* plenitude, through the existence of rules whose function is to fill lacunae. These compensating rules are provided by the *general principles of law* and by *equity*. Therefore there should be no room for the *non-liquet*.

(c) But did the Court pronounce a *non-liquet?* In truth, it is the unfortunate interference of 'elements of fact' in its reasoning (namely, the technological advances which might make possible the manufacture of 'clean' bombs) which unduly troubled certain minds and which stopped the Court on the threshold of a ruling on the prohibition of nuclear weapons. This prohibition already existed in the first clause of paragraph E, and besides imposed itself on the Court in view of the 'unique characteristics' of nuclear weapons whose explosion, as it said, 'by its very nature' releases 'powerful and prolonged' ionizing radiation, which would strike combatants as well as civilian populations, belligerent states as well as neutral states, present as well as future generations.

(d) '*Jura non novit curia?*', wonders Luigi Condorelli. The eminent professor does know, however, that the Court certainly knows the law quite well. It has analysed it perfectly, and its fault may perhaps lie in having on this occasion delivered an Advisory Opinion which stopped at only implicitly condemning the use of nuclear weapons, rather than ruling more overtly on its prohibition.[1]

Let us say that the Court's manner of proceeding arose from, *in this instance, an excessively cautious perception of its judicial policy*. Still, it has often displayed its capacity to go beyond its function of 'stating the law' and has skilfully practised 'normative replacement'. But we must acknowledge the unavoidable reality of the existence of this unfortunate and useless second clause of paragraph E, infiltrating as if by trespass a judgement whose whole philosophy rejects it.

Supposing then that this second clause made clear the existence of a gap in international law and brought on a situation resembling a non-liquet—*quod-non*, in my opinion—then it would be useful to ponder the observations of Judge Vereshchetin, who said

> the case in hand presents a good example of an instance where the absolute clarity of the Opinion would be 'deceptive' and where, on the other hand, its partial 'apparent indecision' may prove useful 'as a guide to action'.[2]

The Lessons to be Drawn from the Opinion

1 The Court has recognized the pertinence of the law of armed conflict, including humanitarian law, prohibiting the use of nuclear weapons

This is a major point on which it is more than ever important to focus attention. The Court has, in my view, fully recognized that the cardinal principles of international humanitarian law, such as

- the distinction between combatants and non-combatants, which prohibits the state to target the civilian population,
- the prohibition to cause superfluous harm to combatants, which makes it clear that the state cannot have unlimited choice as to what weapons it may use,
- the principles drawn from the law of neutrality, which the use of nuclear weapons cannot possibly honour given their radiation and radioactive fallout over space and time,
- the 'Martens clause', which provides that civilian populations and combatants,

Remain,

> under the protection of the laws of humanity and the dictates of the public conscience, render the use of nuclear weapons completely illegal.

Thus it is important that, in any further initiative, its argumentation must bear essentially on the radical incompatibility existing in principle between the use of nuclear weapons and respect for international humanitarian law.

It is true that the Court has declared that there exists no conventional or customary law prohibiting nuclear weapons as such. However, very fortunately and by way of compensation, the whole body of the law of armed conflict, and especially humanitarian law, indirectly prohibit this highly lethal weapon.

It is my concern for the realities that has led me to clearly assert, in the declaration I attached to the opinion, that nuclear weapons seem to me absolutely of a nature to cause indiscriminate victims among combatants and non-combatants alike, as well as unnecessary suffering among both categories. By its very nature the nuclear weapon, a blind weapon, therefore has a destabilizing effect on humanitarian law, the law of discrimination which regulates discernment in use of weapons. The existence of nuclear weapons is therefore a major challenge to the very existence of humanitarian law, not to mention their long-term harmful effects on the human environment, in respect to which the right to life can be exercised. Because of their indiscriminate effects, nuclear weapons constitute the negation of humanitarian law. Nuclear warfare and humanitarian law therefore appear to be mutually exclusive, the existence of the one automatically implying the non-existence of the other. And that remains true no matter how exceptional the situation confronting any eventual user of nuclear weapons.

I would add, especially, that any use of nuclear weapons, even in such a situation, would risk the survival of humanity, because of the inextricable link between terror and escalation in the use of such weapons. In the declaration I appended to the opinion, my interpretation of paragraph E and especially of its second clause was simply summarized by an obvious statement: a 'fragment' cannot be saved if the 'whole' is destroyed; a 'part' cannot be saved at the cost of destroying the 'whole':

> the use of nuclear weapons by a State in circumstances in which its survival is at stake risks in its turn endangering the survival of all mankind, precisely because of the inextricable link between terror and escalation in the use of such weapons. It would thus be quite foolhardy unhesitatingly to set the survival of a State above all other considerations, in particular above the survival of mankind itself.[3]

So we may wonder why the World Court did not stop at this conclusion and purely and simply declare the prohibition of the use of nuclear arms on the grounds of humanitarian law alone. In my opinion, but it is a completely personal opinion, even while recognizing the non-pertinence of taking so-called 'clean' nuclear weapons into account, the Court seems to me to have remained somewhat troubled by the possibility of such weapons, present or future. That is a point that deserves attention for any future initiative, as will be seen.

2 The Court recognized the non-pertinence of taking so-called 'clean' nuclear weapons into account

In the Court's dossier there are, as elements of fact, reports provided by various states concerning the existence of 'low-yield nuclear weapons', 'clean weapons', 'reduced-effect weapons', and 'tactical weapons'. Speculation has been put forward that science has progressed to the point where there presently may exist intelligent nuclear weapons capable of discrimination and, in particular, able to strike combatants while sparing non-combatants.

The Court should not have credited such reports, in particular because it had not received any evidence to prove the existence of nuclear weapons that emit no radiation and have no prolonged effects in space and time. Per the definition of the nuclear weapon provided in paragraph 35, these would no longer be 'nuclear' weapons but rather some new and wholly other type of classical or conventional weapon, lying beyond the 'nuclear threshold'. Weapons of a type releasing less heat or less blast could certainly be invented; they would still remain 'nuclear' weapons so long as they retained their fundamental characteristic of emitting ionizing radiation which is particularly devastating in time and space. If technological progress should eliminate that characteristic, we would no longer be looking at a 'nuclear' weapon.[4]

The Court was correct to consider those reports insufficient, fragmentary, and lacking in probative significance. And in any case, the nuclear weapon, thus 'improved', would not really be a 'nuclear weapon' if its explosive core was 'denatured' by technological advances to the point where it no longer continued to emit its devastating ionizing radiation over decades, even centuries. If certain unique characteristics of a nuclear weapon should disappear through the effect of scientific progress, we would then be in the presence not of a nuclear weapon but of some entirely different weapons. The Court, however, was asked to rule on the nuclear weapon; to rule on a weapon of an entirely different nature would have been beyond its mandate.

It must be one or the other: either it has become possible to build a type of weapon without destructive radiation in time and space, but this would be a different weapon, one not involved in the debate before the Court; or else one has conceived and produced a weapon properly described as 'nuclear' but low-yield, but then that means that its nature has not been modified, that is to say it has still crossed the 'nuclear threshold' that distinguishes it from the classical weapon. Therefore, the reports offered concerning this 'weak' or 'clean' type of weapon in no way change the debate.

Let us read carefully paragraph 35 of the Court's Advisory Opinion; it is particularly instructive and revealing. On what type of weapons has the high international jurisdiction been asked to give its opinion? On 'nuclear weapons, as they exist today', not on some other type of weapon of tomorrow. How are they characterized? By several elements including 'the phenomenon of radiation' which 'is said to be peculiar to nuclear weapons'. Now, 'ionizing radiation', which is the essential element characterizing these weapons, 'is a powerful and prolonged radiation', with an especially long life ravaging the environment and compromising the survival of future generations. Hence the Court's conclusion, in the same paragraph: 'The destructive power of nuclear weapons cannot be contained in either space or time.' It is exclusively on these weapons, and not on some new type (about which, besides, we do not know whether it can lessen the duration in time and the dispersion in space of its devastating effects) that the Court has been asked to rule. In its reasoning, there could be no room for considering some possible 'advances' which, in any case, would place us before weapons quite different from the nuclear arms of today. The impossibility of limiting their effects to military objectives alone necessarily places nuclear weapons in manifest contradiction with the principles and rules of the law of armed conflict and of humanitarian law, and cannot therefore do otherwise than make it a weapon prohibited under international law. Any possible or claimed advances in the conception of the weapon can have no effect on this situation. The Court could only take account of the nuclear weapon's 'unique characteristics,' which it very carefully specified, in particular 'of their destructive capacity, their capacity to cause untold human suffering, and their ability to cause damage to generations to come.'[5]

It was that weapon, and no other, that stood in judgement before the Court.

And for this reason the Court declared, very simply but very clearly, the following:

> The Court does not consider that, in giving an advisory opinion in the present case, it would necessarily have to write 'scenarios', to study various types of nuclear weapons, and to evaluate highly complex and controversial technological, strategic, and scientific information.[6]

3   A 'clean' bomb nonetheless polluting the atmosphere of the Court

The Court therefore, as indicated above, seems to have thrown out the door the question of the 'clean' weapon. But I wonder (and this is of course a completely personal feeling) whether in fact it was able completely to exclude from its thinking this 'clean' bomb that would somehow, providentially, emerge to become compatible with respect for humanitarian law.

I have the impression that this idea of a possible 'advance' which would make the nuclear weapon a 'clean' bomb has not totally vanished from the discourse of the Court, despite its repeated assertions. The Court has not completely cleansed its argumentation of this element that may perhaps have weighed on the minds of some of the judges.

Herein lies the whole problem of paragraph E of the dispositif. That is the Gordian knot of the whole business. Unfortunately this problem of 'clean' or 'low yield' weapons has left something in the atmosphere.

One could, after all, believe in all sincerity that there exists, or could exist in a near future, a 'clean' weapon (but could it still be called 'nuclear'?) that could satisfy the fundamental principles of humanitarian law which call primarily for distinguishing between combatants and non-combatants. It's not entirely impossible. In any case, the Court's consideration of technological advances, without its having to say so, seemed to me to have become something of an underlying argument that allowed the Court to confess its uncertainty as to the legality of these weapons without risking the criticism of one camp or another. And after having asserted, in the first clause of paragraph E, the patent contradiction between the nuclear weapon (as it is known) and humanitarian law, the Court cautiously wondered, in the second clause, whether in view of 'the **elements of fact** at its disposal', it could or could not declare the nuclear weapon legal or illegal.

On this question of technological advances toward making nuclear weapons 'clean' weapons, the judges and the Court were told too much, or not enough, but were not provided with unassailable certainties. The Court was unable to expunge completely and soundly this pseudo-scientific chiaroscuro which, thus distilled, finally managed to seep into some interstices of its reasoning. At least, that is my personal interpretation of the Advisory Opinion rendered.

4 One possible reason for the intrusion of clause 2 of paragraph E into the Court's Opinion

Thus, it is primarily these 'factual elements' of possible advances in the mastery of nuclear weapons that have troubled the Court and left it in a quandary. Yet the Court did not venture so far as to declare, in that second clause, that those factual elements enabled it to say that nuclear weaponry answers perfectly to the requirements of the law of armed conflict and notably to those of humanitarian law. It confined itself to confessing ignorance, and avoiding any statement of support for either this thesis or its opposite.

5 The World Court recognized, unanimously, the existence of an obligation to pursue in good faith and bring to a conclusion negotiations for nuclear disarmament

This is a new and critical point. It is also welcome for easing the sense of dissatisfaction or frustration that international public opinion may have felt at seeing the Court's indecision about declaring nuclear arms either legal or illegal.

Any subsequent initiative meant to lead to the eradication of such weapons should, in my opinion, take into account this important declaration by the Court, and try to reinforce it and make it prevail fully. For this revolutionary pronouncement which, through the grace of its unanimity, has acquired legal value, is still fragile in that a sizeable portion of legal doctrine continues to contest the validity of this courageous declaration.

It is to the credit of the International Court of Justice that not only has it recalled to all the states party their good-faith duty to negotiate nuclear disarmament in accordance with Article VI of the NPT, which they ratified, but also went on to task them with a second, vigorous obligation (to 'bring to a conclusion' these negotiations) which is nothing more nor less than actually to bring about concrete nuclear disarmament.

There was some hesitation within the Court, not because it opposed such good-faith negotiation, but rather because that question had not been explicitly put to the Court in the request for an advisory opinion as formulated by the United Nations General Assembly, so that the Court risked declaring itself 'ultra petita'.7

The precious unanimity of the Court on the double obligation to negotiate and to conclude should not be eroded by the criticisms of the legal doctrine, which, however, should be answered, in order to strengthen this important declaration from the high jurisdiction, as I shall try to do below.

These are the main lessons to be drawn from the Advisory Opinion of 8 July 1996.

The Double Obligation: to Negotiate and to Bring to Conclusion

I **The grounds (customary and conventional) for the obligation to negotiate in good faith**

A The primary and powerful grounds for the obligation to negotiate in good faith are found in the United Nations Charter, which imposes on all member states a general obligation of disarmament, without prejudice to the right of legitimate self-defence. The Charter makes disarmament a means of assuring collective security. The obligation at issue here concerns the states party to the NPT. But it can be said that this obligation in fact commits the entire international community insofar as resolutions of the United Nations General Assembly containing that obligation have on several occasions been adopted unanimously.

B Four decades ago international law articulated a conventional obligation to negotiate in good faith toward complete nuclear disarmament. Article VI of the 1968 Non-Proliferation Treaty mandates that obligation, but this stipulation merely crystallizes, that is to say codifies, what certainly already existed as a *customary obligation,* one whose constituent elements began to take shape starting in the earliest months of existence of the United Nations Organization. Well before 1968, actually, the path to this mandate was carefully paved by several expressions of the conviction in the international community of the necessity for nuclear disarmament. In 1946 already, the very first resolution adopted by the General Assembly of the United Nations provided for the creation of a commission, one mandate of which was to present proposals with a view, *inter alia,* to 'the elimination from national armaments of atomic weapons and all other major weapons adaptable to mass destruction'.[8]

C The question of disarmament, which by the terms of Article 11 of the United Nations Charter enters into the field of competence of the General Assembly, has never since that time ceased to interest that organ. In a great number of its resolutions, the General Assembly has effectively reiterated the necessity for nuclear disarmament, as in 1954 when it determined

> that a further effort should be made to reach agreement on comprehensive and co-ordinated proposals to be embodied in a draft international disarmament convention providing for: ... b) The total prohibition of the use and manufacture of nuclear weapons and weapons of mass destruction of every type, together with the conversion of existing stocks of nuclear weapons for peaceful purposes.[9]

D In 1965, the General Assembly called for the conclusion of a treaty intended to prevent the proliferation of nuclear weapons, and which 'should be a step toward the realization of general and complete disarmament and, more particularly, nuclear disarmament'.[10]

In a following resolution, the General Assembly reaffirmed 'the paramount importance of disarmament for the contemporary world and the urgent need for the achievement of this goal', as well as the imperative to 'exert further efforts towards reaching agreement on general and complete disarmament...'[11]

E The same conviction was also expressed outside the framework of the United Nations. Thus in 1963, three nuclear powers proclaimed

> as their principal aim the speediest possible achievement of an agreement on general and complete disarmament under strict international control in accordance with the objectives of the United Nations which would put an end to the armaments race and eliminate the incentive to the production and testing of all kinds of weapons, including nuclear weapons.[12]

F Not until 1968 was that determination enshrined in the operative portion of a treaty, in which today participation is nearly universal. Article VI of the Treaty on Non-Proliferation of Nuclear Weapons[13] in fact provides that

> Each of the Parties to the Treaty undertakes to pursue negotiations in good faith on effective measures relating to cessation of the nuclear arms race at an early date and to nuclear disarmament, and on a Treaty on general and complete disarmament under strict and effective international control.[14]

G   As was solemnly declared by the states possessing nuclear weapons,

> the non-proliferation of nuclear weapons is not an end in itself but, rather, a means of achieving general and complete disarmament at a later stage.[15]

Their commitment to good-faith negotiation on general and complete disarmament, including nuclear disarmament, was subsequently confirmed on several occasions, as for instance in the Treaty of 11 February 1971[16] forbidding the emplacement of nuclear weapons or other weapons of mass destruction on 'the Seabed and the Ocean Floor and in the Subsoil Thereof', and also in the Treaty on the Limitation of Anti-Ballistic Missile Systems signed on 26 May 1972.[17]

H   The obligation outlined in Article VI of the NPT is to be analysed as a *pactum de negociando*,[18] but one of a particular type—this for reasons both intrinsic and extrinsic. In fact, both by its wording and by its nature as conventional counterpart to another obligation, the obligation to negotiate in good faith stipulated here is shown to be a true international obligation requiring its subjects to adopt a specifically determined conduct in the sense intended by the International Law Commission.

I   The obligation to negotiate nuclear disarmament in good faith is also *specific in its purpose* insofar as it concerns a matter (nuclear disarmament) that concerns, on one hand, the vital interests of a handful of states possessing a nuclear strike force and, on the other, the no less fundamental interests of humankind as a whole. The extreme importance of the stakes for humankind in the issue of nuclear disarmament therefore requires the utmost rigour in assessing the protagonists' conduct regarding the obligation to negotiate such a disarmament in good faith.

J   It is again worthwhile to point out that while, *de facto,* the states which are party to the negotiations on nuclear disarmament all belong to the narrow circle of states that possess nuclear weapons, all the states signatory to the NPT are *de jure* considered to be party to these negotiations.[19] In consequence, any state that is party to the Treaty has the right to demand that the negotiations be conducted in good faith, and thus has the right to invoke, should it occur, any failure of the obligation laid out by Article VI.

K   Though not explicitly and specifically forbidden by international law, nuclear weapons are nonetheless, as we have shown, weapons whose effects are clearly contrary to certain prescriptions of that *corpus juris* of certain rules of humanitarian law. Thus the direct prohibition of the use of nuclear weapons as such lies in a kind of legal grey area: indeed, that interdiction, practically speaking, no longer arises from the domain of *lex ferenda*, but does not yet emerge completely from that of *lex lata*. In the end, international law, and with it the stability of the international order which it is tasked to govern, can only suffer from that uncertainty over the legal status of so fearsome a weapon. It is therefore necessary to put an end to this regrettable legal vagueness, and the complete nuclear disarmament so long promised seems the best way to achieve this result.

L   **In these circumstances, then, we see the paramount importance of Article VI's mandated obligation to negotiate a nuclear disarmament in good faith.** In fact, the legal meaning of that obligation exceeds by far that of a mere obligation of conduct whose content was defined by international jurisprudence in connection with the obligation to negotiate generally; the obligation at issue here is to achieve a particular result. The obligation articulated by Article VI of the NPT is an obligation to achieve a precise result (nuclear disarmament) by adopting a specifically prescribed conduct, the pursuit in good faith of negotiations toward that end.

2   The obligation to negotiate nuclear disarmament in good faith: an obligation to adopt a prescribed conduct

International judges and arbitrators were very early called upon to define the legal meaning of an obligation to negotiate. Thus in the arbitral decision rendered on 4 March 1925 in the *Tacna-Arica (Chile/Peru) Case*, a case in which an agreement was to be negotiated to hold a plebiscite as prescribed by the 1883 Treaty of Ancona, the arbitrator declared that the negotiations were to be conducted in good faith by the parties.[20] He added that in the case before him, the obligation to negotiate was not violated by a party merely because it refused an agreement whose terms it did not judge acceptable; such a finding, he said, would also require a demonstration that the party was trying to prevent the conclusion of any reasonable agreement aimed at organizing the plebiscite.[21]

In the decision of 16 November 1957 in the case of *Lac Lanoux,* the arbitral tribunal recognized the variety of undertakings by states with respect to negotiation, and their scope, even as it ruled that

> the reality of the obligations thus undertaken is incontestable and sanctions can be applied in the event, for example, of an unjustified breaking off of the discussions, abnormal delays, disregard of the agreed procedures, systematic refusals to take into consideration adverse proposals or interests, and, more generally, in cases of violation of the rules of good faith.[22]

The tribunal also gave some general indications as to the conditions that must surround a negotiation, noting that in order for it

> to occur in a favourable climate, the Parties must consent to suspend, for the period of the negotiation, the full exercise of their rights.[23]

In its ruling of 20 February 1969 in the *North Sea Continental Shelf* case, the International Court of Justice did somewhat specify these conditions; it said that the parties

> are under an obligation to enter into negotiations with a view to arriving at an agreement, and not merely to go through a formal process of negotiation as a sort of prior condition for the automatic application of a certain method of delimitation in the absence of agreement; they are under an obligation so to conduct themselves that the negotiations are meaningful, which will not be the case when either of them insists upon its own position without contemplating any modification of it.[24]

Following the Court, the Arbitral Tribunal of the Agreement on German External Debts also clarified the meaning of the obligation to negotiate. In its judgement rendered on 26 February 1972, the Tribunal said that

> both sides would make an effort, in good faith, to bring about a mutually satisfactory solution by way of a compromise, even if that

meant the relinquishment of strongly held positions earlier taken...
Though ... an agreement to negotiate does not necessarily imply an
obligation to reach an agreement, it does imply that serious efforts
toward that end will be made.[25]

In the operative part of its unanimous decision the Tribunal defined the
obligation for parties to engage in negotiations as a commitment 'to confer
with a view to reaching an agreement', and, here echoing the Court, it
specifically stated that these negotiations

shall be meaningful and not merely consist of a formal process of
negotiations. Meaningful negotiations cannot be conducted if either
party insists upon its own position without contemplating any modification of it.[26]

This rapid overview of the international jurisprudence shows us that judges
and the arbitrators have seen in the obligations to negotiate in good faith
submitted to their scrutiny an obligation with a relatively flexible content.
Generally speaking, the obligation to negotiate in fact presents itself as an
obligation prescribing to the interested states the adoption of a certain
conduct in the course of negotiation but not commanding them to reach
a determined result, for instance, bringing to conclusion the agreement
which was the purpose of the negotiation.[27]

Referring back to Article VI of the NPT, such an obligation of conduct
requires parties to that instrument to *give meaning to* the negotiations
on nuclear disarmament; to *reach a mutually satisfactory compromise*,
not insisting on their own position without envisaging any modification
of it; to *make serious efforts* with the goal of *reaching an agreement*.

The circumstances mentioned in the arbitral decision in the *Lac
Lanoux* case could also serve as useful indicators for the good-faith conduct of negotiations in this area. Invoking a single one of these circumstances should suffice to engage the responsibility of one or several
states party to the NPT for failure to fulfil the obligation to negotiate in
good faith. Without denying the great technicality and complexity of the
negotiations in process, the impression that emerges is that these negotiations are not progressing. There is even reason to fear that they are
regressing. A large majority of the states party to the NPT could also
complain of systematic refusals to take account of their proposals or
their interests.

The criteria drawn from international jurisprudence could thus provide yardsticks for assessing the reality of the activation of the obligation of good-faith negotiation prescribed by Article VI of the NPT for, *prima facie,* that obligation can at a minimum, be analysed as an obligation of conduct. But the legal effects of the Article VI obligation do not end there. As a more careful examination of that conventional obligation will show, the Article VI obligation actually has a legal scope much greater than a mere obligation of conduct. As the arbitral panel quite properly indicated in the *Lac Lanoux* case, the scope of the commitments undertaken by states on the occasion of a *pactum negociando*

> varies according to the way they are defined and according to the procedures intended for their execution.[28]

3 The obligation to negotiate nuclear disarmament in good faith: an obligation to adopt a certain conduct to achieve a certain result

While it is true that the obligation to negotiate in good faith has a varying legal scope depending on circumstances, it is useful here to look more closely at the wording of the obligation set out in Article VI of the NPT as well as at the general setting into which it is inserted.

When issues of border delimitation or debt recovery are involved the obligation of good-faith negotiation aims at levelling existing differences, at bringing about a system acceptable to the parties; it takes on a quite particular aspect when it concerns nuclear disarmament. In fact, here it has all the appearance of an obligation to negotiate in order to achieve a very precise result: *nuclear disarmament.* The objective of the negotiation is denuclearization, total nuclear disarmament of the states that are party to the negotiation.

Nuclear disarmament is an objective on which a consensus has existed since 1945, as attested by the number and quality of legal instruments expressing the conviction of the international community as to the importance and necessity of general and complete disarmament, including in the nuclear realm. In itself, this objective can certainly be subject to compromise, but as a series of steps leading toward the final goal; in particular, the focus of negotiations is the schedule to follow for bringing to life the objective which is the purpose of the negotiation.

The obligation to negotiate in good faith for nuclear disarmament can thus be analysed both as a obligation to reach a result and as a veritable obligation of conduct, in the sense of Article 20 in the draft articles on the international responsibility of states elaborated by the International Law Commission. In the terms of the commentary on that provision, what distinguishes obligations termed 'of conduct' or 'of means' from obligations 'of result' is not that the former

> do not have a particular object or result, but that their object or result must be achieved through action, conduct or means 'specifically determined' by the international obligation itself, which is not true of international obligations 'of result'. This is the essential distinguishing criterion for characterizing an international obligation as an obligation 'of conduct' or 'of means'. It is not sufficient, for example, for an obligation to provide, as does Article 33 of the Charter of the United Nations, that States shall settle their international disputes by 'peaceful means', for it to be characterized forthwith as an obligation 'of conduct' or 'of means'. In practice, as the same Article indicates, States remain free to choose the 'peaceful means' which they consider most appropriate for settling the dispute between them.[29]

Also, in substance, in the spirit of the NPT negotiators, Article VI, which lays out the obligation to negotiate nuclear disarmament in good faith, was clearly conceived as the necessary counterpart to the commitment by the non-nuclear states not to manufacture or acquire nuclear weapons; it is without a doubt one of the essential elements of the 'acceptable equilibrium of mutual responsibilities and obligations between nuclear powers and non-nuclear powers' which, according to the General Assembly, was to be established by the Nuclear Non-Proliferation Treaty which it called for in 1965. In 1995, at the time of the fifth Conference of Parties, which decided the extension of the NPT for an indefinite duration, the reciprocal nature of the said obligations was vigorously reaffirmed.[30] Article VI should for this reason be considered an essential provision of the NPT, the breach of which could be considered 'material' in terms of Article 60 of the Vienna Convention on the Law of Treaties[31] and could entail the legal consequences thereto attached.[32]

The states party to the NPT and especially the nuclear states have the obligation to execute in good faith their obligation to negotiate nuclear disarmament in good faith. The good-faith conduct of the negotiations by the nuclear states mandates, among other things, that they not betray the legitimate trust which the non-nuclear states could reasonably have invested in the hope that the promised negotiations would lead swiftly to an agreement on nuclear disarmament. But the progress made so far by states possessing nuclear weapons in commencing good-faith negotiations toward nuclear disarmament do not seem to reach the level of expectations of the countries without such weapons.

On the occasions of the Conferences of Parties organized every five years since the Treaty entered into force, the non-nuclear states have in fact regularly called attention to the absence of implementation of the obligation of good-faith negotiation called for by Article VI of the Treaty. The 1990 Conference of the Parties is symptomatic in this regard insofar as, in the absence of agreement, no final declaration could be adopted, essentially because of the fact that the non-aligned states felt that the nuclear powers were making inadequate efforts toward disarmament.

In its Resolution 984 (1995) of 11 April 1995, the Security Council made a point of '[r]eaffirming the need for all States Party to the Treaty on the Non-Proliferation of Nuclear Weapons to comply fully with all their obligations,' and urged

> all States, as provided for in Article VI of the Treaty on Non-Proliferation of Nuclear Weapons, to pursue negotiation in good faith on effective measures relating to nuclear disarmament and on a treaty on general and complete disarmament under strict and effective international control which remains a universal objective.

The importance attached to the respect for reciprocal obligations stipulated in the NPT had been emphasized some days earlier by the United States government as follows:

> It is important that all Parties to the Treaty on the Non-Proliferation of Nuclear Weapons fulfil their obligations under the treaty. In that regard, consistent with generally recognized principles of international law, Parties to the Treaty on the Non-Proliferation of Nuclear Weapons must be in compliance with these undertakings in order to be eligible for any benefits of adherence to this treaty.[33]

Lastly, in adopting Decision 2 in conjunction with the Treaty's indefinite extension, the Conference of Parties to the Non-Proliferation Treaty, charged with reviewing the Treaty and the question of its extension, which was held from 17 April to 12 May 1995, declared *inter alia* that

> 3   Nuclear disarmament is substantially facilitated by the easing of international tension and the strengthening of trust between

States which have prevailed following the end of the cold war. The undertakings with regard to nuclear disarmament as set out in the Treaty on the Non-Proliferation of Nuclear Weapons should thus be fulfilled with determination. In this regard, the nuclear-weapon States reaffirm their commitment, as stated in Article VI, to pursue in good faith negotiations on effective measures relating to nuclear disarmament.

4   The achievement of the following measures is important in the full realization and effective implementation of article VI, including the programme of action as reflected below:

A   The completion by the Conference on Disarmament of the negotiations on a universal and internationally and effectively verifiable Comprehensive Nuclear-Test-Ban Treaty no later than 1996. Pending the entry into force of a Comprehensive Test-Ban Treaty, the nuclear-weapon States should exercise utmost restraint;

B   The immediate commencement and early conclusion of negotiations on a non-discriminatory and universally applicable convention banning the production of fissile material for nuclear weapons or other nuclear explosive devices, in accordance with the statement of the Special Coordinator of the Conference on Disarmament and the mandate contained therein;

C   The determined pursuit by the nuclear-weapon States of systematic and progressive efforts to reduce nuclear weapons globally, with the ultimate goals of eliminating those weapons, and by all States of general and complete disarmament under strict and effective international control.[34]

Significance of the Addition of 'Good Faith' to Article VI of the NPT

1   General significance of an addition of this kind in any treaty

'Good faith,' writes Robert Kolb, a specialist in this matter,[35] 'constitutes this chemical addition which makes it possible to go from a formal mechanical principle to a concrete, material principle which takes the measure of what is to be executed … or to be done.'

Kolb distinguishes 'good faith' in the subjective or psychological sense from that in the semi-objective sense and finally from that in the objective sense, as a general principle of law. And he sees this last one from different aspects: Under its objective side it protects the legitimate confidence which a certain behaviour has engendered in another person, whatever the real or intelligible intention of its author; under its negative side it protects certain aims anchored in the collective interest against excessive individualistic pretensions (the theory of abusive law); and finally, in a subordinate manner, good faith hinders a subject from profiting from unfair behaviour which acts as a brake on reciprocity and equality.[36]

A   **Good faith, the essential vector of law**

Good faith is a fundamental principle of international law, without which all international law would collapse. Georg Schwarzenberg rightly calls it

> a fundamental principle which can be eradicated from international law at the price of the destruction of international law itself.[37]

Christian Tomashat, however, believes that good faith is an axiom and, as such, has an empirically unverifiable character:

> It stands to reason that good faith … cannot be observed by empirical methods. As an ever-present element of any legal system, it constitutes a rationalization of a certain way of correct conduct required of everyone.[38]

Oscar Schachter has this to say:

> Whether called legal or political, [the] meaning [of good faith] is essentially the same. A significant legal consequence of the 'good faith' principle is that a party which committed itself in good faith to a course of conduct or to recognition of a legal situation would be stopped from acting inconsistently with its commitment or position when other parties have reasonably relied on it.[39]

Oscar Schachter is speaking here of the unilateral undertaking of the state. His point of view is very significant, for if a unilateral act gives rise to a legal effect in all good faith, *a fortiori* a treaty instrument must bind every contracting state. This is the well-known jurisprudence of the International Court of Justice in the *Nuclear Test Case* of 1974 and the case *Military and Para-Military Activities in and against Nicaragua*.[40]

The adage 'Pacta sunt servanda', cited in this abbreviated form, really reads in its integral version 'Pacta sunt servanda bona fide'. Agreements must be respected in good faith.

In the wording of Article 26 of the Vienna Convention, 'Every treaty in force is binding upon the parties to it and must be performed by them in good faith.' Article 31 of the same Convention provides, in its first paragraph, 'A treaty shall be interpreted in good faith ...' This is the codification of an international law principle so fundamental that it counts among the basic principles mentioned in certain legal instruments such as the *Declaration on Friendly Relations* of 24 October 1970[41] or the *Final Act of the Helsinki Conference* of 1 August 1975.[42]

Nor has the International Court of Justice failed to recall it in the following terms

> One of the basic principles governing the creation and perform-ance of legal obligations, whatever their source, is the principle of good faith.[43]

The *Dictionnaire Salmon* specifies that good faith concerns

> the behaviour which the parties are legally obliged to observe in the execution and interpretation of their rights and obligations, whatever their source, based on a general principle of law the obligatory force of which rests on a constant practice and juris-prudence.[44]

In relations between states, good faith occupies exceptional impor-tance. It is the guarantor of international stability, because it allows state A to foresee the behaviour of its partner, state B, and thus makes it possible for the former to align its behaviour with that of the latter. There is a 'standard' of good faith. It is a concept which evolves with changes in international life. It is this standard that determines the obligation and gives it its quality and its dimensions. Resisting proof, good faith is presumed and its opposite, bad faith, is its foil. It excludes fraud, ruses, the intention to hurt, shameful motives, dissimulation, malice and in general every kind of trickery.

B Good faith, the generator of legitimate expectations

Paul Reuter has said

> [A state] created a certain expectation in its partners, and ... it was the non-fulfilment of that expectation that was incompatible with good faith.[45]

The essential characteristic of good faith is that it has legal effects resulting from a legitimate expectation nourished by the contracting state. In international relations, states which are supposed to act in good faith are obliged to take into account, in their behaviour, their respective legitimate expectations. Each of them has with respect to the others a right, created by good faith, not to be deceived in these expectations. Good faith thus gives birth to rights.

One can see straight away that good faith and confidence have a close relationship. Good faith corresponds and responds to legitimate confidence.

C Good faith in the light of trust

Trust plays an important part in all types of relations, between persons as well as between states. Without trust, international society would be a jungle or chaos. Individuals, states and even animals submit themselves to a social order based above all on the exclusion of deceitful behaviour.

In its commentary on the draft of article 26 (then article 23), the International Law Commission has also recalled that good faith is a legal principle which plays an integral part in the rule 'Pacta sunt servanda' and as a result of which an obligation based on a treaty undertaking must not be evaded by a strictly literal interpretation of its clauses.[46]

2 The specific significance of this addition to the NPT

In the particular context of the NPT, one can vigorously affirm that the principle of good faith illuminates the entirety of the negotiations called for by Article VI. In becoming parties to the NPT, all states have agreed to execute in good faith their obligation to pursue in good faith negotiations concerning general and complete disarmament. This means that these states must display good-faith behaviour both in the conduct of the negotiations and while the negotiations last. They must therefore abstain from performing any act which would deprive the treaty on general and complete disarmament of its object and its aim. It is obvious that any act bolstering its nuclear arsenal by a state party to the NPT would be such an act.

Let us examine these aspects more closely.

In order to have an idea of the enrichment which good faith brings to the disarmament negotiations, let us indicate hereafter what kind of conduct this good faith implies and requires:

A Significance of a negotiation qualified as 'in good faith'

A The negotiations must be conducted with good faith as properly to be understood; sustained upkeep of the negotiation over a period appropriate to the circumstances; awareness of the interests of the other party; and a persevering quest for an acceptable compromise.'[47]

B The negotiations to be conducted ... must be guided by the following principles:

- They shall be meaningful and not merely consist of a formal process of negotiations. Meaningful negotiations cannot be conducted if either party insists upon its own position without contemplating any modification of it.

- Both parties are under an obligation to act in such a way that the principles of the Agreement are applied in order to achieve a satisfactory and equitable result.[48]

C The addition of 'good faith' to the negotiation called for by Article VI is in no way a simple redundancy. According to the World Court, its mention, made with a view to a result as capital as nuclear disarmament, confers upon the said negotiation an exceptional importance given the global stakes involved:

The obligation expressed in Article VI of the Treaty on

the Non-Proliferation of Nuclear Weapons includes its fulfilment in accordance with the basic principle of good faith ... The importance of fulfilling the obligation expressed in Article VI ... was also reaffirmed in the final document of the Review and Extension Conference of the parties to the Treaty on the Non-Proliferation of Nuclear Weapons, held from 17 April to 12 May 1995. In the view of the Court, it remains without any doubt an objective of vital importance to the whole international community today.[49]

B Interpretation, in the light of good faith, of the NPT and of all specialized disarmament treaties already concluded

In a domain as vital and also as delicate as progressive nuclear disarmament, the stakes of which are capital, each state party, which is sovereign, understands that it is not bound beyond what it has really agreed to. The principle 'Pacta sunt servanda' must be entirely accepted, but without trampling on the sovereignty of the state party. The Vienna Convention of 1969 on the Law of Treaties includes an essential rule, that of the double respect for the treaty and for the sovereignty of the state party, thanks to a 'good-faith interpretation' of the said treaty, formulated in its article 31, paragraph 1: priority of and submission to the text, but without neglecting the intention of the parties.

Tamerlaine, having negotiated the surrender of a town and having promised to shed no more blood, decided in effect to spill not another drop of blood of the soldiers of the town's garrison, by burying them alive. Good faith prohibits clinging to the meaning of a phrase in order to escape that of the parties.

C Obligation to preserve the object and purpose of the NPT and to respect its integrity

Good faith prohibits every act, behaviour, declaration, initiative tending to deprive the NPT of its object and purpose. It forbids every measure whose effect is to injure the essence of the Treaty. Good-faith behaviour takes the form of a series of obligations 'not to do' or obligations of 'preservation', such as:

A The obligation to refrain from acts incompatible with the object and purpose of the NPT: prohibition to disrupt the general scheme of the NPT; proscription of every initiative the effect of which would be to render impossible the conclusion of the contemplated disarmament treaty;

B The obligation to refrain from enacting, at the national level, laws and rules incompatible with the purpose of the treaty;

C The obligation to refrain from concluding an agreement manifestly incompatible with the purpose of the treaty;

D The obligation to respect the integrity of the treaty; a specialist on the question of good faith in international law has rightly written the following on this subject: 'a treaty must be considered executory in all its provisions, whether they are favourable or unfavourable to the contracting party. Good faith prohibits selectivity according to the interests of the moment.[50]

This rule is perfectly embedded in the doctrine. One could, however, ask whether, when dealing with a question as crucial as nuclear disarmament, it would not be suitable to be more flexible and to practise, with discernment, a certain selectivity in the matters to be resolved, if it appears that such an approach could serve to bring the parties closer to the ultimate purpose of the NPT.

One example of conduct apt to safeguard the object and purpose of the treaty could be the SALT II agreements. The Soviet invasion of Afghanistan occurred at the very moment when the Senate of the United States was getting ready to review these agreements. Fearing that this unfortunate situation might compromise the ratification of SALT II, President Carter asked the Senate to postpone its review until later. And the Department of State published on 4 January 1980 the following declaration, by which the Americans and the Soviets intended to see to the preservation of the object and purpose of the treaty:

> The United States and the Soviet Union share the view that under international law a State should refrain from taking action which could defeat the object and the purpose of a treaty it has signed subject to ratification.

D Obligation to take all positive measures for the realization of the NPT

Good faith requires each state party to take, individually and in concert with every other state, whether or not party to the NPT, all positive measures likely to bring the international community closer to the purpose of the NPT, nuclear disarmament. It imposes on all states parties a general and permanent obligation to act positively, i.e. in a sense which serves the correct fulfilment of the NPT.

With this mention in a treaty concerning a domain as crucial as that of global nuclear disarmament, good faith acquires a more imperative connotation than ever before, since its task thus becomes to protect the fundamental values of the entire international community and to reinforce the international public order.

Robert Kolb writes that the negotiations must take place with a **minimum of** '*fair dealing*'. The International Law Commission has stated:

> The Commission's choice ... had not wished to deprive States of their freedom of action. During negotiations each of the parties expected a minimum of fair dealing on the part of the other. A State remained free to break off negotiations; only acts of bad faith were excluded.[51]

And Robert Kolb adds:

> The interpretation of what good faith requires in this matter must reflect this: it will retain only the irreducible minimum which, according to the nature, the subjects and the object of the negotiation, emerges as the indispensable condition for its reasonable progress.[52]

E General duty to cooperate in good faith

Good faith implies a general obligation of cooperation among states party to the NPT. In the context of the eradication of nuclear weapons, good faith confers upon this duty to cooperate a particular depth and makes it all the more imperative. The states parties must necessarily maintain an appropriate level of consultation in order to cooperate in the solution of the considerable difficulties which will inevitably be encountered in the gigantic endeavour of disarmament.

Virally and Böckstiegel said this in a wholly different context, but it is even more valid for disarmament:

> the parties ... have to work in good faith to resolve any difficulty which may arise in implementing the agreements which bind them. As it was already stressed, such an obligation is a general principle of international law, codified in the Vienna Convention and applicable to every treaty.[53]

The case *Interpretation of the Agreement on 25 March 1951 between the World Health Organization and Egypt* gives an interesting overview of the content of the obligation to cooperate. The duty to cooperate in good faith prescribes

A that every unilateral action be avoided: The World Health Organization and Egypt must consult with each other in good faith in order to arrive at agreement over the modalities of transfer;[54]

B that every precipitous action is impossible: the party which desires transfer must give to the other reasonable notice according to the circumstances.[55]

F General obligation of information and communication

Within the framework of the general obligation to cooperate there exists an obligation to inform that takes on a character of necessity all the more imperative as it is difficult for a state party, acting in good faith, to know perfectly the concerns of another state party. Questions of national defence are in effect marked by the seal of state secrets. This obligation of information naturally does not aim to unveil defence secrets and to profit from doing so in relation to another state party, which would be contrary to good faith.

The obligation to inform arises each time it touches on the correct execution of the NPT. The parties must fairly communicate to each other documents required for an understanding of the matters at issue, or necessary for an understanding of the interests of the other parties.

In certain hypotheses, the silence of a state party looks like a violation of good faith, whenever the circumstances are such that the silence is incompatible with the necessary honesty established between the parties.

G   Obligation to compromise

The NPT is a *'pactum de negociando'*. But,

> [A] *pactum de negociando* is also not without legal consequences. It means that both sides would make an effort, in good faith, to bring about a mutually satisfactory solution by way of a compromise, even if that meant the relinquishment of strongly held positions earlier taken. It implies a willingness ... to meet the other side part way.[56]

H   Prohibition of abuse of process

Abuse of process is generally based on unacceptable conduct. It becomes particularly serious when it manifests itself in an area as crucial as nuclear disarmament. Good faith prohibits abuse of process in all its manifestations such as fraud or deceit. Negotiations intended to derive advantage in any manner from the good faith of others constitute bad faith.

But there is the very difficult and delicate problem of proof.

I   Unjustified termination of good-faith negotiations

The time of negotiation is variable and in the case of nuclear disarmament it can be very long, taking into account the extreme complexity of the problems to be resolved and the exceptional importance of what is at stake. The world knows that negotiations in this field have already lasted for decades although we cannot say that we are on the verge of disarmament.

After the Review Conference of 2005 the world observed an alarming halt in the negotiations. One thing is certain: a manifestly unjustified breaking off of negotiations is radically incompatible with good faith.

J   Building Confidence

I must here ask a little indulgence and understanding for venturing into a complex realm where I lack expertise. The following remarks on the theme of 'confidence-building' will seem excessively simplistic and elementary. I offer them merely by way of indication, because I find it difficult to end this analysis on the obligation to eradicate nuclear weapons without mentioning the overriding factor that is 'confidence-building', which remains the powerful engine of nuclear disarmament.

This said, I know that because of their overly simplified nature, these notes will bring nothing to the great specialists on this question. Such experts will doubtless elevate the discussion on the theme to the appropriate level.

First elementary law: Opacity breeds opacity

In a realm so heavily determinative for the security of each state, the problem of 'confidence-building' assumes a major importance that must be stressed.

Let us approach these complex matters with a few simple ideas. It is clear that the nuclear arms policies of states are among those that, by nature and by definition, require secrecy. The opacity of activities connected to nuclear weapons is an essential element of the nuclear age.

If a state A has reason 'objective or subjective, real or supposed' to think that state B is engaged in experiments, research, testing, or a quantitative or qualitative increase in its weaponry, especially when nuclear materials are involved, it is unimaginable that we would reasonably expect state A to harbour much confidence about state B. It is a simple law that states, 'opacity provokes opacity in return'; it generates it and feeds it. Opacity and secrecy inevitably turn contagious. State A will seek to establish imperiously the same degree of opacity in its activities and behaviour, and go even farther than state B in that direction.

Second elementary law: Opacity breeds arms racing

Arms racing is the obvious manifestation of the law of opacity, feeding on the fear of the Other. States tend constantly toward 'ever more and ever better', drawing them into exhausting and costly escalation.

Another manifestation of opacity consists of the tendency of the state to hide events like nuclear accidents, accidental irradiations of troops, or any event that could expose its activities in the handling of nuclear weapons.

Third elementary law: In the end, transparency generates transparency

Through repeated resolutions, the United Nations General Assembly has regularly called on states for 'Transparency in Armaments' and encouraged states to engage in 'Transparency Talks' to arrive at substantial 'Multilaterally Agreed Transparency Measures'. The doctrine of the United Nations is that such transparency contributes significantly to building and reinforcing confidence and security among states.

The opposite of opacity in nuclear activities (transparency and openness) is likely, if the terrain is favourable to a 'break in the vicious circle of opacity', to bring about similar behaviour by other states. Of course, this does not have the rigour and the automatic nature of a law; transparency by one party can be met by concealment by the other. But this negative behaviour only pays off over the short term, for concealment by the one will snuff out transparency in the other as soon as the latter notices the negative attitude of his partner. There is reason to think that, insofar as it exists, transparency can end by generating a similar behaviour.

This idea does not spring from some irresponsible, sweet naiveté. But it is clear that transparency cannot 'prosper' unless it is fed by converging wills. In other words, transparency cannot survive and grow strong except in conformity with a basic and highly comprehensible law of strict reciprocity.

Fourth elementary law: The tyranny of the 'psychological factor'

As an underlying aspect of 'confidence building', it must not be denied that there exists what I would call a 'complex game of mirrors' fed by a series of images that states send back and forth about their respective armament situations, real or presumed. These images, set up face to face, produce a panorama in which the real and the virtual change at the whim of each state's perceptions of the other, but the psychological factor is always present. The 'complex game of mirrors' is actually fed mainly by reflexes of suspicion, of difficulty with trusting, of permanent reaction against a credulity judged to be too dangerous. Each state develops fears and anxious presumptions about the arms policy of the Other.

So the 'psychological factor' is an element to be treated with very special attention. It is not enough to demand the eradication of nuclear weapons with great efforts of meetings and conferences. Precious and influential, a powerful wave of international public opinion in favour of the abolition of nuclear weapons certainly makes for a positive effect on the mind. But that does not authorize disregard for the importance of the 'psychological factor' that drives a state's leaders and makes abolition directly dependent on the state's ability to overcome its legitimate anxieties.

It is this area too that calls for action, to help a state surmount its fears, action to be coupled with public pressure and the whole arsenal of persuasion.

For nuclear weapons are not weapons of power; they are and they remain weapons of fear above all. Fear of the Other. Fear of being wiped out, for possibly underestimating a mortal danger.

Therefore, it is crucial to reduce subjectivity.

Fifth elementary law: Reduce subjectivity to increase objectivity

To this end, the international community is working to create 'confidence-building measures' (CBMs). As we know, the notion of 'confidence and security-building measures' was broached in 1984–1986 at the Stockholm Conference. It has been developed more deeply over time by the OSCE. CBMs are generally defined as being

> tools that adversarial States can use to reduce tensions and avert the possibility of military conflict.

More thoroughly stated:

> the primary goal of confidence-building measures is to reduce the risk of arms conflict by building trust and reducing misperceptions and miscalculations in international relations, thereby contributing to international peace and security.[57]

These measures are neither substitutes nor preconditions for effective disarmament measures. Their purpose is to create conditions that favour progress toward disarmament.

It is useful to draw attention to various regional experiences with CBMs. The efforts made in the framework of the OSCE are interesting in this regard, for

The system of confidence- and security-building measures in OSCE now constitutes a stable and effective foundation for a culture of cooperation, transparency, and predictability as regards military-political matters for the 55 States Members of the Organization.[58]

Sixth elementary law: Support verification

The measures for reinforcing 'confidence-building' are very numerous, and they depend on circumstances; it would be impossible to list them all. But the exchange of information and communications between states plays a major role. And it is in this area that the ability to verify the truth of reported information can play a role. The more that communications can be confirmed by appropriate verification techniques, the more subjectivity will regress, to the benefit of objectivity.

Obviously, monitoring remains the most difficult problem to resolve. All of human imagination, all of the results drawn from the machine, have never truly sufficed. Almost every method has been tried, from exterior oversight through seismic, hydro-acoustic, or ultra-sound instrumentation, to unannounced on-site inspections, and notably including mutually accepted espionage, from space or through the work of international institutions like the IAEA, which has been enlisted notably to detect the diversion of civilian technologies to military purposes.

Disarmament generally occurs in stages, each of them meticulously monitored. A state is unwilling to move on to a next stage unless it is fully satisfied that its partner's preceding stage has been properly monitored. This system is seen mainly in agreements for the definitive destruction of a some particular weapon and the machines that produced it.

The panorama of various experiments in disarmament certainly shows the range of verification possibilities that states have conventionally accepted. For instance, in the framework of the 1959 Washington Treaty on the Antarctic, states have an absolute obligation to 'denounce' any state, whether or not party to the Treaty, that fails to respect the denuclearization and demilitarization of that region. Another example is the London Club (Nuclear Suppliers Group) created in 1975, which brings together all the exporters of technologies considered sensitive, for better cooperation among themselves and better control of the final destination of their products. The Helsinki Treaty of 24 March 1992, called the 'Open Skies'

Treaty, authorizes aerial overflight of states for purposes of verification. But clearly, such an option would in fact only be available to the large powers that have the sophisticated technologies to carry out such over-flights.

We may also remark that at the level of the IAEA, the main virtue of a diplomatic instrument known as the 'Additional Protocol', to which the nuclear powers seek ratification from states not having nuclear weapons, resides in the fact that this text sets out a very heavy and detailed arsenal of measures meant to obtain an exceptionally rigorous and thorough verification of a non-nuclear-weapon state's nuclear activities.

In this very sensitive area, we should also cite the 'transparency measures' listed in Article 7 of the Ottawa Convention of 4 December 1997 on the prohibition of anti-personnel mines. The member states must, when they have finished destroying these devices, not only send reports to the Secretary-General of the United Nations, but also cooperate with any on-site monitoring by 'fact-finding missions' carried out at the request of either the suspected state or the Assembly of States Party to the Convention.

A reading of some treaties shows states' great attachment to the problem, and the minute detail with which their plenipotentiaries have worked it out. For instance, the Comprehensive Nuclear-Test-Ban Treaty of 24 September 1996 contains an Article IV comprised of (and this is completely symptomatic) no fewer than 68 paragraphs devoted to monitoring and verification.

Yet it is clear that the need to nourish confidence by the exchange of information and communications contains its own limits. In a number of agreements there occurs a so-called 'confidentiality' clause, by which the parties commit not to make public the content of these exchanges. Thus: 'Each Party undertakes not to release to the public the information provided pursuant to the agreement except with the express consent of the Party that provided such information.'[59]

Seventh elementary law: The legal status of CBMs between necessary rigidity and desirable flexibility

The legal status of 'confidence-building measures' is generally rather imprecise. It is the product of two contradictory lines of force. On the one hand, state A must feel that the confidence-building measure chosen by state B is a reliable measure, binding on the state taking it, such that state A, concerned with trustworthiness, would like to see said measure given a legal status that is firm and thoroughly binding on state B. But on the other hand, the imprecision surrounding the legal status of the measure would have the advantage of offering the states greater flexibility, which might encourage them to consider and accept such a measure.

But everything depends on circumstances. If, according to some hypotheses, the CBMs have the nature of an international treaty, by definition binding on the parties, this can only come about through the express will of the states concerned.

In the framework of negotiation for some aspects of disarmament, it is rather absence of rigidity (flexibility) that seems to be sought. The legal status of written or oral communications or of proposals offered by a state in the course of negotiations is put in question. In such a case, as in others, good faith must serve as guide, and Judge Mosler is right to declare that 'the legal effect to be attributed to conduct exhibited during negotiations depends on the circumstances in which these actions take place.'[60]

Indeed, it is in order to protect confidentiality that the International Court of Justice has often ruled that the proposals a state may make in the course of negotiations cannot bind it definitively, especially when those negotiations have not come to a conclusion.[61]

As declared in the document presented by Greece for the European Union, and cited above,

> The building of confidence is a dynamic process, and a gradual step-by-step approach.[62]

The steps have different levels of importance. The most significant ones in nuclear disarmament have been made outside the United Nations. Today more than ever, it is important to attribute a more decisive role to the United Nations in the coherent, democratic conduct of an integrated process of nuclear disarmament, with a realistic and reasonable schedule. The need is clear for more effective and consistent involvement of the United Nations throughout the process, going beyond the simple labours of the sessions of the Disarmament Commission.

Postscript

As a post-script to my Geneva speech above, and for the use of all those in Scotland wishing to ensure full compliance with international humanitarian law, I would like to stress that the International Court of Justice in its Advisory Opinion of 8 July 1996, did not have at its disposal adequate elements of fact to permit concluding with certainty whether a specific nuclear weapon system would be contrary to the principles and rules of the law applicable in armed conflict. The Court was asked to rule on a general question of use and threat of use of nuclear weapons. If the Court had been asked to rule on the legality of a specific nuclear weapons system or doctrine the conclusion we arrived at might well have been much clearer.

I have been asked to give a personal opinion on the legality of a nuclear weapons system that deploys over 100 nuclear warheads with an approximate yield of 100 kt per warhead. Bearing in mind that warheads of this size constitute around eight times the explosive power of the bomb that flattened Hiroshima in 1945 and killed over 100,000 civilians, it follows that the use of even a single such warhead in *any* circumstance, whether a first or second use and whether intended to be targeted against civilian populations or military objectives, would inevitably violate the prohibitions on the infliction of unnecessary suffering and indiscriminate harm as well as the rule of proportionality including with respect to the environment. In my opinion, such a system deployed and ready for action would be unlawful.

In accordance with evidence heard by the Court, it is clear that an explosion caused by the detonation of just one 100 kt warhead would release powerful and prolonged ionising radiation, which could not be contained in space or time, and which would harmfully affect civilians as well as combatants, neutral as well as belligerent states, and future generations as well as people targeted in the present time. In view of these extraordinarily powerful characteristics and effects, any use of such a warhead would contravene international and humanitarian laws and precepts. In other words, even in an extreme circumstance of self-defence, in which the very survival of a State would be at stake, the use of a 100 kt nuclear warhead (regardless of whether it was targeted to land accurately on or above a military target) would always fail the tests of controllability, discrimination, civilian immunity, and neutral rights and would thus be unlawful.

In my opinion, any state that aids and abets another country, in the deployment and maintenance of nuclear warheads of 100 kt or comparable explosive power would also be acting unlawfully.

The modernisation, updating or renewal of such a nuclear weapon system would also be a material breach of NPT obligations, particularly the unequivocal undertaking by the nuclear-weapon states to 'accomplish the total elimination of their nuclear arsenals leading to nuclear disarmament' and the fundamental Article VI obligation to negotiate in good faith on cessation of the arms race and on nuclear disarmament, with the understanding that these negotiations must be pursued in good faith and brought to conclusion in a timely manner.

Recent Developments in the Illegality of Nuclear Weapons

DR JOHN BURROUGHS

A FEW DAYS AGO, in Berlin, I told Judge Weeramantry that my topic for this conference is *Recent Developments in the Illegality of Nuclear Weapons*. He commented that since nuclear weapons have always been illegal, I should think of my topic as *Recent Developments in **Communicating** the Illegality of Nuclear Weapons*.

Indeed, in its 1996 Advisory Opinion, the International Court of Justice (ICJ) was at pains to explain that the rules of international humanitarian law applying to nuclear weapons largely pre-date the nuclear age.

> PARA. 78
>
> humanitarian law, **at a very early stage**, prohibited certain types of weapons either because of their indiscriminate effect on combatants and civilians or because of the unnecessary suffering caused to combatants, that is to say, a harm greater than that unavoidable to achieve legitimate military objectives.' (Emphasis added.)

> PARA. 86
>
> nuclear weapons were invented after most of the principles and rules of humanitarian law applicable in armed conflict had already come into existence; the Conferences of 1949 and 1974–1977 left these weapons aside, and there is a qualitative as well as quantitative difference between nuclear weapons and all conventional arms. However, **it cannot be concluded from this that the established principles and rules of humanitarian law applicable in armed conflict did not apply to nuclear weapons. Such a conclusion would be incompatible with the intrinsically humanitarian character of the legal principles in question which permeates the entire law of armed conflict and applies to all forms of warfare and to all kinds of weapons, those of the past, those of the present and those of the**

future. In this respect it seems significant that the thesis that the rules of humanitarian law do not apply to the new weaponry, because of the newness of the latter, has not been advocated in the present proceedings. (Emphasis added.)

I do not think it is entirely a digression to observe that a clear implication of the ICJ's reasoning is that the US atomic bombings of Hiroshima and Nagasaki were unlawful.

But let me nonetheless review some of the developments in international law relating to nuclear weapons since the 1996 opinion.

1 US National Academy Of Sciences

I start not with a legal authority, but a scientific one, a body extremely knowledgeable about the effects of nuclear weapons and doctrines regarding their use. In a 1997 book, *The Future of US Nuclear Weapons Policy*, the Committee on International Security and Arms Control of the US National Academy of Sciences well summarized the implications of the ICJ's opinion. The Committee stated:

> [T]he ICJ unanimously agreed that the threat or use of nuclear weapons is strictly limited by generally accepted laws and humanitarian principles that restrict the use of force. Accordingly, any threat or use of nuclear weapons must be limited to, and necessary for, self defense; it must not be targeted at civilians, and be capable of distinguishing between civilian and military targets; and it must not cause unnecessary suffering to combatants, or harm greater than that unavoidable to achieve military objectives. **In the committee's view, the inherent destructiveness of nuclear weapons, combined with the unavoidable risk that even the most restricted use of such weapons would escalate to broader attacks, makes it extremely unlikely that any contemplated threat or use of nuclear weapons would meet these criteria.**[1]

2 International Criminal Court

Negotiations on the Rome Statute of the International Criminal Court were completed in 1998, and the Statute entered into force in 2002. The statute sets forth 'serious violations of the laws and customs applicable in international armed conflict, within the established framework of international law' (Art. 8(b)).

The substantive provisions of the Statute were negotiated on the basis that they would reflect the present state of law binding on all states. It thus stands as a consensus-based statement of presently binding law defining war crimes. The United Kingdom is also a party.

A **Discrimination:** Article 8(b)(i) forbids 'Intentionally directing attacks against the civilian population as such or against individual civilians not taking direct part in hostilities'.

The International Court of Justice identified as customary the following rule:

'States must never make civilians the object of attack and must consequently never use weapons that are incapable of distinguishing between civilian and military targets'. (para. 78)

In the view of the International Committee of the Red Cross (ICRC), the prohibition on attacks on civilians covers the use of indiscriminate weapons. The Red Cross pointed out: 'The Court thus equated the use of indiscriminate weapons with a deliberate attack upon civilians.'[2]

B **Rule of proportionality:** Rome Statute Art. 8(b)(iv)) prohibits: 'Intentionally launching an attack in the knowledge that such attack will cause incidental loss of life or injury to civilians or damage to civilian objects or widespread, long-term and severe damage to the natural environment which would be clearly excessive in relation to the concrete and direct overall military advantage anticipated'.

This is sometimes known as the rule of proportionality, as applied to methods of warfare as opposed to the general response to another state's armed attack. It was not addressed specifically by the ICJ, perhaps because it was thought too flexible for the context of nuclear weapons, as it involves balancing. Nonetheless, it is central to the way the UK and USA now practise warfare, and deserves examination.

What we have recently been emphasizing at the Lawyers Committee on Nuclear Policy (LCNP) is that compliance with this rule, and others, requires the ability to control the weapon or method of warfare used.[3]

An Air Force publication on the law of armed conflict states in part:

> Weapons are not unlawful simply because their use may cause incidental casualties to civilians and destruction of civilian objects. Nevertheless, particular weapons or methods of warfare may be prohibited because of their indiscriminate effects.... [S]ome weapons, though capable of being directed only at military objectives, may have otherwise uncontrollable effects so as to cause disproportionate civilian injuries or damage. Biological warfare is a universally agreed illustration of such an indiscriminate weapon.[4]

Nuclear weapons are not capable of being controlled in this fashion. A related provision is found in the 1977 Protocol I to the Geneva Conventions. Article 51, provides:

4 Indiscriminate attacks are prohibited. Indiscriminate attacks are:

a those which are not directed at a specific military objective;

b those which employ a method or means of combat which cannot be directed at a specific military objective;

c those which employ a method or means of combat the effects of which cannot be limited as required by the Protocol; and consequently, in each such case, are of a nature to strike military objectives and civilians or civilian objects without distinction.[5]

Limiting effects requires that the weapons be capable of being controlled. Again, that is not possible with nuclear weapons, above all due to the radiation effects.

C **Protection of the environment:** It is also noteworthy that the Rome Statute Art. 8(b)(iv) prohibition of disproportionate attacks includes effects on the environment within the balancing test. This is also stated in the ICJ opinion. While noting that environmental law does not 'deprive a State of the exercise of its right of self-defense under international law because of its obligations to protect the environment,' the ICJ stated: 'Nonetheless, **States must take environmental considerations into account when assessing what is necessary and proportionate in the pursuit of legitimate military objectives.**'[6] With the Rome Statute, that requirement became more entrenched. It is important to the illegality of threat and use of nuclear weapons, because it may come into play even in cases of attacks which arguably do not affect civilian populations and civilian infrastructure.

The ICJ also observed:

> that Articles 35, paragraph 3, and 55 of Additional Protocol I [to the Geneva Conventions] provide additional protection for the environment. Taken together, these provisions embody **a general obligation to protect the natural environment against widespread, long-term and severe environmental damage**; the prohibition of methods and means of warfare which are intended, or may be expected, to cause such damage; and the prohibition of attacks against the natural environment by way of reprisals. [§] These are powerful constraints for all the States having subscribed to these provisions.[7]

As the years go by, those provisions also become part of customary international law, applicable even to those states not party to Protocol I or which, as in the case of the United Kingdom, ratified subject to the reservation that rules 'introduced' by the Protocol (new rules) do not apply to nuclear weapons.

D **Crimes against humanity:** The Rome Statute also defines the following as a crime against humanity (Article 7): murder, extermination, and other inhumane acts of a similar character, when committed as part of a widespread or systematic attack directed against any civilian population. This is the modern version of the crime against humanity prosecuted at Nuremberg. While not really a 'recent development', it certainly demonstrates the entrenchment of the prohibition of crimes against humanity. Any use of nuclear weapons would involve war crimes. However, because nuclear weapons really are beyond the scope of warfare, and because of its rhetorical power, it is important to also state that use of nuclear weapons is a crime against humanity. This may serve as useful language for a future agreement or perhaps a UN Security Council resolution, as Rebecca Johnson has suggested.[8] It is also significant that crimes against humanity can be committed in time of peace as well as time of war, opening the door for arguments that peacetime preparations to commit such crimes are unlawful.

3 **Reprisal and the International Criminal Tribunal for the Former Yugoslavia:** The ICJ framed the prohibition of inflicting indiscriminate harm in categorical form, stating that it is a 'fundamental' and 'intransgressible' rule that states must '**never** use weapons that are incapable of distinguishing between civilian and military targets'.[9]

While the Court elsewhere declined to pass on the legality of nuclear reprisals, its statement of the prohibition effectively rules them out. The categorical nature of the principle protecting civilians was affirmed by the Trial Chamber of the International Criminal Tribunal for the Former Yugoslavia in a decision reconfirming Milan Martic's indictment for ordering rocket attacks on Zagreb which killed and wounded civilians.[10] Applying humanitarian law including Article I Common to all Geneva Conventions, which sets forth minimum standards of customary international law, the Trial Chamber stated that 'no circumstances would legitimize an attack against civilians even if it were a response proportionate to a similar violation perpetrated by the other party'.[11]

4 **1968 Nuclear Non-Proliferation Treaty**

Article VI of the Nuclear Non-Proliferation Treaty (NPT) states: 'Each of the Parties to the Treaty undertakes to pursue negotiations in good faith on effective measures relating to cessation of the nuclear arms race at an early date and to nuclear disarmament, and on a treaty on general and complete disarmament under strict and effective international control.'

In paragraph 105(2)F of the 'dispositif' setting forth its answers to the General Assembly, the Court unanimously concluded:

'There exists an obligation to pursue in good faith and bring to a conclusion negotiations leading to nuclear disarmament in all its aspects under strict and effective international control.'

The Court's statement of the disarmament obligation is now the authoritative interpretation of Article VI.

Article VI must be understood in the context of the entire treaty. The NPT is the only security treaty that permits two classes of members: states acknowledged to possess nuclear weapons and states barred from acquiring them. One hundred and eighty-eight states are members. Only three countries are outside the regime, all nuclear-armed: India,

Pakistan, and Israel. In addition, North Korea's status is in limbo; it has announced its withdrawal, and may have a few nuclear weapons. The NPT strikes a bargain between non-nuclear-weapon states, which are prohibited from acquiring nuclear arms and are guaranteed access to peaceful nuclear technology, and nuclear-weapon states, which are required to negotiate nuclear disarmament in good faith. In the post Cold War era, the 1995 and 2000 NPT Review Conferences and the 1996 International Court of Justice opinion established that the NPT requires the achievement of symmetry by obligating the nuclear-weapon states to implement a programme culminating in the elimination of their arsenals.

In 1995, the year that the NPT was due to expire, the indefinite extension of the treaty was agreed as part of a larger package that included a set of commitments known as the *Principles and Objectives for Nuclear Non-Proliferation and Disarmament*. The Principles and Objectives set forth measures for implementation of the Article VI disarmament obligation. They include negotiation of a Comprehensive Test Ban Treaty (CTBT) by 1996, commencement of negotiations on a treaty banning production of fissile materials for use in weapons, and the 'determined pursuit by the nuclear-weapon States of systematic and progressive efforts to reduce nuclear weapons globally, with the ultimate goal of eliminating those weapons.'

The 2000 NPT Review Conference further specified what the Article VI disarmament obligation requires. Its Final Document sets forth *practical steps for the systematic and progressive efforts to achieve nuclear disarmament* (Practical Steps). Implementation of this comprehensive agenda would result in the achievement of a nuclear-weapon-free world.

Among its crucial elements were:

I   an 'unequivocal undertaking by the nuclear-weapon States to accomplish the total elimination of their nuclear arsenals', confirming the ICJ's interpretation of Article VI;

II affirmation of principles of transparency, verification, and irreversibility for the reduction and elimination of nuclear arsenals;

III bringing the Comprehensive Test Ban Treaty into force and observing the moratorium on nuclear test explosions pending its entry into force; and

IV a diminishing role for nuclear weapons in security policies to minimize the risk that these weapons ever be used and to facilitate the process of their total elimination.

Under well-established rules of treaty interpretation set forth in the Vienna Convention on the Law of Treaties, the 2000 Practical Steps together with the 1995 Principles and Objectives constitute agreement and practice subsequent to the adoption of the NPT authoritatively applying and interpreting Article VI.

The Vienna Convention is widely acknowledged as stating customary rules of international law. Article 31(3) of the Vienna Convention, entitled 'General Rule of Interpretation', provides that in addition to the text and preamble of a treaty,

> there shall be taken into account ... (a) any subsequent agreement between the parties regarding the interpretation of the treaty or the application of its provisions; (b) any subsequent practice in the application of the treaty which establishes the agreement of the parties regarding its interpretation.

The 2000 NPT Review Conference Final Document states that the 'Conference agrees' on the Practical Steps. Further, the agreement was reached in the context of a proceeding authorized by Article VIII of the NPT

> to review the operation of this Treaty with a view to assuring that the purposes of the Preamble and the provisions of the Treaty are being realized.

This is the most natural setting for states to make authoritative applications and interpretations of the NPT.

In addition to constituting *agreements*, the Principles and Objectives and Practical Steps are part of a *practice* of the Parties to the NPT that has been consistent over the course of the treaty's life, dating back to its inception. After the treaty was opened for signature on 1 July 1968, the Soviet Union and the United States placed specific measures before the predecessor to today's Conference on Disarmament, the Eighteen Nation Disarmament Committee, where the NPT had been negotiated. Under a heading taken from Article VI, they proposed an agenda including, the cessation of testing, the non-use of nuclear weapons, the cessation of production of fissionable materials for weapons use, the cessation of manufacture of weapons and reduction and subsequent elimination of nuclear stockpiles...[12]

Disarmament measures have been the subject of discussion at every Review Conference since then. In short, the Practical Steps, as an application of Article VI, are an essential guide to its interpretation. They identify criteria and principles that are so tightly connected to the core meaning of Article VI as to constitute requirements for compliance with the NPT and more generally the disarmament obligation stated by the ICJ.

Article VI and the commitments made in 1995 and 2000 enjoin reduction and elimination of nuclear arsenals. They are wholly incompatible with planning and implementation of maintenance and modernization of nuclear forces for decades to come. What are their implications for threat and use of nuclear weapons? If a state has accepted an undertaking to eliminate its arsenal, and a diminishing role for nuclear weapons in security policies to minimize the risk of their use, the strong implication is that threat and use are illegitimate; the NPT thus reinforces international humanitarian law in this respect.

5   Good Faith

The International Association of Lawyers Against Nuclear Arms recently has sought to better define what the 'good faith' referred to in Article VI requires. It is also a fundamental principle of international law that treaties are to be implemented in good faith. With others we organized an excellent conference on 1 May 2008 in Geneva on this subject. Judge Bedjaoui gave the keynote address, and some of what he said on good faith is available in the paper prepared for today's Conference.

At the most basic level, good faith means keeping promises and working sincerely and cooperatively to achieve agreed objectives. Good faith requires meeting the NPT commitments made in 1995 and 2000 or, when appropriate, developing alternative means of fulfilling Article VI. Judge Bedjaoui stated that good faith requires refraining from acts incompatible with the object and purpose of the NPT and proscribes every initiative the effect of which would be to render impossible the conclusion of the contemplated disarmament treaty. Replacement and modernization of nuclear arsenals looking ahead for decades falls in the category in an act incompatible with the NPT's object and purpose. As to the negotiations required by Article VI, they must first of all be commenced! Once commenced, Judge Bedjaoui explained, good faith requires their sustained upkeep, awareness of the interests of the other party, and a persevering quest for an acceptable compromise.

I think that the concept of good faith deserves emphasis and further development. Not only is it required to make progress in the nuclear sphere and others, notably that of climate protection. It also is one that is well suited to public advocacy and public understanding. Citizens can demand that their governments act in good faith to stop nuclear arms racing and accomplish the elimination of nuclear forces.

6 UN Security Council (UNSC) Resolution 1540 (2004)

UNSC resolution 1540 is aimed at requiring states to prevent non-state actor trafficking in and acquisition of nuclear, chemical, biological weapons and associated materials and parts. It also, however, calls upon all States to:

> promote the universal adoption and full implementation, and, where necessary, strengthening of multilateral treaties to which they are parties, whose aim is to prevent the proliferation of nuclear, biological or chemical weapons. (operative paragraph 6a)

Also, a preambular provision recalls,

> the Statement of its President adopted at the Council's meeting at the level of Heads of State and Government on 31 January 1992 (S/23500), including the need for all Member States to fulfil their obligations in relation to arms control and disarmament and to prevent proliferation in all its aspects of all weapons of mass destruction. (preambular paragraph 2)

As a whole, UNSC resolution 1540 is binding upon all states. It was adopted under Chapter VII of the UN Charter pursuant to which the Security Council maintains international peace and security. While the provisions relating to disarmament are phrased in precatory terms — 'calls upon' — arguably they too are binding, given the context.

So 'non-state actors', the subject of the resolution, can have a positive role as well, for example as citizens in demanding that their government meet the NPT obligations reinforced by the resolution.

7 Addressing the threat of use of nuclear weapons

I am not aware of developments in the law since the ICJ opinion. Already, the fact that the use of nuclear weapons would be unlawful under the law of armed conflict necessarily means that any specific threat to use nuclear weapons would be unlawful. This arises from the established rule of the law of armed conflict that it is unlawful for a state to threaten to use force that it would be unlawful in fact to use.

As stated by the International Court of Justice,

> If an envisaged use of weapons would not meet the requirements of humanitarian law [including discrimination], a threat to engage in such use would also be contrary to that law.

Clearly, a *'threat'* contrary to the UN Charter and humanitarian law will be considered to have occurred in a concrete situation, like an ongoing war, where one state signals to another: 'If you do not do X or refrain from Y, we will resort to the use of nuclear weapons.' That is true even where the demand itself is lawful, for example 'do not invade our territory'. However, clearly identifiable threats of this kind, while they have occurred, are somewhat rare and hard to establish. (Interestingly, governments do not like to openly threaten use of nuclear weapons in specific circumstances.)

What about long-running declared policies giving governments the option of use of nuclear weapons in certain circumstances? What about the long-standing nuclear threat vs. nuclear threat claimed to be at the core of 'strategic stability' by the United States and Russia? It can certainly be plausibly argued that these are 'unlawful' threats. The ICJ opinion gives some support to this argument. While declining to make a formal pronouncement on the policy of 'deterrence', the Court concluded that the policy would be unlawful under the United Nations Charter if use of nuclear weapons in self-defence pursuant to the policy would violate the principles of necessity and proportionality. This is an area where further analysis is needed, or, much better, clear international agreements or decisions. It is certainly the case that on-going, declared policies of deterrence are contrary to the commitment to a 'diminishing role for nuclear weapons in security policies to minimize the risk' of their use by the 2000 NPT Review Conference, and are generally inconsistent with the obligation of good faith negotiation of disarmament.

What we sometimes lose sight of, and what I will end with, is that doctrines of so-called 'deterrence' (even if they will indefinitely not result in use of the weapons) are wholly incompatible with achievement of the world governed by principles of peace, law and disarmament promised by the UN Charter. One of the aims of the Charter, as stated in its preamble, is 'to establish conditions under which justice and respect for the obligations arising from treaties and other sources of international law can be maintained'.

Anti-Nuclear Scotland

ROSEANNA CUNNINGHAM MSP

I AM AN SNP member of the Scottish Parliament, and thus a member of the governing party. This has been quite important over the last 18 months as it changes somewhat the way in which the Government in Scotland has related to issues like nuclear weapons and to nuclear energy.

Since May 2007, when our last Parliamentary election was, there has been a change of government in Scotland and we now have a minority government situation and my party is by one seat the main party and has formed a minority government. My party has been over many, many decades resolutely anti nuclear weapons and anti nuclear energy. The two issues have become somewhat linked over the years. It was inevitable that the new Government in Scotland would want to say things about nuclear weapons regardless of the fact that that really is a matter which is supposed to be Westminster's particular remit. It was inevitable given that we had such a different view of the situation that we would want to take the opportunity to make that difference of view heard, in our view to reflect what we considered to be the majority opinion in Scotland, which has been anti-Trident all along and to take what steps we could take as a Government in the context of a situation where we did not have the direct powers over nuclear weapons that Westminster has.

As a result of that, a Working Group was set up in October 2007 (a Scotland Without Nuclear Weapons Working Group) and it has a number of remits. It has a remit to look at the economic impact because, as you are aware, there is often a question of the associated jobs, and there is a need to consider what the decision would mean and to identify options for alternative employment. It would be our argument that if you were not spending money on Trident nuclear weapons then you could spend it on developing real alternatives including employment beyond what exists at the base, and that that would be a far better way to spend that money. There is a remit also to look at international legal opinions and that of course is very interesting in an international context and a lot of that relates to the international criminal law of the issue of war crimes and Scotland's potential culpability that might be held to be applied to the use of nuclear weapons; and although as a devolved Parliament Scotland does not have a direct decision-making power over the use or non-use of nuclear weapons (and indeed I suppose one interesting thing internationally is whether, in fact, the UK has a decision-making power itself) nevertheless there are arguments about culpability that may apply to Scotland. There is also a remit on the Non-Proliferation Treaty and a remit to look at peace and reconciliation.

Another remit, that is turning out to be a very interesting one, is looking at the legislative framework, because it transpires that although it may be rather more mundane and workaday, it might have the biggest impact. We explored some of that in connection with nuclear energy and also with nuclear weapons; we could use environmental law, planning law and issues relating to transport in order to effect a different attitude towards the siting of nuclear weapons. Although the Scottish Parliament does not have power over nuclear weapons, nor indeed does it have power over nuclear power stations, the fact is it does have planning powers. And those planning powers for example have already been explored in connection with potential nuclear reactors to the extent that at present it looks very unlikely that new nuclear reactors will be built in Scotland, although I note an emerging debate in some quarters that argue that in those circumstances those powers should be taken away from the Scottish Parliament, so effective do people think they might be.

Now those same powers (the environmental, planning, transport powers) are not big, glamorous powers; they are not big debates about war crimes, about international legal opinions. But ironically they may turn out to be actually more effective powers and I think we would want this to go forward. In a sense, it is over to the practising lawyers to be really imaginative about how they look at ways in which some of these issues can be dealt with, how we can block or put obstacles in the way of nuclear weapons. Not using the big, glamorous debates and arguments, not even using the criminal law, but actually using the common or garden variety of laws and by-laws that may already be in existence.

It is an interesting area but it's a very important one for Scotland because it is the way in which we could express the view of the Scottish people. There has been a debate in the Scottish Parliament about this and I am glad to say that the anti-Trident view won by a substantial majority in the Parliament, so that we have a stated view now that is the Scottish Parliament's view, not just the Government's view. And we think that is important because even those statements, while they themselves do not necessarily bring about immediate change, nevertheless add to the argument, add to the understanding of the people that we are simply not going to allow this to go without opposition.

This is a quick update on where we are in Scotland, a proactive Government on this issue notwithstanding not having direct powers to deal with it, but an interesting and imaginative exploration of what use can be made of other powers that might not immediately come to mind. And I suppose if there is one lesson to learn from the Scottish experience it is that you can overlook some very simple ways to deal with some of these issues and I would not want anyone to do that.

A Scottish Perspective

JANET FENTON

THERE IS A PARTICULAR Scottish perspective on nuclear disarmament, and a distinct and separate tradition and system of law in Scotland that is separate from England. This is why it was important to hold this Conference on *Trident and International Law: Scotland's Obligations* in Edinburgh, close to the Scottish Parliament.

Defence (and in a separate clause, nuclear weaponry) is reserved to the UK government at Westminster according to the 1998 Scotland Act which established and defined the devolved Parliament in Scotland. But Scotland is in a unique position in the world. In the words of Professor William Walker of St Andrew's University, 'there is a unique situation in Scotland. There are nuclear weapons in a land where the mood of the Parliament and of the country is opposed to them'.[1] This is a statement of fact, rather than opinion, and notwithstanding the limitation of the Scottish Government's devolved responsibility, it does indicate that there are distinct opportunities, responsibilities and interpretations that must be considered in Scotland by Scottish institutions.

The Edinburgh Peace and Justice Centre works through responding to the expressed wishes of the community it serves across Scotland. Through our experience of doing that, we have no doubt that nuclear weapons are an anathema to the vast majority of the Scottish people, within and beyond the Peace Movement. An opinion poll carried out by ICM early in 2007 found that almost two thirds of Scots opposed the plan to replace Trident. That figure rose to 73 percent if the price tag was set at £50 billion, which many consider an under-estimation of what it would actually cost.

Since the UK Government first chose the nuclear weapon route and Scotland was landed with the task of playing host to nuclear weapons, there has been, over this 50 year period, much learning about the nature and dangers attached to nuclear weapons which has engendered discussion, debate, protest, civil disobedience and direct action. Civic society, faith groups and the trade union movement consider them to be illegal, immoral and unaffordable.

Cardinal Keith O'Brien, the leader of the Catholic Church in Scotland, has stated,

> We here in Scotland have a duty to lead the way in campaigning for change, because we have the shameful task of housing these horrific weapons. With the Trident nuclear weapon system fast becoming obsolete, ... now is the time for all men and women ... to raise our voices. Enter this debate and demand that these weapons of mass destruction be replaced, but not with more weapons. Rather...with projects that bring *life* to the poor.[2]

A Church of Scotland minister, the Rev. David McLachlan, stated,

> My own denomination, the Church of Scotland, has for many years argued against the possession and threatened use of nuclear weapons... a united front with Catholic and Protestant churches sounding the same message.[3]

Matt Smith, the Secretary of Scotland's largest trade union, UNISON, agreed:

> We have a world of unmet needs – of poverty and hunger – of war and destruction. There are so many needs that we have to fund, replacing Trident is not one of them. At a time that Government here and in the UK are looking for the most efficient use of public money, it is clearly a very poor use of that money to spend it on new nuclear weapons. We call on the government to draw back from this step, and on our representatives in Parliament to vote against it.[4]

Scotland's for Peace is a comparatively new organisation, established since devolution, with partners coming from right across Scottish civic society. Its aim is stated as,

> We desire that Scotland should be known for its contribution to international peace and justice, rather than as a launch-pad for waging war.[5]

Its first objective 'to persuade the majority of Scottish MPs and MSPs to speak out publicly against the replacement of Trident'[6] has already been achieved. The widespread support it has reflects the mood of the country to which Professor Walker refers.

The mood of the Scottish Parliament is equally clear. Despite their reserved status, nuclear weapons and the proposed replacement of Trident became a major campaigning issue in the last Scottish Parliamentary election.7 And now, the Scottish Government is opposed to them. On 14 June 2007, when the Scottish Parliament debated the issue, it took a clear position against renewing Trident, with a motion congratulating the majority of Scots MPs for voting against a replacement system in March. The (amended) motion, which also called on the UK Government to reconsider Trident replacement, was backed by 71 MSPs to 16, with 39 abstentions. We rejoiced in the good sense of the Scottish people, and the fruit of our peace-building efforts over many years. It was an affirmation of our obligations under the Non-Proliferation Treaty and our work over so many years through the World Court Project to establish and uphold International Law.

In addition to the principled stand of the Labour 'rebels' who joined the majority of MSPs in voting in favour of that motion, Bill Butler, Malcolm Chisholm, Marlyn Glen and Cathy Peattie, the vote highlighted the bizarre position of the Labour party in Scotland, since not one single Labour MSP voted to collude with the Labour Government at Westminster's flagrant violation of International Law.

During the debate on 14 June 2007, Minister for Parliamentary Business Bruce Crawford stated:

> In our election manifesto, we stated that Scotland should be free to remove nuclear weapons from our shores. Short of the full responsibilities of independence, the Government will reflect on the views of the majority of Scots and carefully consider which aspects of the plans to replace Trident impact on devolved areas. We will do what we can, using those responsibilities, to persuade the UK Government to change its stance. We also intend to hold a summit with key stakeholders to agree a joint position against Trident and get the best ideas and proposals from an alliance of people from throughout Scottish life who oppose the son of Trident. We will stand up for our beliefs and do all that we can to represent Scottish opinion on these vital matters.[8]

Scotland has a unique legal system that is separate from the rest of the UK. This system of law pre-dates the Acts of Union in 1707. The preceding Union of the Crown in 1603, when James VI of Scotland inherited the English crown, had really meant that two crowns rested on the head of one monarch. In 1707, following anxiety about how Scotland would react to the the lack of a direct successor to Queen Anne and anxious about an attempt to restore a Catholic monarchy, the English Parliament had prohibited all Scottish imports to England unless the Scots accepted the Hanoverian succession. While the Scots were fearful of being swallowed up by England, which had happened to Wales some 400 years earlier, they needed the advantage in free trade within the new British common market and reluctantly agreed, but insisted on retaining independence with respect to Scotland's legal and religious systems.

Neither side was completely happy with the two Acts of Union, one proposed and voted in by the Scots Parliament and the other by England's. Many Scots shared the view of Robert Burns, that the Scottish MPs were 'bought and sold for English gold' when coinage, taxation, sovereignty, trade, parliament and flag became one. Nevertheless, this was how Scotland came to keep its legal system and its Presbyterian Kirk while, for the next 300 years, it gave up its Parliament in exchange for 45 seats in the House of Commons and 16 seats in the House of Lords.

This history also explains the importance of Scotland's independent legal system to its governance under devolution:

> And that no Causes in Scotland be cognoscible by the Courts of Chancery, Queens-Bench, Common-Pleas, or any other Court in Westminster-hall; And that the said Courts, or any other of the like nature after the Union, shall have no power to Cognosce, Review or Alter the Acts or Sentences of the Judicatures within Scotland, or stop the Execution of the same.[9]

Scots law has two main sources, enacted law and common law. Enacted law has the authority of a body with legislative powers. Enacted law can come from many sources, including Royal proclamation or order, Acts of Parliament, European legislation, or local authority by-laws. The question for the conference was where the International Court of Justice stands in this regard. In his authoritative Introduction to Scots Law, Angus MacCulloch stated:

> Common law derives it authority from the courts and is based on Scots legal tradition. Both forms of law have equal authority and often operate in the same areas. Under the theory of the 'supremacy of Parliament', as partially recognised in Scotland, enacted law will override common law, but common law cannot override an enacted law.[10]

Common law develops through the judgements of the courts, through precedent. This involves examining the decisions of the courts in similar cases. Common law initially derived from the Roman law and Canon law, the law of the church. Scots law deals with two streams of activity, civil law and (what concerns us here) criminal law, which deals with matters between the individual and the state.

The criminal courts are, in ascending order of authority: The District Court, the Sheriff Court, and the High Court of Justiciary. The doctrine of 'precedent' means that the decision of a higher court will be binding on a lower court. According to MacCulloch,

> The High Court of Judiciary and the House of Lords are not bound by their own decisions. The decision of an English court is never binding upon a Scottish court. The decisions of the House of Lords sitting as an English court will be of a persuasive nature in a Scottish case.[11]

Early in 2007, Trident Ploughshares contacted the Edinburgh Peace and Justice Centre and together we organised a delegation to make a submission to the Lord Advocate, Eilish Angolini, on the legality of nuclear weapons, with particular regard to the replacement of Trident. The response from the Lord Advocate's office was that the Lord Advocate's responsibility was to give advice to the Scottish Government, and therefore she would not be responding to our submission. By the time that this response was received, Bruce Crawford's promised summit had taken place in Glasgow in October 2007, and the Scottish Government's Working Group on Scotland without Nuclear Weapons was being established.

The increase in the number of seats held by the Scottish National Party and the formation of an SNP Government should not blind us to the fact that the nuclear weapons in Scotland are a problem for MSPs (and Scottish MPs) across the political spectrum. When the SNP declined to take part in the Calman Commission on Reviewing Devolution,[12] because it would not consider complete independence for Scotland, there were still a range of those making submissions who considered that Scotland's interests would be better served if control of weapons of mass destruction was devolved.

It is important to understand that our cultural identity as Scots, our history and language and legal system, is not the monopoly of any Nationalist movement. Scots writer Sir Walter Scott was an ardent unionist who worked tirelessly to support the parliament at Westminster and the monarchy, and yet he still wrote:

> Breathes there the man, with soul so dead,
> Who never to himself hath said,
> This is my own, my native land!
> Whose heart hath ne'er within him burn'd,
> As home his footsteps he hath turn'd,
> From wandering on a foreign strand!
> …
> O Caledonia! stern and wild,
> Meet nurse for a poetic child!
> Land of brown heath and shaggy wood
> Land of the mountain and the flood,
> Land of my sires! what mortal hand
> Can e'er untie the filial band,
> That knits me to thy rugged strand![13]

We can be, and are, global citizens as well as Scots with a responsibility to play our part in building real human security.

> The Secretary of State for Defence undertakes to inform the Scottish Ministers of all relevant draft legislation, executive functions he proposes to exercise, and policy developments in sufficient time for the policy and practical implications for devolved matters to be examined and representations made as appropriate.

Thus states the Concordat between the Scottish Ministers and the UK Secretary of State for Defence. This surely implies that the implications of Trident replacement for devolved matters is the legitimate concern of the Scottish Government. Any risk attaching to renewing Trident would remain a significant factor until at least 2055.

The Ministry of Defence recognises, in its own safety case, that it is possible that an accident on public roads involving the convoys carrying fully armed nuclear warheads could result in a nuclear explosion.[14] At the least, any major accident would be likely to cause the dispersal of plutonium and other radioactive substances over a wide area. The Scottish Government is responsible for emergency planning. Scottish Ministers are responsible for monitoring the work of local authorities and emergency services in risk assessment and planning.[15] A nuclear accident would involve police and other services in the protection of the public, appropriate health advice, distribution of potassium iodide tablets, agriculture and fishing restrictions and precautions for handling radiation-contaminated casualties.

In the event of a nuclear attack as an act of war or terrorism, it would be likely that several thermonuclear weapons would be detonated at Faslane and or Coulport with immediate and devastating effect in Scotland. Other targets could include waterways where nuclear submarines might be located, or roads where warheads might be being transported. Civil defence is devolved.

These possibilities make it clear that there is an obligation on the part of the UK Government towards Scotland that is separate from the rest of the UK. Additionally, the resistance towards nuclear weapons in Scotland means that there are regular protests, with impact on policing, which is devolved, and people who are willing to risk arrest for nuclear disarmament activities, which has an impact on the judicial and prison systems. In the year preceding the Scottish Government's Summit on making Scotland Nuclear Free, there were 1150 arrests at Faslane. However, these resulted in only 66 prosecutions, with most of the cases being dropped, despite the Procurators Fiscal stating in almost every case that they found that there was 'sufficient evidence to bring the arrestees to court'. Many people with respect for Scots law feel that the selective application of the law for political purposes is weakening it.

The Scotland Act defines both Defence and the Control of Weapons of Mass Destruction as matters reserved to the UK Government at Westminster. To say that this means that neither are the concern of the Scottish Government or Parliament is at best simplistic; such an analysis fails to address appropriately any of the legitimate concerns of the Scottish people through their legal institutions or their elected representatives.

Our hope is that this Conference on Trident and International Law: Scotland's Obligations, and the publication of its proceedings, will enable us to accelerate the process whereby nuclear weapons are banished from Scotland, in order that this will act as a lever towards their global elimination, and replacement with a system of real human security that respects life, cultural identity and diversity.

The United Kingdom's Nuclear Deterrent: Current and Future Issues of Legality

PHILIPPE SANDS QC AND HELEN LAW

Introduction

1   We are asked to advise Greenpeace on the following issues relating to the United Kingdom's Trident nuclear deterrent (Trident):[1]

   i   The compatibility with international law, in particular the *jus ad bellum,* international humanitarian law ('IHL') and Article VI of the Treaty on the Non-Proliferation of Nuclear Weapons ('NPT'), of the current UK strategy on the use of Trident. In particular, the use, or threat of use, of nuclear weapons against non-nuclear states in order to deter attacks against 'vital interests', including UK forces overseas threatened with chemical or biological weapons;

   ii   The compatibility with IHL of deploying the current Trident system;

   iii   The compatibility with IHL and Article VI NPT of the following options for replacing or upgrading Trident:

   a   Enhanced targeting capability;

   b   Increased yield flexibility;

   c   Renewal of the current capability over a longer period.

2   We are asked to advise on these issues in the context of the current international debate on nuclear non-proliferation, including in particular North Korea and Iran. The UK has indicated that the future of Trident may depend on the outcome of the Iranian situation.[2] It supported UN Security Council Resolution 1696, of 31 July 2006, in which the UNSC expressed its intention to use Chapter VII measures against Iran to enforce the requirements of the Resolution and of the IAEA, should compliance not be forthcoming. Politically, therefore, it may be of particular importance that the UK is seen to be adhering to

its obligations under the NPT, including in particular those relating to Article VI.[3]

3   The common theme throughout this opinion is the nature and extent of the obligations under the *jus ad bellum,* IHL, and Article VI NPT. For clarity, we have explained our understanding of these obligations at the outset of this opinion, before considering the specific issues on which we are asked to advise. We also want to make clear that any final opinion we express will necessarily depend on the precise facts. For obvious reasons these cannot be available to us at this time.

Summary of Advice

4   In our opinion, and for the reasons we set out below:

i   The use, or threat of use, of nuclear weapons in self-defence will be unlawful under the *jus ad bellum* where it fails to meet the requirements of necessity and proportionality. Where their use is contemplated in response to a threatened rather than actual attack, the additional requirement of imminence must be fulfilled. Given the devastating consequences inherent in the use of the UK's current nuclear weapons, we are of the view that the proportionality test is unlikely to be met except where there is a threat to the very survival of the state. In our view, the 'vital interests' of the UK as defined in the *Strategic Defence Review* are considerably broader than those whose destruction threaten the survival of the state. The use of nuclear weapons to protect such interests is likely to be disproportionate and therefore unlawful under Article 2(4) of the UN Charter.

ii   It is difficult to conceive of any circumstances in which the use of nuclear weapons in self-defence to deter future chemical or biological attacks on UK forces overseas could be proportionate and therefore lawful. In particular, the use of nuclear weapons in the context contemplated in 2002 by Mr Hoon in relation to Iraq would, on the facts available, be unlawful.

iii   We find it hard to envisage any scenario in which the use of Trident, as currently constituted, could be consistent with the IHL prohibitions on indiscriminate attacks and unnecessary suffering. Further, such use would be highly likely to result in a violation of the principle of neutrality.

i Article VI of the NPT places an obligation on all state parties,

ii **to achieve** a precise result, nuclear disarmament in all its aspects, by adopting a particular course of conduct, namely, the pursuit of negotiations on the matter in **good faith**.[4]

iii Article VI is a provision essential to the accomplishment of the object of the NPT, nuclear disarmament, breach of which will be material. Acts or omissions which render nuclear disarmament remote or impossible, or which undermine its attainment, will be inconsistent with Article VI NPT.

Accordingly:

a A broadening of the deterrence policy to incorporate prevention of nonnuclear attacks so as to justify replacing or upgrading Trident would appear to be inconsistent with Article VI;

b Attempts to justify Trident upgrade or replacement as an insurance against unascertainable future threats would appear to be inconsistent with Article VI;

c Enhancing the targeting capability or yield flexibility of the Trident system is likely to be inconsistent with Article VI;

d Renewal or replacement of Trident at the same capability is likely to be inconsistent with Article VI; and

e In each case such inconsistency could give rise to a material breach of the NPT.

The Relevant Obligations under the *Jus Ad Bellum*, IHL and Article VI NPT

The *jus ad bellum*

5 The *jus ad bellum* regulates the lawfulness of the use of force by one state against another. Article 2(4) of the UN Charter states the central tenet:

'All Members shall refrain in their international relations from the threat or use of force against the territorial integrity or political independence of any state, or in any other manner inconsistent with the Purposes of the United Nations'.

The same threshold of legality applies to a threatened use of force as it does to an actual use:

> If the envisaged use of force is itself unlawful, the stated readiness to use it would be a threat prohibited under Article 2, paragraph 4. ... The notions of 'threat' and 'use' of force under Article 2, paragraph 4, of the Charter stand together in the sense that if the use of force itself in a given case is illegal, for whatever reason, the threat to use such force will likewise be illegal. In short, if it is to be lawful, the declared readiness of a State to use force must be a use of force that is in conformity with the Charter. ... no State, whether or not it defended the policy of deterrence, suggested to the Court that it would be lawful to threaten a use of force if the use of force contemplated **would be illegal**.[5]

The mere possession of nuclear weapons, when not accompanied by a specific threat against the territorial integrity or political independence of a state, does not amount to a threat within the meaning of Art. 2(4).[6]

6 Any use or threat of force is unlawful unless it falls within a recognised exception to Article 2(4), of which one is self-defence. Article 51 of the UN Charter states:

> Nothing in the present Charter shall impair the inherent right of individual or collective self-defence if an armed attack occurs against a Member of the United Nations, until the Security Council has taken measures necessary to maintain international peace and security. Measures taken by Members in the exercise of this right of self-defence shall be immediately reported to the Security Council and shall not in any way affect the authority and responsibility of the Security Council under the present Charter to take at any time such action as it deems necessary in order to maintain or restore international peace and security.

The provisions in Article 2(4) and Article 51 reflect customary international law.[7] In September 2005 Heads of State and Heads of Government reaffirmed that, the relevant provisions of the Charter are sufficient to address the full range of threats to international peace and security.[8]

7   The right to act in self-defence is circumscribed by a number of conditions, usefully summarised in the *Principles of International Law on the Use of Force by States in Self-Defence*, adopted in October 2005 by a group of 13 international law academics and practitioners under the auspices of the International Law Programme at Chatham House ('the Chatham House Principles').[9] We adopt the approach set forth in the Principles. Two conditions are key:

    i Measures taken in self-defence must be **necessary** in order to respond to the armed attack; and

    ii They must be a **proportionate** response to that attack.[10]

8   Necessity is a strict objective standard,[11] and one that must be determined at the time of the decision to take the measures. Necessity in the context of self-defence requires a close temporal nexus between the attack and the response: any delay in response will undermine the credibility of the need to respond at all. It also requires that that there be no other way of eliminating the danger, other than the measures taken.[12] In our view necessity is not, however, a fixed or static concept; it must take account of *inter alia* technological developments so that – together with the notion of imminence – its application today might be different from when the UN Charter was adopted in 1945.[13] Chatham House Principle 3 summarises the requirements as follows:

> Force may be used in self-defence only when this is necessary to bring an attack to an end, or to avert an imminent attack. There must be no practical alternative to the proposed use of force that is likely to be effective in ending or averting the attack.

The commentary to Principle 3 states that:

> In applying the test of necessity, reference may be made to the means available to the state under attack; the kinds of forces and the level of armament to hand will be relevant to the nature and intensity of response that it would be reasonable to expect, as well as the realistic possibilities of resorting to non-military means in the circumstances.[14]

9 Proportionality is to be assessed on an ongoing basis throughout the course of the measures taken, and must consider the entirety of those measures.[15] Chatham House Principle 5 summarises the requirements as follows:

> The exercise of the right of self-defence must comply with the criterion of 'proportionality'.
>
> • The force used, taken as a whole, must not be excessive in relation to the need to avert or bring the attack to an end.
>
> • The physical and economic consequences of the force used must not be excessive in relation to the harm expected from the attack.

The commentary to Principle 5 states:

> The ICJ has confirmed that it is a well-established rule of customary international law that a use of force in self-defence must be 'proportional to the armed attack and necessary to respond to it.' This requires that the level of force used is not greater than that necessary to end the attack or remove the threat. As such it is another way of looking at the requirement of necessity.
>
> The proportionality requirement has been said to mean in addition that the physical and economic consequences of the force used must not be excessive in relation to the harm expected from the attack. But because the right of self-defence does not allow the use of force to 'punish' an aggressor, proportionality should not be thought to refer to parity between a response and the harm already suffered from an attack, as this could either turn the concept of self-defence into a justification for retributive force, or limit the use of force to less than what is necessary to repel the attack.

10 Also relevant to the ambit of this opinion is the use of force in response to an anticipated rather than ongoing attack. On this issue, we share the opinion of the Attorney General, Lord Goldsmith, that

> international law permits the use of force in self-defence against an imminent attack but does not authorise the use of force to mount a pre-emptive strike against a threat that is more remote.[16]

What amounts to 'imminent' is a question of fact to be judged on the circumstances of each case. Any use of self-defence in these circumstances must, of course, fulfil the usual requirements of necessity and proportionality. Principle 4 of the Chatham House Principles provides:

'A state may use force in self-defence against a threatened attack only if that attack is 'imminent'.'

There is a risk of abuse of the doctrine of anticipatory self-defence, and it needs to be applied in good faith and on the basis of sound evidence. But the criterion of imminence must be interpreted so as to take into account current kinds of threat and it must be applied having regard to the particular circumstances of each case. The criterion of imminence is closely related to the requirement of necessity.

- Force may be used only when any further delay would result in an inability by the threatened state effectively to defend against or avert the attack against it.

- In assessing the imminence of the attack, reference may be made to the gravity of the attack, the capability of the attacker, and the nature of the threat, for example if the attack is likely to come without warning.

- Force may be used only on a proper factual basis and after a good faith assessment of the facts.'

The commentary to Principle 4 provides, *inter alia,* as follows:

The concept of 'imminence' reflects the Caroline formulation of 'instant, overwhelming, leaving no choice of means, and no moment for deliberation'. In the context of contemporary threats imminence cannot be construed by reference to a temporal criterion only, but must reflect the wider circumstances of the threat.

There must exist a circumstance of irreversible emergency. Whether the attack is 'imminent' depends upon the nature of the threat and the possibility of dealing effectively with it at any given stage. Factors that may be taken into account include: the gravity of the threatened attack (whether what is threatened is a catastrophic use of WMD; capability) for example, whether the relevant state or terrorist organisation is in possession of WMD, or merely of material or component parts to be used in its manufacture; and the nature of the attack, including the possible risks of making a wrong assessment of the danger. Other factors may also be relevant, such as the geographical situation of the victim state, and the past record of attacks by the state concerned.

The criterion of imminence requires that it is believed that any further delay in countering the intended attack will result in the inability of the defending state effectively to defend itself against the attack. In this sense, necessity will determine imminence: it must be necessary to act before it is too late. There is a question as to whether 'imminence' is a separate criterion in its own right, or simply part of the criterion of 'necessity' properly understood. As an additional criterion however it serves to place added emphasis on the fact that a forcible response in these circumstances lies at the limits of an already exceptional legal category, and therefore requires a correspondingly high level of justification.

To the extent that a doctrine of 'pre-emption' encompasses a right to respond to threats which have not yet crystallized but which might materialise at some time in the future, such a doctrine (sometimes called 'preventive defence') has no basis in international law.

International Humanitarian Law

11 The UK does not dispute that customary IHL applies to nuclear weapons to the same extent as it does to conventional warfare.[17] There are three principles of IHL central to the debate on the legality of the UK's current and future nuclear capability:

a   The prohibition on indiscriminate weapons;

b   The prohibition on the use of weapons which cause unnecessary suffering;

c   The principle of neutrality.

12 The first two rules have been found by the ICJ to represent 'intransgressible principles of customary international law.'[18] A state is required to comply with them even when acting in self-defence, notwithstanding that its very survival is at risk.[19] The ICJ has since clarified that they are obligations owed *erga omnes*.[20]

The Prohibition On Indiscriminate Weapons

13 It is a basic principle of customary IHL that a state must not carry out indiscriminate attacks. It is an embodiment of the obligation to distinguish between the civilian population and combatants.[21] In its

Advisory Opinion on nuclear weapons the ICJ did not define the precise scope of the prohibition. However, in our view, the correct reading of the ICJ Opinion, and of the broader principle of distinction, supports the conclusion that there are two limbs to the prohibition:

i   Not to use weapons which are incapable of being targeted on military objectives;

ii   Not to use weapons which are capable of being targeted, but whose effects upon civilians cannot be controlled.

14 Our reasons for this conclusion are:

i   The purpose of the principle of distinction would be significantly undermined if it permitted a state to use a weapon which was in theory capable of being targeted, in so far as the point of explosion could be determined, but the effects of which were so unpredictable as to make this targeting largely ineffective in ensuring a distinction between military and civilian objects.

ii   The ICJ itself was concerned with the *effect* of a particular weapon, not just its targeting capability:

> ... humanitarian law, at a very early stage, prohibited certain types of weapons because of their indiscriminate effect on combatants and civilians...[22]

15 In our opinion, a definition of the prohibition which overlooked the second limb identified at paragraph 13(ii) would be artificial and unduly limited. We find support for our conclusion both in Additional Protocol I to the Geneva Conventions ('API'), Article 51(4),[23] and in the comments of Louise Doswald-Beck, Professor of International Law and Director of the University Centre for International Humanitarian Law, who has stated:

> ... the majority of state practice introduces a second condition for what could be considered an indiscriminate weapon: if the effects of a weapon, once targeted accurately at a military objective, are uncontrollable, the weapon is indiscriminate.[24]

The Prohibition on Weapons which cause Unnecessary Suffering

16 The ICJ said of this principle:

> ... it is prohibited to cause unnecessary suffering to combatants: it is accordingly prohibited to use weapons causing them such harm or uselessly aggravating their suffering. In application of that second principle, States do not have unlimited freedom of choice of means in the weapons they use.

> ... humanitarian law, at a very early stage, prohibited certain types of weapons ... because of the unnecessary suffering caused to combatants, that is to say, a harm greater than that unavoidable to achieve legitimate military objectives.[25]

17 The prohibition requires a state to first assess and then balance the likely suffering caused by a weapon against the military advantage gained by its use.

The Principle of Neutrality

18 This principle, which forms part of customary international law, places an obligation on states not to cause damage to neutral territory during attacks on a belligerent state:

> The inviolability of neutral territory also means that the neutral states must not be affected by collateral effects of hostilities. The parties to the conflict have no right to cause damage to neutral territory through hostilities themselves. Therefore, there is no rule of admissible collateral damage to the detriment of the neutral state. If the effects of attacks directed against targets on the territory of a party to the conflict are felt on neutral territory, they are unlawful.[26]

Article VI of the Treaty on Non-Proliferation of Nuclear Weapons

19 The NPT was adopted on 12 June 1968 in New York. The United Kingdom, the United States and the Russian Federation were named

as the depositary states. In accordance with Article IX, it entered into force when the fortieth state, in addition to the depositories, ratified its provisions on 5 March 1970. To date, 189 states have ratified the NPT, of which one has withdrawn (North Korea in 2003). The significance of the NPT is aptly summarised by the United Nations' Weapons of Mass Destruction Branch:

> The NPT is a landmark international treaty whose objective is to prevent the spread of nuclear weapons and weapons technology, to promote cooperation in the peaceful uses of nuclear energy and to further the goal of achieving nuclear disarmament and general and complete disarmament. The Treaty represents the only binding commitment in a multilateral treaty to the goal of disarmament by the nuclear-weapon States.[27]

20 The scope of the Article VI obligations remains the subject of considerable debate. The provision states:

> Each of the Parties to the Treaty undertakes to pursue negotiations in good faith on effective measures relating to cessation of the nuclear arms race at an early date and to nuclear disarmament, and on a Treaty on general and complete disarmament under strict and effective international control.

21 The basic principles of treaty interpretation are set out in Articles 31 and 32 of the Vienna Convention on the Law of Treaties ('VCLT'). Although the VCLT does not have retrospective effect, and therefore does not directly apply to the NPT, the central tenets of interpretation which it encapsulates have been held by the ICJ to reflect customary international law.[28] Accordingly and in addition to the text of the NPT, the purposes of the preamble,[29] the materials produced at the subsequent review conferences[30] and the *travaux preparatoires*[31] are relevant to interpreting Article VI.

22 The preamble and the materials produced at the review conferences are 'primary' sources of interpretation. The *travaux preparatoires* assume a 'secondary', supplementary role, and should only be relied on where the primary sources leave the meaning ambiguous or obscure, or lead to a result which is manifestly absurd or unreasonable.[32]

23 The preamble to the NPT states, in relevant part:

> Declaring their intention to achieve at the earliest possible date the cessation of the nuclear arms race and to undertake effective measures in the direction of nuclear disarmament...
>
> Desiring to further the easing of international tension and the strengthening of trust between States in order to facilitate the cessation of the manufacture of nuclear weapons, the liquidation of all their existing stockpiles, and the elimination from national arsenals of nuclear weapons and the means of their delivery pursuant to a Treaty on general and complete disarmament under strict and effective international control...

24 The review conferences are held in accordance with Article VIII(3) NPT, and serve to ensure that the purposes of the preamble and the provisions are being realised. Their significance has been underlined by the ICJ:

> The importance of fulfilling the obligation expressed in Article VI of the Treaty on the Non-Proliferation of Nuclear Weapons was also reaffirmed in the final document of the Review and Extension Conference of the parties to the Treaty on the Non-Proliferation of Nuclear Weapons, held from 17 April to 12 May 1995.[33]

25 The most significant conference to date was that held in 2000, where the parties agreed a series of 'practical steps for the systematic and progressive efforts to implement article VI of the Treaty'.[34] Of particular relevance are steps 5, 6 and 9:

> 5   The principle of irreversibility to apply to nuclear disarmament, nuclear and other related arms control and reduction measures.
>
> 6   An unequivocal undertaking by the nuclear weapon States to accomplish the total elimination of their nuclear arsenals leading to nuclear disarmament, to which all States parties are committed under article VI. ...
>
> 9   Steps by all the nuclear-weapon States leading to nuclear disarmament in a way that promotes international stability, and based on the principle of undiminished security for all:
>
>   • Further efforts by the nuclear-weapon States to reduce their nuclear arsenals unilaterally;

- Increased transparency by the nuclear weapon States with regard to the nuclear weapons capabilities and the implementation of agreements pursuant to article VI and as a voluntary confidence building measure to support further progress on nuclear disarmament;
- The further reduction of non-strategic nuclear weapons, based on unilateral initiatives and as an integral part of the nuclear arms reduction and disarmament process;
- Concrete agreed measures to further reduce the operational status of nuclear weapons systems;
- A diminishing role for nuclear weapons in security policies to minimize the risk that these weapons will ever be used and to facilitate the process of their total elimination;
- The engagement as soon as appropriate of all the nuclear-weapon States in the process leading to the total elimination of their nuclear weapons.'

26 These 'progressive efforts' add detail to the somewhat general obligation in Article VI NPT, and are relevant to interpreting the ambit of that provision. They make it clear that the obligation in Article VI is considerably wider than mere negotiation, and includes a specific and independent duty on each state to take steps towards disarmament. This is apparent from the language used: 'reduce their nuclear arsenals unilaterally', 'unilateral initiatives'. The inclusion in Step 9 of an obligation on nuclear-weapon states to act with increased transparency with regard to their weapons capabilities is of particular note for the matters we consider in this opinion.

27 In so far as they are relevant, the *travaux preparatoires* of the NPT serve to confirm the importance of the obligation to achieve nuclear disarmament in Article VI. The negotiating history reveals the significance that the non-nuclear states placed upon the inclusion of nuclear disarmament in Article VI, and their dissatisfaction with earlier drafts which had only included references to 'cessation of the arms race' in the preamble.[35]

28 The view that Article VI creates a specific obligation of nuclear disarmament and not just an obligation to negotiate was emphasised by the ICJ in *Legality of the Threat or Use of Nuclear Weapons*:

> The legal import of that obligation goes beyond that of a mere obligation of conduct; the obligation involved here is an obligation to achieve a precise result, nuclear disarmament in all its aspects, by adopting a particular course of conduct, namely, the pursuit of negotiations on the matter in good faith... This two-fold obligation to pursue and to conclude negotiations formally concerns the 182 States parties to the Treaty...[36]

29 Acts or omissions by state parties which run counter to the objectives of Article VI, as elucidated in particular by the 2000 Review Conference, will therefore amount to a violation of an international legal obligation imposing an identifiable result. Breaches of Article VI *'may be demonstrated by acts and failures to act which, taken together, render the fulfilment of specific treaty obligations remote or impossible.'*[37]

30 Taking into account all of the above, Article VI can be seen to impose the following obligations:

    i To undertake to pursue negotiations in good faith on effective measures to end the nuclear arms race at an early date;

    ii To undertake to pursue negotiations in good faith on effective measures relating to nuclear disarmament;

    iii To undertake to pursue negotiations in good faith on a treaty for general and complete disarmament.

31 In our opinion, these obligations, and in particular the requirement to act in good faith, would be breached by, *inter alia,* the following:

    i An act or omission by a state party to the NPT which would render the attainment of the objective of nuclear disarmament remote or impossible;

    ii An act which undermines the overall objective of nuclear disarmament, as elucidated by the 2000 Review Conference.

32 Article VI is at the very crux of the NPT's purpose. In our view, it is a 'provision essential to the accomplishment of the object or purpose of the treaty.'[38] Accordingly, breach of it would be material within the meaning of customary international law, as codified by the VCLT, Article 60.

33 A state cannot defend its own actions or inactions by reference to any failure by another state party, unless it is alleged that the failure amounted to a material breach warranting termination or suspension, and only then when the proper process is adhered to.[39] Alternatively, a state may elect to withdraw from the NPT in accordance with its international legal obligations, as is permitted by Article X, if it considers that extraordinary events require it to do so. However, in the absence of any such formal action to terminate, suspend or withdraw from the NPT, its obligations remain binding upon each state party in their entirety.

The Legality of the UK's Current Strategy on the use of Nuclear Weapons

The Trident system

34 Trident is a three-component nuclear missile system, and comprises the UK's strategic nuclear deterrent. The three elements are:[40]

i **The platform**: Trident operates from Vanguard-class nuclear-powered submarines, of which there are currently four in service. Each submarine has 16 missile tubes. At any given time, one of the four submarines is on patrol, forming the Continuous-at-Sea Deterrent Cycle.

ii **The missile**: the submarines carry Trident II D5 submarine-launched ballistic missiles, which have a range of between 6,500km and 12,000km, depending on their payload. The missiles are accurate to within a few metres, and each can carry up to 12 warheads. However, subsequent to the 1998 *Strategic Defence Review*, each submarine is currently limited to 48 warheads, implying no more than 3 warheads per missile. It is thought that some missiles are armed with a single warhead, to be used on a sub-strategic basis.[41]

iii **The warhead**: public information is limited as to the precise nature of the warheads used in Trident. However, they are thought to be closely related to the American W76 thermonuclear warhead, which has a yield of approximately 100 kilotons ('kt').[42] A 100kt explosion has a lethal distance[43] of approximately 5km, such that the area of lethal damage will extend to some 74.2km². The UK has an estimated total stockpile of approximately 185 nuclear warheads.

According to the Atomic Weapons Establishment's 2000 Annual Report, Trident is capable of being fired at two yields, although the precise size is not specified.[44] It is believed that different yields are achieved,

> by choosing to detonate a warhead's unboosted primary, which would produce a yield of 1 kiloton or less, or by choosing to detonate the boosted primary, which would produce a yield of approximately a few kilotons.[45]

It therefore remains unclear whether there is capability to fire at two or three different yields, and what precisely those yields are.[46] For present purposes, it is noted that a 1kt explosion has a lethal distance of approximately 2.9km².

The lethal distance of a nuclear explosion accounts only for the immediate damage, and not for the residual radiation released in the fall-out. It must first be noted that it is impossible to predict the full effect of nuclear fall-out because 'where the fall-out goes will depend on the winds'.[47] However, the following is one estimation of the likely fall-out from a 1kt nuclear explosion on the assumption of a particular wind speed:

> Assuming a 24km per hour wind, ionising radiation levels from radioactive fallout within an area of about 15km2 would be high enough to cause radiation sickness in the short term to those exposed in the open, and in some cases to those in buildings. This area would extend to some ten kilometres downwind and would have a maximum width of about 2km. Furthermore, radiation levels in an area of about 400km2 would be such that certain counter-measures would have to be taken to protect people from the long-term effects of exposure to radiation, for example, fatal cancers. This area would extend to some 80km downwind.[48]

35 Trident is intended to fulfil two roles within the UK defence policy: strategic and sub-strategic.[49] Strategic strikes are those which involve *'a full-scale attack against an adversary in which all or a significant part of the available Trident force would be launched.'*[50]

In contrast, a sub-strategic strike is one involving the *'launch of one or a limited number of missiles against an adversary as a means of conveying a political message, warning or demonstration of resolve.'*[51] A more graphic description of the role and effect of a sub-strategic strike was given by a Ministry of Defence official in 1996:

> The limited and highly selective use of nuclear weapons in a manner that fell demonstrably short of a strategic strike, but with a sufficient level of violence to convince an aggressor who had already miscalculated our resolve and attacked us that he should halt his aggression and withdraw or face the prospect of a devastating strategic strike.[52]

Trident is not currently held out as fulfilling a tactical role, 'where weapons are used for a military purpose against enemy units on the battlefield'.[53]

The UK's current strategy on the use of Trident

36 In this section of our opinion, we consider the legality of the current UK stance on the use of nuclear weapons, as encapsulated in two statements.

37 The first is the 1998 *Strategic Defence Review*, which provides:

> ... while large nuclear arsenals and risks of proliferation remain, our minimum deterrent remains a necessary element of our security. ... This does not depend on the size of other nation's arsenals but on the minimum necessary to deter any threat to our **vital interests.**[54]

As to what constitute the UK's 'vital interests':

> We are a major European state and a leading member of the European Union. Our security is indivisible from that of our European partners and Allies. We therefore have a fundamental interest in the security and stability of the continent as a whole and in the effectiveness of NATO as a collective political and military instrument to underpin these interests. This in turn depends on the transatlantic relationship and the continued engagement in Europe of the United States.
>
> But our **vital interests are not confined to Europe.** Our economy is founded on international trade. ...[55]

38 The second statement is reflected in a series of comments by the then Defence Secretary, Mr Hoon, in 2002:[56]

> In March, Hoon said, in the context of Iraq: 'I am absolutely confident, in the right conditions, we would be willing to use our nuclear weapons.'

... a few days later Hoon gave more particulars to Jonathan Dimbleby, insisting that the nuclear option would be taken pre-emptively, if we thought British forces were about to be attacked by Iraqi chemical or biological weapons.[57]

> A British government must be able to express their view that, ultimately and in conditions of extreme self-defence, nuclear weapons would have to be used.[58]

39 Mr Hoon's comments are to be taken as representing the views of the Government. In the *Nuclear Tests Case* the ICJ found that the comments of the French President

> and members of the French Government acting under his authority up to the last statement made by the Minister of Defence ... constitute a whole. Thus, in whatever form these statements were expressed, they must be held to constitute an engagement of the State, having regard to their intention and to the circumstances in which they were made.[59]

40 These statements reveal an apparent willingness to use nuclear weapons against non-nuclear states in order to deter attacks on 'vital interests', where those interests include conventional UK forces overseas under threat from biological or chemical warfare.

The use of nuclear weapons against non-nuclear states in response to threats against the UK's 'vital interests', including forces overseas

41 It is apparent from Mr Hoon's comments, made as Defence Secretary, that the policy of the British Government is to countenance the use of nuclear weapons in self-defence against a threatened attack by a non-nuclear state.[60] As we stated above, in our opinion, the use of force in response to a threatened attack may be lawful, but only where the following three requirements are met:

i   The threat posed is imminent;

    ii   The response is necessary;

    iii The response is proportionate.

42 It must also be recalled that:

> A weapon that is already unlawful per se, whether by treaty or custom, does not become lawful by reason of it being used for a legitimate purpose under the Charter.[61]

43 Therefore, if a particular nuclear weapon is inherently incapable of meeting the requirements imposed by IHL, its use in self-defence will not be lawful: a weapon's inherent illegality is not corrected by virtue of the right to act in self-defence. Our conclusions on the legality under IHL of deploying Trident as it is currently constituted can be found at paragraphs 59, 63 and 64, below. In this section, we only consider issues of compatibility with the *jus ad bellum*.

Imminence

44 The imminence of a threat can only be judged by reference to a specific factual situation. Accordingly, it is impossible to form an opinion in the abstract as to whether this criterion is fulfilled. However, we re-affirm the view that there must be an immediate threat in the circumstances that prevailed, and not a threat that was more remote or hypothetical: see paragraph 10, above. We note also the debate ignited by the USA's suggestion in its National Security Strategy, published during the period prior to the invasion of Iraq, that the use of force was permissible even where the imminence of the threat had not been determined:

> The United States has long maintained the option of pre-emptive actions to counter a sufficient threat to our national security. The greater the threat, the greater is the risk of inaction – and the more compelling the case for taking anticipatory action to defend ourselves, even if uncertainty remains as to the time and place of the enemy's attack. To forestall or prevent such hostile acts by our adversaries, the United States will, if necessary, act pre-emptively.[62]

45 It is our strong view that there is no rule of international law which would permit the use of force, regardless of whether it was by nuclear

or conventional weaponry, in circumstances where the intention is to forestall an unascertained future attack, rather than to prevent an imminent and identifiable threat.[63]

Necessity and proportionality

46 We stated our understanding of these requirements at paragraphs 8–9, above. Accordingly, any use of nuclear weapons in self-defence which exceeds that which is strictly and objectively necessary and proportionate will be unlawful. Use of force which is excessive to that required to respond to a real threat will be disproportionate.

47 The ICJ has provided some indication of the threshold that would have to be met in relation to nuclear weapons:

> ... in view of the current state of international law, and of the elements of fact at its disposal, the Court cannot conclude definitively whether the threat or use of nuclear weapons would be lawful or unlawful in an extreme circumstances of self-defence, in which the very survival of a State would be at stake.[64]

48 In his separate Declaration, President Bedjaoui made it clear that this should not 'in any way be interpreted as leaving the door open to the recognition of the *lawfulness of the threat or use of nuclear weapons.*'[65] In our opinion, the ICJ's statement tends to support the view that where the *'very survival'* of a state is not at stake it would be difficult to envisage the necessity and proportionality – and hence legality – of the use of nuclear weapons. Relatedly, we wish to be clear that we are not concluding that whenever the 'very survival' of a state is at stake *any* scale of nuclear response will be lawful. The presence of a threat to state survival does not, in our view, absolve the threatened state from its obligation to confine its response to that which is necessary and proportionate[66], and in compliance with IHL.

49 In considering whether the UK could act lawfully in using nuclear weapons to respond to a threatened attack, it must be recalled that the current Trident system uses warheads with a yield of approximately 100kt (although capable, it is thought, of being deployed with approximately 1 or 5kt yields, with some modification[67]). A weapon of this size has a lethal distance of approximately 74.2km².[68] By way of example,

six of the most central London boroughs have population densities in excess of 10,000 people per square kilometre,[69] so that a 100kt nuclear explosion in an area with a similar population density would likely have a lethal extent encompassing several hundred thousand people.

50 Given the long-term and extreme devastation and loss of life likely to be caused by a response using the UK's current nuclear weaponry, we are of the view that the threat posed must, as the ICJ intimated, be one that goes to the very survival of the state. By this we mean an action which threatens the existence, not merely the effectiveness, of the most essential economic and political components of the state. Alternatively, an action which would kill or incapacitate a significant percentage of the UK's population may threaten the state's survival, although substantial loss of life on its own is unlikely to be enough to merit deployment of nuclear weapons. We are of the opinion that the 'vital interests' outlined in the 1998 *Strategic Defence Review*, in particular those outside the jurisdiction of the UK, could not lawfully be protected by way of a nuclear strike. The *Strategic Defence Review* is, in our view, over broad and not easily reconcilable with the approach taken by the ICJ.

51 We are asked to consider specifically the scenario of using nuclear weapons to deter an imminent biological or chemical attack on UK forces overseas. Whilst the seriousness of such a threat or attack is very great and should not be underestimated, in our view it falls short of the threat to state survival envisaged by the ICJ as **potentially** justifying a nuclear response in self-defence. This is especially so given that the UK does not currently have tactical nuclear weapons capability.[70] The use of nuclear weapons in this situation is therefore likely to be sub-strategic, intended to convey a political message, and involving the use of one or a small number of warheads[71] which would inevitably have an impact upon non-military personnel and property. Indeed, the Government appears to accept that significant civilian causalities and devastation would be the likely consequence of such an attack:

JONATHAN DIMBLEBY: You also told the select committee that you doubted whether Saddam Hussein would be deterred by that threat. If you did then use British nuclear weapons against Iraq because he was not deterred, **you would in effect be punishing the people of Iraq for what Saddam Hussein had done with annihilation.**

GEOFF HOON: **What we would be doing is defending ourselves and the British people against a threat from Saddam Hussein,** I said in extreme conditions of self-defence we would need to do that. You're suggesting somehow that we're talking about retaliation, we are talking about reserving the right to protect our own people from attack by Saddam Hussein. ...

JONATHAN DIMBLEBY: If Britain was to use its own weapon of mass destruction one nuclear weapon **you would in effect be obliterating the lives of hundreds of thousands of people in Iraq,** you would have destroyed Iraq, the countries around, Turkey, in the Gulf, Jordan, Saudi Arabia, Israel, could very easily be horrifically affected by nuclear fall out. I put it to you that in reality no British government would ever, against the threat that you described, deploy that weapon of mass annihilation.

GEOFF HOON: **That is why these are in only the most extreme circumstances where there is a direct threat to our forces and to our people from weapons of mass destruction but it is important that we do not rule that out,** it is important that we do not allow an appalling dictator like Saddam Hussein to know precisely what our response might be.[72]

52 Mr Hoon did not challenge the view that the use of nuclear weapons he envisaged would cause the damage suggested by his interviewer. In our opinion, the use of nuclear weapons in this situation could not comply with the requirements of self-defence and would be in breach of the UK's obligations under Article 2(4) of the UN Charter, as well as IHL. It would be unlawful.[73]

The Lawfulness under IHL of the current Trident System

53 In this part of our opinion we consider whether Trident, as currently constituted, is capable of being deployed in a manner compatible with IHL. We have already outlined our understanding of the relevant IHL obligations. We do not consider in this section the context in which the weapons may be deployed i.e. self-defence, which is discussed elsewhere in this opinion.

Compatibility with the prohibition on indiscriminate weapons

54 We stated above, at paragraph 13, our understanding of the requirements of this prohibition. We concluded that, in order to meet the obligations it imposes, a weapon must be capable of being targeted and its effects must be capable of being predicted and controlled sufficiently so as to be able to discriminate between combatants and civilians.

55 The UK has continually maintained that nuclear weapons are capable of complying with this obligation. In its written statement to the ICJ in the *Legality of the Threat or Use of Nuclear Weapons* the UK said:

> The reality ... is that nuclear weapons might be used in a wide variety of circumstances with very different results in terms of likely civilian casualties. In some cases, such as the use of a low yield nuclear weapon against warships on the High Seas or troops in sparsely populated areas, it is possible to envisage a nuclear attack which caused comparatively few civilian casualties. It is by no means the case that every use of nuclear weapons against a military objective would inevitably cause very great collateral civilian casualties.[74]

56 In our opinion, this position fails to give sufficient regard to all consequences of a nuclear explosion. It is certainly possible to envisage a nuclear strike on the high seas or in a sparsely populated area in which the lethal distance of the immediate explosion will be sufficiently limited so as to be able to discriminate between combatants and civilians. We would add, however, that the UK has never sought to expressly limit its policy on the use of nuclear weapons to such situations, and its recent statements in relation to Iraq do not limit the potential use of nuclear weapons to these circumstances. We accept that the UK has made general statements saying that it will act compatibly with its legal obligations,[75] but it has nonetheless countenanced the use of nuclear weapons to deter non-nuclear attacks on UK forces overseas, and in circumstances where massive civilian loss of life is highly likely.[76] Moreover, it did not seek then to argue that the weapon would only be used in a sparsely populated area, or even to rebut the suggestion that civilian casualties would be vast.

57 More important, however, is the failure to give sufficient regard to the secondary, but unique aspect of a nuclear explosion: the radioactive fall-out. It cannot sensibly be argued that this is currently capable of either prediction or limitation. The ICJ assessed these effects as follows:

> ... nuclear weapons are explosive devices whose energy results from the fusion or fission of the atom. By its very nature, that process, in nuclear weapons as they exist today, releases not only immense quantities of heat and energy, but also powerful and prolonged radiation. According to the material before the Court, the first two causes of damage are vastly more powerful than the damage caused by other weapons, while the phenomenon of radiation is said to be peculiar to nuclear weapons. These characteristics render the nuclear weapon potentially catastrophic. **The destructive power of nuclear weapons cannot be contained in either space or time.** They have the potential to destroy all civilization and the entire ecosystem of the planet.
>
> The radiation released by a nuclear explosion would affect health, agriculture, natural resources and demography over a very wide area. Further, the use of nuclear weapons would be a serious danger to future generations. Ionizing radiation has the potential to damage the future environment, food and marine ecosystem, and to cause genetic defects and illness in future generations.
>
> ... methods or means of warfare, which would preclude any distinction between civilian and military targets, or which would result in unnecessary suffering to combatants, are prohibited. In view of the unique characteristics of nuclear weapons, to which the Court has referred above, the use of such weapons in fact seems **scarcely reconcilable with respect for such requirements.**[77]

58 Further explanation and support for the uncontrollable and unpredictable nature of nuclear weapons can be found in the comments of Dr Douglas Holdstock, a member of Medact's Nuclear Hazards Group and a retired hospital physician with experience of radiation protection:

> As well as prompt radiation, a nuclear explosion creates large amounts of highly radioactive material by fission of uranium or plutonium. In addition, if the explosion is low in the atmosphere or at ground level, so that the fireball is in contact with the

ground, solid material is sucked into it and irradiated also creating radioactive isotopes.

The fate of this material depends upon particle size and weather conditions. Much of it is deposited in an approximately cigarshaped area down-wind of the explosion. The various forms of radiation sickness ... would result, the most severe of course closest to the explosion site. The extent of the fall-out would depend on the size of the explosion and wind speed. After the first multimegaton H-bomb explosion at Bikini Atoll in the Pacific in 1954, the plume extended for over 400km, most of the islanders in atolls 200km from Bikini were affected by radiation-induced illnesses including cancers. Some of these atolls were still uninhabitable 25 years later.

... Some of the irradiated material is carried high into the stratosphere and comes down slowly over a wide area as delayed fall-out.

... [Q] What would be the effects on civilians if a single 'tactical Trident' warhead were detonated in the Arctic or the Sahara?

It probably wouldn't do very much physical damage. The surrounding area would become desert (if it were not desert already). The fallout would be mainly in uninhabited areas, but some would go high up into the stratosphere, carried by the wind and come down all over the earth. Civilian deaths could not be ruled out.

[Q] What would be the effects of using a nuclear device at sea?

A tidal wave-like effect. Irradiated water would not be as dangerous as irradiated debris. But radiation would get into the foodchain (through fish). Internal radioactivity, through inhalation of radioactive fall-out or through ingestion of affected food, is much worse than external effects. It would produce cancers and could produce birth defects. References to severely deformed babies in the Bikini Islands could well have been caused by the fact that people at a lot of fish in that region.[78]

59 In our opinion, there is ample evidence on which it can be concluded that the harmful effects of the nuclear weapons currently held by the UK are inherently unpredictable and uncontrollable. We conclude that there must be a presumption that the use of the UK's current nuclear

weaponry, whether with 1kt or 100kt yields, would breach the prohibition on the use of indiscriminate weapons.

Compatibility with the prohibition on unnecessary suffering

60 A nuclear explosion produces both immediate radiation and radioactive fall-out. Exposure to either can cause radiation sickness. The closer to the explosion site, the higher the degree of radiation. The stronger the radiation, the more severe the sickness. In larger nuclear explosions, the heat and blast will generally kill more people than the immediate radiation. However, smaller 1kt nuclear events cause less lethal blast and heat damage, and the preponderance of fatalities will be caused by radiation.[79]

61 Acute radiation sickness has three forms, which are dependent on the level of radiation received:[80]

    i   The neurological syndrome is caused by the highest doses of radiation. It leads to coma and rapid death;

    ii The gastrointestinal syndrome is caused by a lesser dose. It causes severe vomiting, intestinal ulceration and copious diarrhoea, and has a very high mortality rate;

    iii The bone marrow is affected in the third form of acute sickness, caused by lower levels of radiation. This leads to a lowering of white blood cells and blood clotting agents. In itself this can be fatal. It also predisposes the victim to infection and reduces the ability to heal other injuries sustained in a nuclear explosion. This may render fatal injuries which were otherwise survivable.

62 Those who do survive acute radiation sickness, and those who are exposed to radiation, but who do not develop acute symptoms, are at increased risk of leukaemia and other cancers for several years thereafter.

63 It is indisputable that the various forms of acute radiation sickness, and the long-term effect of exposure to high levels of radiation, cause considerable and prolonged suffering. We also note the view, shared by an increasing number of commentators, that there is no military purpose for nuclear weapons which is incapable of being achieved

by conventional weaponry.[81] In our opinion, the unique suffering caused by radiation from a nuclear explosion, and potentially coupled with an absence of true military necessity, is such as to render the use of the nuclear weapons currently held by the UK inherently in violation of the prohibition on unnecessary suffering.

Compatibility with the principle of neutrality

64 The inability to predict or control the geographical or temporal consequences of nuclear fall-out is readily apparent. It is also clear that nuclear fall-out causes considerable damage to the natural environment as well as to humans: on this we reiterate the conclusions of the ICJ, quoted at paragraph 57, above. In our opinion, it is therefore difficult to envisage any circumstances in which the use of Trident would not breach the principle of neutrality by causing damage to neutral states.

The legality of replacing or upgrading Trident

65 The Government has stated that a decision will be taken on the future of Trident during the current Parliament. In June 2005, the then Defence Secretary Dr Reid accepted that enhancements to the UK's nuclear capability could breach the NPT obligations:

> ... the answer depends on what we do: if we replace the existing system with a massive increase in our capability, that may not be compatible; if we reduce capability, that may well be compatible. So the answer to the question is precisely as I said: it could well be in line with our existing obligations.[82]

66 There are a number of options open to the UK, of which the following are most relevant:

i   Not to replace Trident. There are approximately 18 years of Trident's projected 30 year life span remaining, during or at the end of which the UK would relinquish its nuclear deterrent;

ii To upgrade the current Trident system, for example by enhancing its targeting capabilities;

iii To replace Trident with a new system of the same or similar capabilities;

iv To replace Trident with a new system using smaller yields.

67 In our view, there is no inherent legal difference between an 'upgrade' and a 'replacement', both of which would involve enhancing the current system. The question is one of substance and not form: whether the changes are such as to be incompatible with the UK's obligations under Article VI NPT and IHL.

68 On this basis, we consider the options in terms of their substantive impact on the UK's nuclear posture and capability, rather than their form as an upgrade or replacement. From the current debate, we consider the following to be the most relevant possibilities:

i   Enhanced targeting systems, permitting more accurate deployment of nuclear weapons;

ii Increased yield flexibility, incorporating a 'mini-nuclear capability' for explosions of 1–5kt;

iii Renewal of the current capability over a longer period.

69 Before we consider the legality of these three possibilities, there are some issues relating to the underlying policy of the UK's nuclear deterrent which we think are relevant to the current debate. We deal with these issues first, and then consider the three possibilities outlined above. We do not consider in this opinion the issue of any upgrades that may already have been made to the UK's nuclear weaponry, and which do not bear on the legality of future upgrades or renewals.

The policy underlying Trident

70 Trident was initially developed in the context of the Cold War, and was intended to fulfil the 'Moscow criteria': **'the ability to threaten to inflict sufficient damage** on Moscow and a number of other Soviet cities at any time of the day, 365 days of the year'.[83] Since the end of the Cold War, this particular context and purpose has become redundant. Robin Cook MP, the former Foreign Secretary, said in July 2005:

> No other credible nuclear threat has stepped forward to replace the Soviet Union as a rationale for the British nuclear weapons

system. To be sure, two or three other nations have emerged with a crude nuclear capability, but none of them has developed the capacity or the motivation to attack Britain. ... the collapse of the cold war has removed even the theoretical justification for our possessing strategic nuclear weapons.[84]

71 In 1993 the then Defence Secretary, Malcolm Rifkind, stated:

Of course complete and general nuclear disarmament remains a desirable ultimate goal and we must continue to make what progress we can towards it. But nuclear weapons cannot be disinvented... And reflect on the course of events, should at some distant point in the future a new East/West threat arise... We would be at risk of seeing, in such circumstances, a race to be the first to recreate nuclear weapons... Would a Europe in which the prospect of a nuclear rearmament race existed be genuinely more stable?[85]

72 In December 2003 the Ministry of Defence stated: *'There are currently no major conventional military threats to the UK or NATO...'*[86] Similarly, the 1998 *Strategic Defence Review* concluded that *'there is today no direct military threat to the United Kingdom or Western Europe. Nor do we foresee the re-emergence of such a threat. But we cannot take this for granted.'*[87]

73 The Government maintains that nuclear weapons form an important part of the UK's defence policy, although not in order to counter the terrorist threat.[88] Dr Reid, then Defence Secretary, said in January 2006:

It is perfectly true that there are new threats arising from terrorism, but that does not mean that the old threats have disappeared. It is equally true that the type of forces that we would need to develop to counter-terrorism, such as special forces, extra surveillance and extra mobility, are not necessarily nuclear weapons. That nuclear weapons are not a response to the threat of terrorism does not mean, however, that we should, for instance, get rid of special forces because they are not a response to the threat of nuclear weapons. The truth is that we need a range of responses to a range of threats.[89]

The legitimacy of the policy justifications for replacing or upgrading Trident

74 The Government has stated that it will set out the factors it believes are relevant to the necessary current and any possible future minimum nuclear deterrent for the UK when it publishes a White Paper.[90] Until then, the following is representative of the Government's stance:

i The nuclear deterrent is not dependent on the size of nuclear arsenals held by other states;

ii The nuclear deterrent is not retained because of the status it accords the UK in its international relations;

iii It is retained because of its role in deterring acts of aggression, insuring against the re-emergence of major strategic military threats, preventing nuclear coercion and preserving peace and stability.[91]

75 This can be distilled into two principal bases on which the UK is likely to justify any upgrade to or replacement of Trident:

i Deterrence;

ii Insurance against a possible future threat.

Deterrence

76 The UK has consistently argued that it is necessary to retain a nuclear capability as a deterrent. In its response to the Defence Committee's Eighth Report of Session 2005–06, the Government reiterated the following statement initially made in the December 2003 Defence White Paper 'Delivering Security in a Changing World':

> However, the continuing risk from the proliferation of nuclear weapons, and the certainty that a number of other countries will retain substantial nuclear arsenals, mean that our minimum nuclear deterrent capability, currently represented by Trident, is likely to remain a necessary element of our security.[92]

77 The Government's stated justification for a nuclear deterrent is therefore the possession of nuclear weapons by other states. It does not, on its face, appear to be predicated on the possession of conventional, chemical or biological weaponry by other states.

78 However, these statements must be read in light of Mr Hoon's comments, as Defence Secretary, in 2002 that the UK would use nuclear weapons to deter chemical or biological attacks on UK forces overseas.[93] They must also be read in light of Dr Reid's comments, as the Minister of State for the Armed Forces, made in 1997:

> The role of deterrence, to which the right hon. Member referred, must not be overlooked. Even if a potential aggressor has developed missiles with the range to strike at the United Kingdom, and nuclear, **biological or chemical warheads** to be delivered by those means, he would have to consider—he would do well to consider—the possible consequences of such an attack.
>
> ... Although such despots often appear indifferent to the suffering of their own peoples, I see no sign that they are indifferent to the survival of their regimes and the preservation of their personal positions. Deterrence has a bearing on both those matters.
>
> It seems unlikely that a dictator who was willing to strike another country with weapons of mass destruction would be so trusting as to feel entirely sure that that country would not respond with the power at its disposal. Any state contemplating such an assault on a NATO member would have to consider the implications very carefully.[94]

79 If this reflects the actual Government policy on Trident, that it is necessary for deterrence of both nuclear and non-nuclear weapons of mass destruction (WMD), this raises concerns as to the ambit of the deterrence doctrine and the impact on the UK's compliance with Article VI NPT.

80 We considered above, at paragraphs 30–31, the obligations imposed by Article VI. The conflict of an expanded deterrence policy with these obligations is two-fold:

> i   The expansion of the policy basis on which nuclear weapons can be retained undermines the disarmament objective of Article VI NPT, and is therefore inconsistent with the treaty obligation. It is contrary to the steps agreed by the parties to the NPT at the 2000 conference which includes: 'A **diminishing role** for nuclear weapons in security policies to minimise the risk that these weapons

will ever be used and to facilitate the process of their total elimination.'[95]

ii If nuclear deterrence is justified by the UK on the basis of non-nuclear WMD, and not just nuclear WMD, this is a significant extension of the previous rationale. It is also a basis on which the UK can argue, indefinitely, for the retention of nuclear weapons. This has the potential to thwart the good faith in negotiating nuclear disarmament that the UK is obliged to show under Article VI NPT, by rendering disarmament a more remote prospect.

81 In our opinion, any extension of the deterrence doctrine to include threats posed by non-nuclear WMD would be inconsistent with the rationale of Article VI NPT.

82 The Government has not argued to date that deterrence requires the UK to have a tactical nuclear capability. Were this to become part of the Government's justification in the forthcoming White Paper, we would repeat our view that any expansion of the policy basis on which nuclear weapons can be retained is a breach of Article VI NPT.

Insurance against possible future threats

83 The UK has not, as yet, sought to justify retention of a nuclear deterrent on the basis of any **specific** threat or act of aggression. Instead, it appears to be predicated in part on an inability to rule out any future threats.[96]

84 In its response to the Defence Committee's Eighth Report of Session 2005–06, the Government stated:

The debate about the future of the UK's nuclear deterrent is less about the security position now than about the extent to which we can be confident about the nature of the risks and threats to our defence and security interests that we might face over the next 20–50 years.[97]

85 The difficulty with this rationale is that we cannot now and will not in the future be able to predict what threats the UK will face 20–50 years hence. If this inability to predict future risks forms the basis of

the Government's policy on upgrading or replacing Trident, we will never be in a position to rule out the need for a nuclear deterrent. Essentially the argument is one for permanent retention. As Professor Colin Gray has argued:

> ... in 2006, we can no more predict the strategic history of the 21st Century, than our predecessors in 1906 could predict what the 20th Century would bring.[98]

86 This leads to an obvious conflict with the UK's obligations under Article VI NPT, the requirements of which we outlined above, at paragraphs 30–31. The UK is required to negotiate in **good faith** on **effective measures** to **achieve nuclear disarmament**. If the position of the UK is that a nuclear deterrent remains necessary whilst there is the unascertainable risk of a future threat developing, this amounts to a *de facto* acceptance that the UK will never fully disarm. In our opinion, this can only negate the good faith with which the UK is required to negotiate in order to achieve precisely the aim that its policy will never permit: complete nuclear disarmament by the UK and other states.[99]

87 In our opinion, any justification for upgrading or replacing Trident predicated on the risk of some possible (but unknown) future threat is inherently incompatible with Article VI NPT. This conclusion applies regardless of the precise nature of the proposed upgrade or replacement because it belies a more general failure to observe the good faith obligation.

Enhanced targeting systems

88 The US Navy is carrying out a Life Extension Programme (LEP) to its Trident systems, two aspects of which are:

i Equipping guidance systems with GPS and 'three-axis flat system' for steering the re-entry vehicle. This is a significant upgrade designed to increase accuracy...

ii ... a new guidance system using updated technologies...[100]

89 The legal consequences of the UK taking steps such as these, which are intended to improve the accuracy of the targeting and guidance

systems of nuclear weapons, must be considered both in relation to IHL and Article VI NPT.

90 Dealing first with IHL, we concluded above, at paragraphs 59, 63 and 64, that it should be presumed that use of Trident as currently constituted would breach the prohibitions on indiscriminate weapons, and on unnecessary suffering, and would be likely to breach the neutrality principle. We reached this view on the basis, primarily, of the uncontrollable and devastating effects of the radiation released in a nuclear explosion that would follow the use of Trident. In our opinion, improving the targeting accuracy of nuclear weapons will have little or no effect on this aspect of their consequences and therefore on their compatibility with IHL.

91 Moreover, it is our view that enhancing the targeting capability of the UK's nuclear weaponry undermines the objectives of the NPT, and Article VI in particular. We reach this view on the basis that, *inter alia,* such steps:

  i   Would go against the principle of irreversibility in nuclear disarmament and arms controls which the NPT parties adopted at the 2000 Review Conference, in that it would improve and enhance the UK's nuclear deterrent, rather than diminishing it;[101]

  ii Are likely to increase the circumstances in which the UK's nuclear weapons would be used, in particular in establishing a tactical capability where precision targeting would be of most use, contrary to the obligation to pursue a diminishing role for nuclear weapons in security policies, and to specifically reduce non-strategic weaponry.[102]

92 We concluded above, at paragraph 31, that any steps which undermined the overall objective of nuclear disarmament, or which rendered that objective remote, would be inconsistent with Article VI NPT. Accordingly, and in our opinion, enhancement of the targeting capability of the UK's nuclear deterrent, particularly in the context of a broadening of deterrence policy, would be likely to breach Article VI NPT.

Increased yield flexibility

93 The possibility of developing a nuclear warhead with a wider range of yield options to replace Trident has been the subject of some speculation.[103] This would allow 'more 'useable' smaller weapons to be deployed against more 'precise' targets.'[104] Were such weapons to be developed, it is likely they would fulfil a tactical role which Trident does not currently offer. In assessing the legality of such a development, it must be recalled that the UK is already thought to have the capability to fire Trident warheads modified so as to give yields of 1 or 5kt.[105]

94 It is not immediately clear to us that the development of smaller and more useable nuclear weapons with yields from 1kt upwards would diminish the prospects for breaches of IHL that use of the current Trident weapons is likely to engender (as discussed above, at paragraphs 54–64). Although the radiation released from a 1kt explosion is relatively small in comparison to a larger weapon, it is nonetheless incapable of control and apt to cause indiscriminate harm and unnecessary suffering.[106] Accordingly, it is our view that the use of a nuclear weapon with increased yield flexibility will not necessarily be lawful under IHL, and the overwhelming likelihood is that it would not be.

95 Again, it is our opinion that developing an increased flexibility in yields, in particular to permit tactical deployment, is an enhancement to the current Trident system that undermines the objectives of the NPT. We acknowledge that Trident is capable of being fired at lower yields, but it is apparent that this is a relatively limited capability, giving only two options in addition to the 100kt full yield. In our view, a more flexible system would:

i   Enhance the role of nuclear weapons in the UK's security policy;

ii   Lead to an increase in the UK's non-strategic weapons capability.

96 Both these consequences appear contrary to the practical steps adopted by the state parties to the NPT at the 2000 Review Conference.[107] In our opinion, a system with enhanced yield flexibility will undermine the principle of irreversibility and the obligation to move towards disarmament, in so far as it signifies a technical advance rendering the

use of nuclear weapons more, and not less, likely. For these reasons, we conclude that any such system would be inconsistent with the obligations owed under Article VI NPT.

Renewal of the current capability over a longer period

97 Even those who are sceptical of the imperative nature of the obligations in Article VI, accept that:

> ... the broad thrust of article VI ought to be recognized as among the factors carrying some weight in the scales against renewal, and in **particular against renewal at unchanged or increased magnitude.**[108]

98 In our opinion, this underestimates the strength of the obligations imposed by Article VI. We do not share the view that:

> ... it cannot plausibly be maintained that a legal imperative rests upon the United Kingdom – which has repeatedly affirmed its willingness to abandon capability when all others do – to do so unilaterally, regardless of action by others.[109]

99 It is apparent from the steps agreed at the 2000 Review Conference that the obligation on the nuclear-weapon states under Article VI is **unilateral** as well as **collective**:

> Further efforts by the nuclear-weapon States to reduce their nuclear arsenals **unilaterally.**[110]

100 We accept that this does not impose a complete obligation to disarm, or even an absolute obligation to reduce. However, in our view, it does prohibit steps which are inconsistent with 'further efforts to reduce'. Such steps would have the effect of undermining the overall objective of disarmament and the good faith obligation in relation to negotiations under Article VI.

101 In our opinion, a decision to renew the existing capability, especially on the policy bases of deterrence and insurance considered above, would be incompatible with the taking of 'further steps to reduce' the UK's nuclear arsenal. It renders disarmament more remote and is likely to undermine the good faith obligation. Accordingly, it is likely to be a material breach of Article VI.

Conclusion

102 We have considered three main issues in this opinion: the legality of the UK's strategy on the use of nuclear weapons, the compatibility of the use of Trident with IHL, and the legality of replacing or upgrading the current system.

103 We have concluded that there are serious concerns in all three areas. In particular, we are concerned that the UK has stated a willingness to use nuclear weapons in situations which appear to be outside the doctrine of self-defence as currently recognised under international law. Moreover, it is very difficult to reconcile the indiscriminate and uncontrollable effects of using the Trident system with the UK's obligations under IHL.

104 In relation to the future of Trident, our concerns are twofold. First, we are concerned about the broadening in policy which may be relied on to justify any renewal, replacement or upgrade. Second, we are concerned about the legality of the specific technical options for such renewal, replacement or upgrade. In our view, there are several bases on which expanding either policy or capability may breach the obligations owed by the UK under Article VI of the NPT.

The Maintenance and Possible Replacement of the Trident Nuclear Missile System

RABINDER SINGH QC AND PROFESSOR CHRISTINE CHINKIN

Introduction and Summary of Advice

1   We are asked to advise Peacerights on the legality under international law of the United Kingdom's actions with respect to the Trident nuclear missile system.[1] The question on which our advice is sought is whether the UK is in breach of international law through maintenance of the Trident system or the replacement of that system by one with a similar yield. More specifically advice is sought on (i) whether Trident or a likely replacement to Trident breaches customary international law and (ii) whether the replacement of Trident would breach the Non-Proliferation Treaty 1967 (NPT), article VI.

2   In our opinion, for the reasons which are set out below:

i   The use of the Trident system would breach customary international law, in particular because it would infringe the 'intransgressible' requirement that a distinction must be drawn between combatants and non-combatants.

ii   The replacement of Trident is likely to constitute a breach of article VI of the NPT.

iii   Such a breach would be a material breach of that treaty.

The UK's obligations under customary International Law

3   Since there is no immediate question of the use of Trident the question is whether its possession or replacement is contrary to customary international law. Possession of Trident has been justified by the government in the following terms:

> The justification of Trident is as an instrument of deterrence

with the possibility of its use only in the 'extreme circumstances of self-defence.[2]

4   The language of 'extreme circumstances of self-defence' is taken from the *Legality of the Threat or Use of Nuclear Weapons* advisory opinion of the International Court of Justice (ICJ) where the Court concluded by the President's casting vote that:

> in view of the current state of international law, and of the elements of fact at its disposal, the Court cannot conclude definitively whether the threat or use of nuclear weapons would be lawful or unlawful in an extreme circumstance of self-defence, in which the very survival of a State would be at stake.[3]

5   The Court did not determine that the threat or use of such weapons would be lawful or unlawful but said that it could not definitively rule on the subject. President Bedjaoui, who made the casting vote, explained that para.105. 2. E of the *dispositif* must not 'in any way be interpreted as leaving the way open to the recognition of the lawfulness of the threat or use of nuclear weapons'.[4]

6   The Court emphasised that the *dispositif* must not be read alone for the Court's reply to the question put to it 'rests on the totality of the legal grounds set forth by the Court ... each of which is to be read in the light of the others'.[5]

7   Included within the legal grounds analysed by the ICJ was the affirmation that for a particular instance of the threat or use of force to be lawful it must not be contrary to either the laws regulating the lawfulness of recourse to force (*jus ad bellum*) or the international laws of war (*jus in bello*). It stated that:

> a use of force that is proportionate under the law of self-defence, must, in order to be lawful also meet the requirements of the law applicable in armed conflict which comprise in particular the principles and rules of humanitarian law.[6]

8   The UK did not challenge this legal principle and stated before the Court that:

> The legality of the use of nuclear weapons must therefore be assessed in the light of the applicable principles of international law regarding the use of force and conduct of hostilities, as is the case with other methods and means of warfare.[7]

UK obligations under the *Jus Ad Bellum*

9   UN Charter, article 51 provides that self defence is an exception to the prohibition of the use of force contained in the UN Charter, article 2 (4). It is also an exception under customary international law. The International Law Commission (ILC) Articles on Responsibility of States for Internationally Wrongful Acts,[8] article 21 reiterates that: 'The wrongfulness of an act of a State is precluded if the act constitutes a lawful measure of self-defence in conformity with the Charter of the United Nations.'

10   In the *Legality of the Threat or Use of Nuclear Weapons* the ICJ clarified some aspects of the application of the prohibition of the use of force and self-defence to the use or threat of nuclear weapons.

11   First, the Court coupled the threat of force with its use. The Court stated that:

> Whether a signalled intention to use force if certain events occur is or is not a 'threat' within Article 2, paragraph 4 of the Charter depends upon various factors. If the envisaged use of force is itself unlawful, the stated readiness to use it would be a threat prohibited under Article 2, paragraph 4. ... no State, whether or not it defended the policy of deterrence suggested to the Court that it would be lawful to threaten force if the use of force contemplated would be illegal.[9]

12   Thus where a use of force is prohibited under UN Charter, article 2 (4), a threat to use that same force is also prohibited. If a use of force allegedly in self-defence would violate the principles of necessity and proportionality so too would the threat of use of such force.

> In any of these circumstances the use of force, and the threat to use it, would be unlawful under the law of the Charter.[10]

13   Second, this same assertion makes it clear that any use of nuclear weapons in lawful self-defence is subject to the conditions of necessity and proportionality.

> In plain English, the conditions of necessity and proportionality require that the use of nuclear weapons in self-defence could be envisaged only to meet an attack of comparable gravity that could not be neutralized by any other means.[11]

14 These requirements of necessity and proportionality have been confirmed by the ICJ to constitute customary international law:

> For example it [the UN Charter] does not contain any specific rule whereby self-defence would warrant only measures which are proportional to the armed attack and necessary to respond to it, a rule well established in customary international law.[12]

15 Necessity is a justification precluding the unlawfulness of a wrongful act in exceptional circumstances. Under the International Law Commission (ILC), Articles on Responsibility of States for Internationally Wrongful Acts[13], article 25, necessity may not be invoked unless the act:

   a is the only means for the State to safeguard an essential interest against a grave and imminent peril;

   b does not seriously impair an essential interest of the state or states towards which the obligation exists, or of the international community as a whole.

16 This article was in draft form at the time of the ICJ decision in the *Gabcikovo-Nagymaros* case. Nevertheless the ICJ relied upon it, reiterated its negative wording and its emphasis on the exceptional nature of the plea. It affirmed the basic principles: the act contrary to an international obligation must have been occasioned by an essential interest of the State which is the author of the act; the interest must have been threatened by a 'grave and imminent' peril; the act being challenged must have been the only means of safeguarding the interest; the act must not have seriously impaired an essential interest of the state towards which the act is directed; and the state the author of the act must not have 'contributed to the occurrence of the state of necessity.' The ICJ also stated that these conditions reflect customary international law.[14]

17 The assessment of necessity must be made at the time the decision is made to commit the otherwise unlawful act. In the *Legality of Nuclear Weapons* the Court did not elaborate on the requirement of necessity, perhaps because of the abstract nature of the question put to it. In the *Oil Platforms* case the Court construed necessity strictly and with specific application to the facts in question. It determined that US

attacks on the oil platforms could not be justified as acts of self-defence and also were not necessary to that state's security interests under the Treaty of Amity, 1955, article xx (1) (d).

18 The assessment of proportionality is ongoing throughout any use of force. It requires determining the amount of force that can be legitimately used to achieve the goal. The ICJ also assessed the requirement of proportionality strictly in the *Oil Platforms case*. In determining the proportionality of the US attacks the Court held that it could not 'close its eyes to the scale of the whole operation, which involved inter alia the destruction of two Iranian frigates and a number of other naval vessels and aircraft'.[15]

UK obligations under International Humanitarian Law

19 In the *Threat or Use of Nuclear Weapons* the Court advised that:

> It is undoubtedly because a great many rules of humanitarian law applicable in armed conflict are so fundamental to the respect of the human person and 'elementary considerations of humanity' as the Court put it in its Judgment of 9 April 1949 in the Corfu Channel case (ICJ Reports 1949, p.22), that the Hague and Geneva Conventions have enjoyed a broad accession. Further these fundamental rules are to be observed by all States whether or not they have ratified the conventions that contain them, because they constitute intransgressible principles of international customary law.[16]

20 The Court affirmed this paragraph in the advisory opinion on the *Legal Consequences of the Construction of a Wall in the Occupied Palestinian Territory* (2004) ICJ Reports, para. 157. The expression 'intransgressible' is not part of the usual vocabulary of customary international law and the ICJ appears to be bestowing these principles with some especially weighty status. Vincent Chetail argues that: 'the Court intended to emphasize the importance of humanitarian norms for international law and order as a whole and the particularity of such norms in comparison with the other ordinary customary rules of international law.'[17]

21 Condorelli argues that 'the solemn tone of the phrase, and its wording, show that the Court intended to declare something much more incisive

and significant, doubtless in order to bring the fundamental rules so described closer to *jus cogens*'. Condorelli continues that: 'In other words, the circumstances eliminating unlawfulness that apply in other sectors of the international legal order (such as the victim's consent, self-defence, counter-measures or a state of necessity) cannot be invoked in this particular case.'[18] Professor Cassese has said in this context that 'intransgressible' means 'peremptory in nature as the ICJ held in Threat or Use of Nuclear Weapons (at para. 79)'.[19]

22 Clearly the Court regarded the relevant principles of international humanitarian law as of extreme significance. President Bedjaoui stated from this that a use of force even exercised in the extreme circumstances in which the survival of a state is in question cannot allow a state to exonerate itself from compliance with these intransgressible norms of international humanitarian law.[20]

23 Further in the *Wall* case the Court affirmed the greater authority of these rules by noting that they 'incorporate obligations which are essentially of an *erga omnes* character.'[21] Obligations owed *erga omnes* are the 'concern of all states' and all states have a 'legal interest in their protection'.[22]

24 The particular rules that are bestowed with this intransgressible nature are:
- the principle of distinction between combatants and non-combatants (civilians);
- prohibition of weapons that cause superfluous injury or unnecessary suffering;
- the residual principle of humanity from the Martens Clause.[23]

25 The principle of distinction between combatants and civilians is central to certain international crimes within the jurisdiction of the Rome Statute of the International Criminal Court. Under the Rome Statute of the International Criminal Court, 1998 article 8 (2) (b) (iv): 'Intentionally launching an attack in the knowledge that such attack will cause incidental loss of life or injury to civilians or damage to civilian objects or widespread, long-term and severe damage to the natural environment which would be clearly excessive in relation to the concrete and direct overall military advantage anticipated' is a serious

violation of the laws and customs applicable in international armed conflict. So too is: 'Attacking or bombarding, by whatever means, towns, villages, dwellings or buildings which are undefended and which are not military objectives;'.[24]

Legality of the possession or replacement of Trident under the *Jus Ad Bellum* and *Jus In Bello*

26 The Court's inability to give a definitive answer to the question put to it in the *Threat or Use of Nuclear Weapons* was based both on its assessment of the current state of international law and on the 'elements of fact at its disposal.' Its determination was made in the abstract without reference to a specific incident of maintenance or replacement of a specific weapons system in the hands of any particular state. Even then, referring to the 'principles and rules of law applicable in armed conflict' it found that: 'In view of the unique characteristics of nuclear weapons, ..., the use of such weapons in fact seems scarcely reconcilable with respect for such requirements.'[25]

27 To determine the legality of the possession or replacement of a particular system requires contextual analysis in any particular case. Thus the possession or replacement of Trident must be assessed against the two bodies of treaty and customary law (*jus ad bellum* and *jus in bello*) and in light of the factual circumstances of its capabilities and the context of its possession. The 'intransgressible' principles described above have been distilled into three core questions that need to be asked in making a contextual determination such as that with respect to Trident:

1 'Would the use of a nuclear weapon in the particular circumstances inflict **unnecessary** suffering upon combatants?

2 Would the use of a nuclear weapon in the particular circumstances be directed against civilians, or indiscriminate, or even if directed against a military target, be likely to cause disproportionate civilian casualties?

3 Would the use of a nuclear weapon in the particular circumstances be likely to cause disproportionate harmful effects to a neutral state?'[26]

28 The UK Trident system currently consists of four Vanguard class

nuclear powered submarines each carrying up to 16 US Trident II D 5 missiles. There are around three nuclear warheads mounted on every missile making about 48 warheads carried on each submarine. At least one is on patrol at all times. Trident nuclear warheads are 100 to 120 kilotons each. Even one kiloton, a 'nuclear mini-bomb' 'would flatten all buildings within half a kilometre with up to 50 per cent fatalities up to I kilometre'.[27] 'The fireball of a detonated trident warhead is said to have a diameter of half a mile across while the heat and blast extend miles further.' 'A low-yield Trident warhead would reduce a whole town to rubble.'[28] Each warhead can be aimed at a different target and each has at least eight times the explosive power of the bomb which was dropped on Hiroshima on 6 August 1945.

29 The first Trident submarine entered service in 1994 with the others coming into service progressively over the next five years. Its life span is approximately 30 years and so it could remain operational until approximately 2025. In light of the lead time for a replacement for the current Trident system to become operational (about 14 years) a decision is now due. The government has indicated that a decision about replacement will be made during the current Parliament.[29] The Defence Secretary, John Reid MP, has said that the options are to replace Trident with another submarine-launched missile system, or a ship or air-launched system, or even a land-based system.

30 In light of the blast, heat and radio-active effects of a detonation of a Trident warhead, in our view, it is impossible to envisage how the intransgressible requirement of the principle of distinction between combatants and non-combatants or the requirement of proportionality in the *jus ad bellum* could be met. The use of a Trident warhead would be inherently indiscriminate. Even if aimed at a military target it cannot distinguish between that and civilians within its range. Radioactive effects are not contained by time or space. Accordingly the use of a single Trident warhead in any circumstance, whether a first or second use and whether targeted against civilian populations or military objectives would inevitably be indiscriminate in effect, inflicting **unnecessary** civilian suffering and disproportionate civilian casualties and **disproportionate** harmful effects to a neutral state.

31 In the *Threat or Use of Nuclear Weapons* the Court stated that: 'If the envisaged use of force is itself unlawful, the stated readiness to use it would be a threat prohibited under Article 2, paragraph 4.' The former Defence Secretary, Mr Hoon, has stated that 'in the right conditions we would be willing to use our nuclear weapons.'[30] In the later 4 April 2005 statement he referred to *'extreme circumstances of self-defence'* although he omitted the further qualification of the ICJ: 'in which the very survival of a State would be at stake.' The former statement was made in the context of questions about a UK response to the use of weapons of mass destruction against our forces **in the field.** This assertion was repeated on television where Mr Hoon stated that the government 'reserved the right to use nuclear weapons if Britain or British troops were threatened by chemical or biological weapons.'[31] In our view, threats to British troops in the field even with weapons of mass destruction could not be said to threaten the survival of the state and thus would not come even within the ICJ's ambivalent *dispositif* in the *Threat or Use of Nuclear Weapons.*

32 Mr Hoon has stated that the government must make clear its willingness to use nuclear weapons:

> for that to be a deterrent, a British government must be able to express their view that ultimately and in conditions of extreme self-defence, nuclear weapons would have to be used. And: It is therefore important to point out that the Government have nuclear weapons available to them, and that – in certain specified conditions to which I have referred – we would be prepared to use them.[32]

33 As he was then Secretary of State for Defence Mr Hoon's words can be taken to be the government's position. In the *Nuclear Tests cases* the ICJ stated that the statements of the President of France 'and members of the French Government acting under his authority up to the last statement made by the Minister of Defence … constitute a whole. Thus in whatever form these statements were expressed, they must be held to constitute an engagement of the State, having regard to their intention and to the circumstances in which they were made.'[33] It is clear that his various statements represent the UK position. They were repeated, recorded in Hansard and expressed on television. He

explicitly stated that he was expressing the position of the UK government.

34 Since it is impossible to envisage how the intransgressible requirement of the principle of distinction between combatants and non-combatants or the requirement of proportionality in the *jus ad bellum* could be met by the use of Trident, even if the strict requirements of necessity for self defence were met, it is hard to see how its use could ever conform with the requirements of international law relating to the *jus ad bellum* or *jus in bello*.

35 As a footnote it is worth noting General Comment No. 14 of the Human Rights Committee on the right to life. In the *Threat or Use of Nuclear Weapons* the Court considered that whether a particular loss of life through the use of a certain weapon in warfare violated the right to life under human rights law would fall to be determined by reference to the law applicable in armed conflict, not the human rights provisions. Nevertheless the words of the Human Rights Committee are strong:

'4 It is evident that the designing, testing, manufacture, possession and deployment of nuclear weapons are among the greatest threats to the right to life which confront mankind today. This threat is compounded by the danger that the actual use of such weapons may be brought about, not only in the event of war, but even through human or mechanical error or failure.

5 Furthermore, the very existence and gravity of this threat generates a climate of suspicion and fear between States, which is in itself antagonistic to the promotion of universal respect for and observance of human rights and fundamental freedoms in accordance with the Charter of the United Nations and the International Covenants on Human Rights'.[34]

Conformity of the possession or replacement of Trident with the Treaty on the Non-Proliferation of Nuclear Weapons (NPT), Article VI

UK obligations under the NPT, Article VI

36 Regardless of the legality under customary international law of the possession or replacement of Trident the UK has entered into treaty obligations with respect to negotiation of disarmament. In particular the NPT, article VI states that:

> Each of the parties to the Treaty undertakes to pursue negotiations in good faith on effective measures relating to cessation of the nuclear arms race at an early date and to nuclear disarmament and on a treaty on general and complete disarmament under strict and effective control.

37 The importance of Article VI has been recognised by commentators. It has been called 'the single most important provision of the treaty, however, from the standpoint of long-term success or failure of its goal of proliferation prevention'.[35]

38 It is necessary to determine the extent of UK obligations under this Article and whether actions to extend the life of Trident or to replace it with another system would be in accordance with it. At the 2005 Review Conference the UK Ambassador asserted that: 'We abide by the undertakings we have given to non-proliferation, to the peaceful uses of nuclear energy and, under Article VI of the Treaty, to those on disarmament.'[36] The UK thus accepts its obligations under the NPT, article VI so determination of whether it is in breach of those obligations requires:

- determination of the scope of those obligations through interpretation of Article VI in accordance with principles of treaty interpretation; and
- determination of whether maintaining or seeking to replace Trident are in conformity with those obligations.

The Vienna Convention on the Law of Treaties

39 The principles relating to the law of treaties are largely codified in the Vienna Convention on the Law of Treaties, 1969, 1155 UNTS (VCLT). The United Kingdom is a party to the VCLT (ratified 25 June 1971), which came into force on 27 January 1980. The VCLT does not have retroactive effect (article 4) and therefore does not apply to the original NPT, 1967 which came into force on 5 March 1970.

40 However some provisions of the VCLT have been explicitly accepted by the ICJ as constituting customary international law, including those on material breach and interpretation.[37]

Principles of Treaty Interpretation

41 The VCLT, articles 31–33 provide the basic principles of treaty interpretation that are widely accepted as constituting customary international law.[38] Interpretation of the NPT, article VI will therefore be in accordance with these articles.

42 VCLT, article 31 (1) provides that: 'A treaty shall be interpreted in good faith in accordance with the ordinary meaning to be given to the terms of the treaty in their context and in the light of its object and purpose.'

43 There are two sets of materials that may be relevant to interpreting the terms of the NPT and its object and purpose: the initial negotiation history (*travaux preparatoires*) and the documents and resolutions of the subsequent Review Conferences. The two reflect very different moments in time. The former evidences the intentions of the original Treaty parties and reflects the cold war politics of the time while the latter reflect the ongoing concerns of all the parties to the Treaty, non-nuclear-weapon states as well as nuclear-weapon states.

44 The VCLT requires that the words of a treaty are interpreted in their context and in the light of its object and purpose. The NPT, article VIII (3), makes explicit that the purposes of the Treaty are to be found in the preamble (five yearly reviews must take place 'with a view to assuring that the purposes of the preamble and the provisions of the

treaty are being realised'). This brings the Preamble more firmly into the obligatory provisions of the Treaty.

45 The preamble of a treaty is in any case part of the treaty's context for the purpose of interpretation. The VCLT, article 31 (2) makes it clear that: 'The context for the purpose of the interpretation of a treaty' includes 'its preamble and annexes'. Further VCLT, article 31 (3), specifies that: 'There shall be taken into account, together with the context: (a) any subsequent agreement between the parties regarding the interpretation of the treaty or the application of its provisions; (b) any subsequent practice in the application of the treaty which establishes the agreement of the parties regarding its interpretation; ...' A Declaration of a Review Conference adopted by consensus would come within the wording of article 31 (3) (a) and is thus an appropriate source of interpretation of the obligations of the NPT.

46 Reference to the use that can be made of a treaty's *travaux preparatoires* (preparatory work) is made in VCLT, article 32. Article 32 states that: 'Recourse may be had to supplementary means of interpretation, including the preparatory work of the treaty and the circumstances of its conclusion, in order to confirm the meaning resulting from the application of article 31, or to determine the meaning when the interpretation according to article 31: (a) leaves the meaning ambiguous or obscure; or (b) leads to a result which is manifestly absurd or unreasonable.'

47 Article 32 makes preparatory work relevant only as a secondary source of interpretation, to be referred to when there is ambiguity, or where the approach under article 31 leads to a manifestly absurd or unreasonable result. This is a lesser status than that accorded to the preamble and any subsequent agreement between the parties by article 31. This is confirmed by the heading given to each of the two articles. Article 31 is headed 'General rule of interpretation' while article 32 is headed 'Supplementary means of interpretation'.

48 Accordingly, if there is any disparity between them greater weight should be given to the Declarations of the Review Conference than to the preparatory work of the NPT in determining the scope of obligations under the Treaty text today.

Negotiation History of the NPT

49 Turning first to the negotiation history, a commitment to disarmament was a major concern of non-nuclear-weapon states. India, Brazil, Scandinavian states, Canada, the then UAR and Germany 'brought strong pressure upon the Co-chairmen to obtain some statement within the treaty concerning nuclear disarmament.'[39] The August 1967 draft included reference to *'cessation of the arms race'* only in its preamble. An earlier version of Article VI was brought within the body of the Revised Draft Treaty on Non-Proliferation of Nuclear Weapons, 18 January 1968. Sweden in particular insisted on strengthening Article VI by broadening the commitment of the nuclear-weapon states to seek disarmament agreements. In the General Assembly debate on the draft treaty further objections were made (for example by Brazil, India) to the lack of tangible commitment to nuclear disarmament by nuclear-weapon states. Article VI was further revised before its inclusion in the adopted Treaty.[40]

50 This drafting history of Article VI is important as it shows the linkage between the commitment to non-proliferation and the obligations of all states to pursue negotiations towards nuclear disarmament. Article VI was an integral part of the NPT package, not just an 'add-on'. Its importance to the objectives of the Treaty is indicated by the preamble, paras 8–12. These include the 'intention to achieve at the earliest possible date the cessation of the nuclear arms race' and 'to undertake effective measures in the direction of nuclear disarmament.'

NPT Review Conference 2000

51 Turning to the Review Conferences it is clear that the commitment to disarmament remains strong. The Review Conferences take place in accordance with the terms of the NPT, article VIII (2) which provides for the holding of a Conference of Parties to the Treaty 'to review the operation of this treaty with a view to assuring that the purposes of the Preamble and the provisions of the Treaty are being realised.' The provision for a Review Conference is separate from both the articles for amendment (article VIII (1)) and for extension of the Treaty (article X (2)). The objective of the Review Conference is to

determine compliance with the purposes of the Treaty as expressed in the preamble and its provisions.

52 The Final Document of the Review Conference 2000[41] reiterated the importance of the commitment to disarmament in a number of its statements. In its Review of the operation of the Treaty the Conference noted that the overwhelming majority of states entered into their legally binding commitments not to acquire nuclear weapons 'in the context, *inter alia* of the corresponding legally binding commitments by the nuclear-weapon states to nuclear disarmament in accordance with the Treaty.'[42] Further the Conference reaffirmed that the 'strict observance' of the provisions of the Treaty remains central to achieving the shared objectives of preventing under any circumstances, the further proliferation of nuclear weapons and preserving the Treaty's vital contribution to peace and security.[43]

53 The 2000 Review Conference also agreed a landmark series of practical steps for the systematic and progressive efforts to implement NPT, Article VI and paras 3 and 4 (c) of the 1995 Decision on 'Principles and Objectives for Nuclear Non-Proliferation and Disarmament'. Step 6 is especially relevant: 'An unequivocal undertaking by the nuclear-weapon states to accomplish the total elimination of their nuclear arsenals leading to nuclear disarmament, to which all States parties are committed under article VI.'

54 Step 9 provides the basis for 'Steps by all the nuclear-weapon states leading to nuclear disarmament in a way that promotes international stability...

- Increased transparency by the NWS with regard to the nuclear weapons capabilities and the implementation of agreements pursuant to Article VI...

- Concrete agreed measures to further reduce the operational status of nuclear weapons systems.[44]

55 While NPT, article VI applies to 'Each of the Parties to the Treaty' these steps adopted by the 2000 Review Conference make explicit that there are particular obligations on the nuclear-weapon states.

56 A number of points can be made about the weight to be accorded to

the documents of the 2000 Review Conference. First, a Declaration of the Review Conference is not a formal amendment to the NPT in the terms of article VIII (1) and does not have formally legally binding effect. However, Review Conferences are included within the NPT as an integral part of the structure for reviewing state compliance and resolutions adopted represent the expressed will of the states parties. Security Council resolution 1172, 6 June 1998 recalled the 'Principles and Objectives for Nuclear Non-Proliferation and Disarmament' adopted by the 1995 Review Conference, which are themselves the basis of the steps agreed at the 2000 Conference.

57 Further the ICJ has given weight to the documentation of the NPT Review Conference process when it noted that the 1995 Review Conference had reaffirmed the importance of fulfilling the obligation of the NPT, article VI in its determination that the obligation 'remains without any doubt an objective of vital importance to the whole of the international community today.'[45] These factors all support the conclusion that the documents of such bodies have juridical significance 'as a source of authoritative interpretation of the treaty.'[46] This is also in line with the VCLT, article 31 (3) (a) as noted above.

58 Second, the language of the 2000 Review Conference is in many instances strong in its reiteration of the states parties' obligations under the NPT. For example, the Conference notes the 'reaffirmation' of the states parties' commitment to Article VI[47]; the 'unequivocal undertaking by the nuclear-weapon states'[48]; the agreement for 'concrete agreed measures to further reduce the operational status of nuclear weapons systems' (Part I, Article VI, para. 15.9). Concreteness of language has been identified as one of the factors for determining when non-binding statements become normative.[49]

59 Third, the Conference agreed steps for the 'systematic and progressive efforts to implement Article VI.' This is important as Article VI is imprecise in the nature of the obligation other than the requirement of good faith. There are no specified conditions or qualifications for taking those steps. In the context of obligations under human rights treaties the Committee on Economic, Social and Cultural rights noted that the similar phrase 'progressive realization' in the Covenant on Economic, Social and Cultural Rights, article 2 'must be read in the

light of the overall objective, ... of the Covenant ... It thus imposes an obligation to move as expeditiously and effectively as possible towards that goal. Moreover, any deliberately retrogressive measures in that regard would require the most careful consideration and would need to be fully justified by reference to the totality of the rights provided for in the Covenant'.[50]

60 By analogy the assertion of practical steps for systematic and progressive efforts towards implementation of the NPT, article VI requires positive action towards that end by the nuclear-weapon states and implies that retrogressive measures would be contrary to the Treaty's objective and wording. This view is supported by the emphasis given by the ICJ that the Article VI obligation must be carried out in accordance with the basic principle of good faith.

61 Thus the importance of Article VI to the objects and purposes of the NPT and to the reciprocal obligations of nuclear weapon and non-nuclear-weapon states is confirmed by the negotiation history of the NPT and reinforced by the reaffirmation of its significance by the 2000 Review Conference. The Security Council too has expressed the importance of this international regime in resolution 1172, 6 June 1998 which reaffirmed 'its full commitment to and the crucial importance of the [NPT] ... as the cornerstones of the international regime on the non-proliferation of nuclear weapons and as essential foundations for the pursuit of nuclear disarmament.'

62 The inability of the 2005 Review Conference to agree a consensus statement does not detract from the continued applicability of the 2000 Review Conference, especially the practical steps for the 'systematic and progressive efforts to implement Article VI.' Of particular interest in this regard is the statement by the Head of the UK Delegation. He noted that 'non-proliferation and disarmament are inter-linked in achieving the Treaty's goals' and that the UK continues 'to implement the decisions of past review conferences, including those taken at the Review and Extension Conference in 1995 and the last Review Conference in 2000.' He also noted that as a nuclear-weapon state the UK has particular obligations under Article VI and that it continued to support the disarmament provisions agreed at the 1995 and 2000 Review Conferences.[51]

Obligation to Negotiate in Good Faith

63 Between the 1995 and 2000 Review Conferences the ICJ in *The Legality of the Threat or Use of Nuclear Weapons* 1996 advisory opinion unanimously asserted in *dispositif* paragraph 105. 2. F that:

> There exists an obligation to pursue in good faith **and bring to a conclusion** negotiations leading to nuclear disarmament in all its aspects under strict and effective control. (Emphasis added)

64 The Court based this conclusion on NPT, article VI and confirmed that the obligation contained in article VI, as reaffirmed by the 1995 Review Conference 'remains without any doubt an objective of vital importance to the whole of the international community today.'[52] As the words we have emphasised in the quotation in paragraph 63 above make clear, the Court has interpreted the obligation in article VI to include not merely an obligation to pursue negotiations in good faith but also to bring those negotiations to a conclusion.

65 The Court asserted that this obligation goes beyond that of a 'mere' obligation of *conduct* for it is an obligation to achieve a precise *result*: 'nuclear disarmament in all its aspects ... by the pursuit of negotiations on the matter in good faith.'[53]

66 The Court also noted Security Council resolution 984, 11 April 1995 which reaffirmed the 'need for all States parties to the [NPT] to comply fully with all their obligations'[54]

67 Commentators have noted the importance of the obligation contained in the NPT, Article VI. 'It is important to note that the NPT is the only existing international treaty under which the major nuclear powers are legally committed to disarmament.'[55] The affirmation and extension of this obligation by the Court has also been noted. Richard Falk asserted that the obligation to negotiate to achieve nuclear disarmament was not necessary for the Court's judgement but that it went out of its way to assert this unanimously. 'This emphasis in the advisory opinion on the obligatory character of Article VI of the Nuclear Proliferation Treaty appears to represent common legal ground between nuclear and non-nuclear-weapon states.'[56] Marin Bosch notes that Article VI is the 'only treaty provision in which NWS

have undertaken a legal obligation to negotiate nuclear disarmament agreements'.[57]

68 The wording of NPT, article VI, the assertion of the importance of the obligation by the ICJ, and by the 2000 Review Conference along with practical measures for its implementation all make clear that the obligations of nuclear-weapon states parties to the NPT, including the UK are:

- to undertake to pursue negotiations in good faith on effective measures relating to cessation of the nuclear arms race;
- to undertake to pursue negotiations in good faith on effective measures relating to nuclear disarmament, and to bring them to a conclusion; and
- on a Treaty on general and complete disarmament.

69 The Treaty obligation is thus not to disarm as such, but a positive obligation to pursue in good faith negotiations towards these ends, and to bring them to a conclusion. Good faith is the legal requirement for the process of carrying out of an existing obligation. In the *Nuclear Tests cases* the ICJ described the principle of good faith as 'one of the basic principles governing the creation and performance of legal obligations'.[58] The obligation of good faith has been described as not being one 'which obviously requires actual damage. Instead its violation may be demonstrated by acts and failures to act which, taken together, render the fulfilment of specific treaty obligations remote or impossible.'[59] In the context of an obligation to negotiate in good faith this would involve taking no action that would make a successful outcome impossible or unlikely.

70 Would a UK policy with respect to extend or replace Trident be in accordance with this obligation?

Breach of Treaty: Law of State Responsibility

71 Questions of breach of a treaty are determined both by treaty law and by the principles on state responsibility. The International Law Commission (ILC), Articles on Responsibility of States for Internationally Wrongful Acts,[60] article 12, defines the existence of a breach of an international obligation as occurring 'when an act of that State

is not in conformity with what is required of it by that obligation, regardless of its origin or character.' The International Court of Justice has asserted that such breach includes 'failure to comply with treaty obligations.'[61] Whether there has been such failure is determined by asking whether the behaviour in question 'was in conformity' with the treaty requirements.[62]

72 There are indicators that the UK intends to replace (or extend the life of) its Trident weapon system. Statements have been made that indicate that the government is not looking at the non-nuclear weapon option. For example the Defence White Paper, Delivering Security in a Changing World (December 2003) reiterates the conclusion from the Strategic Defence Review 1998 that: 'We should maintain a minimum nuclear deterrent based on the Trident system.'[63] At paragraph 3.11 it states that the government's policy on nuclear weapons remains as set out in the 1998 Strategic Defence Review. The Labour Party Manifesto 2005 states that 'We are also committed to retaining the independent nuclear deterrent.'[64]

73 There have also been actions in conformity with this stance, for example the 2004 renewal of the Mutual Defence Agreement between the UK and the US. At that time President Bush stated that: 'The United Kingdom intends to continue to maintain viable nuclear forces. ... I have concluded that it is in our interest to continue to assist them in maintaining a credible nuclear force.'[65]

74 Enhancing nuclear weapons systems, possibly without going through parliamentary processes, is, in our view, not conducive to entering into negotiations for disarmament as required by the NPT, article VI and evinces no intention to 'bring to a conclusion negotiations leading to nuclear disarmament in all its aspects'. It is difficult to see how unilateral (or bilateral) action that pre-empts any possibility of an outcome of disarmament can be defined as pursuing negotiations in good faith and to bring them to a conclusion and is, in our view, thereby in violation of the NPT, article VI obligation.

Breach of Treaty: the VCLT

75 The analysis has proceeded under the definition of breach provided by the International Law Commission's Articles on State Responsibility. Breach is also included in the VCLT. However the VCLT deals only with 'material' breach. The Articles on State Responsibility provisions are not limited to material breach and are applicable to any breach of a treaty.

76 In addition to determining that the UK is in breach of the obligations of the NPT, article VI under the ILC, Articles on State Responsibility, we also consider whether such behaviour amounts to material breach under the VCLT, article 60.

77 The VCLT, article 60 (3) defines a material breach as occurring in one of two ways: 'A material breach of a treaty, for the purposes of this article, consists in: (a) a repudiation of the treaty not sanctioned by the present Convention; or (b) the violation of a provision essential to the accomplishment of the object or purpose of the treaty.'

78 The UK has not repudiated the NPT and has indeed reaffirmed it as in the words of Ambassador Freeman cited above.

79 Therefore, if there is any material breach it must be under VCLT, article 60 (3) (b), that is whether there is behaviour that violates a provision 'essential to the accomplishment of the object or purpose of the treaty.' The object and purpose of the NPT as spelled out in its preamble include 'to undertake effective measures in the direction of nuclear disarmament'.

80 The linkage between the principles of non-proliferation and the obligation to negotiate towards disarmament shown by the negotiation history (discussed in paras 14–5 above) indicate that Article VI is a provision 'essential to the accomplishment of the object or purpose of the treaty.' The non-nuclear-weapon states required commitments from the nuclear-weapon states as part of their willingness to accept non-nuclear status under the NPT and failure to comply with article VI thus, in our view, constitutes material breach.

Deterrence: The Legal Context

PROFESSOR NICK GRIEF

ANY ANALYSIS OF the legal context of nuclear deterrence must begin with Articles 2(4) and 51 of the UN Charter. Article 2(4) prohibits the threat or use of force against the territorial integrity or political independence of a State, or in any other manner inconsistent with the purposes of the UN. Article 51 preserves 'the inherent right of individual or collective self-defence if an armed attack occurs against a Member of the United Nations...'

In the *Nuclear Weapons Case* (July 1996)[1] the International Court of Justice (ICJ) held that there is a symbiotic relationship between 'use' and 'threat':

> The notions of 'threat' and 'use' of force under Article 2, paragraph 4, of the Charter stand together in the sense that if the use of force itself in a given case is illegal (for whatever reason) the threat to use such force will likewise be illegal. In short, if it is to be lawful, the declared readiness of a State to use force must be a use of force that is in conformity with the Charter...[2]

In March 2001 Scotland's Appeal Court, the High Court of Justiciary, rejected the contention that the general deployment of Trident in pursuit of a policy of deterrence constituted a 'threat' to use it.[3] But the Scottish Court's assessment is arguably at odds with the ICJ's analysis:

> Possession of nuclear weapons may indeed justify an inference of preparedness to use them. In order to be effective, the policy of deterrence... necessitates that the intention to use nuclear weapons be credible. Whether this is a 'threat' contrary to Article 2, paragraph 4, depends upon whether the particular use of force envisaged would be directed against the territorial integrity or political independence of a State, or against the Purposes of the United Nations or whether, in the event that it were intended as a means of defence, it would necessarily violate the principles of necessity and proportionality. In any of these circumstances the use of force, and the threat to use it, would be unlawful under the law of the Charter.[4]

As the ICJ made clear, moreover, the law of the UN Charter is not the only law which must be considered. Even if a State has the right to use force in self-defence under *jus ad bellum* (the law governing recourse to armed force), in using force it must comply with *jus in bello* (the law applicable in armed conflict), in particular International Humanitarian Law (IHL):

> The proportionality principle may thus not in itself exclude the use of nuclear weapons in self-defence in all circumstances.[5] But at the same time, a use of force that is proportionate under the law of self-defence, must, in order to be lawful, also meet the requirements of the law applicable in armed conflict which comprise in particular the principles and rules of humanitarian law.[6]

What are these principles and rules?

> The cardinal principles contained in the texts constituting the fabric of humanitarian law are the following. The first is aimed at the protection of the civilian population and civilian objects and establishes the distinction between combatants and non-combatants; States must never make civilians the object of attack and must consequently never use weapons that are incapable of distinguishing between civilian [objects] and military targets. According to the second principle, it is prohibited to cause unnecessary suffering to combatants: it is accordingly prohibited to use weapons causing them such harm or uselessly aggravating their suffering. In application of that second principle, States do not have unlimited freedom of choice of means in the weapons they use.[7]

The ICJ held that the fundamental rules of IHL 'are to be observed by all States whether or not they have ratified the conventions that contain them, because they constitute intransgressible principles of international customary law.'[8]

In the light of those principles, the Court clearly doubted whether nuclear weapons could ever be used lawfully. In view of 'the unique characteristics of nuclear weapons, and in particular their destructive capacity, their capacity to cause untold human suffering and their ability to cause damage to generations to come', it observed that the use of such weapons 'seems scarcely reconcilable' with respect for the law of armed conflict, 'at the heart of which is the overriding consideration of humanity'.[9] It also questioned whether the so-called 'limited use' of smaller, low-yield, tactical nuclear weapons as advocated by some States 'would not tend to escalate into the all-out use of high yield nuclear weapons'.[10]

However, the Court considered that it did not have sufficient elements to enable it to conclude with certainty that the use of nuclear weapons would necessarily be at variance with IHL in any circumstance. It also said that it could not lose sight of the fundamental right of every State to survival, and thus its right to resort to self-defence, in accordance with Article 51, when its survival is at stake; and that it could not ignore the 'policy of deterrence', which it observed that an appreciable section of the international community had adhered to for many years.[11]

Accordingly, whilst the ICJ held that the threat or use of nuclear weapons would generally violate the rules of international law applicable in armed conflict, in particular the principles and rules of IHL,[12] it could not,

> conclude definitively whether the threat or use of nuclear weapons would be lawful or unlawful in an extreme circumstance of self-defence, in which the very survival of a State would be at stake.[13]

The UK Government misinterpreted the Court's carefully worded position, and subsequently argued that the ICJ's advisory opinion did not:

> require a change in the United Kingdom's entirely defensive deterrence policy. We would only ever consider the use of nuclear weapons in the extreme circumstance of self-defence which includes the defence of our NATO allies.[14]

But this wrongly assumes that the ICJ acknowledged an *in extremis* exception to the general prohibition of threat or use. Not only did the Court **not** say that nuclear weapons may be used *in extremis*, but President Bedjaoui had clearly emphasised that the Court's position did not amount to recognising an *in extremis* exception to the general prohibition of threat or use.[15] If anything, the text and tenor of the advisory opinion indicate a strong inclination towards illegality in all circumstances.

It may theoretically be possible for a single Trident warhead to be used against a remote military target with only slight 'collateral' damage. However, in view of their blast, heat and especially their radiation effects, which could not be limited as required by IHL, the use of such warheads in any realistic military scenario would surely violate the requirements of the international law applicable in armed conflict; particularly the intransgressible principles of IHL. Those principles are arguably *jus cogens*, peremptory norms of international law from which no derogation is permitted.[16]

Furthermore, such norms generate strong interpretative principles[17] which prevent the Nuclear Non-Proliferation Treaty (NPT) from being construed as legitimising the possession and deployment of nuclear weapons. Yet the UK Government claim that the NPT allows the UK to have nuclear weapons since the treaty recognises it as 'a nuclear-weapon State'.[18] It is true that Article IX.3 of the NPT defines such a State as 'one which has manufactured and exploded a nuclear weapon or other nuclear explosive device prior to 1 January 1967'. But that is simply a factual definition for the purposes of the NPT. It does not legitimise the possession and deployment of nuclear weapons as a means of warfare. To construe the NPT as if it did is not 'good faith' interpretation or compliance as required by the law of treaties,[19] especially in view of the ICJ's interpretation of Art VI. The Court concluded its advisory opinion by unanimously holding:

> There exists an obligation to pursue in good faith and bring to a conclusion negotiations leading to nuclear disarmament in all aspects under strict and effective international control.[20]

Some people say that in trying to deal with nuclear deterrence and proliferation we are beyond the limits of law. But we are not: law must play a decisive role as the embodiment of normative values. The rule of law is a fundamental principle of civilised society and respect for the rule of law is an essential prerequisite of international order. The original sense of the rule of law is obedience to law: 'Powerful people and people in government just like anybody else should obey the law.'[21] This was the sense in which Sir Stephen Wall used the phrase in a lecture on the Iraq conflict which he delivered at Chatham House in November 2004:[22]

> I believe that, in Britain, we allowed our judgment of the dire consequences of inaction to override our judgment of the even more dire consequences of parting from the rule of law. We have to be firm in our adherence to that rule of law, even if it sometimes means parting company with the United States and adhering to the United Nations as the only defence against the rule of might that we have.

Similarly, in a lecture in November 2006, Lord Bingham, then the senior

Law Lord, stated that the principle of the rule of law requires compliance by the State with its obligations in international law as well as with its obligations under domestic law. He added: 'I do not think this proposition is contentious.'[23]

Either we have the rule of law or we do not. As Judge Shi declared in the *Nuclear Weapons Case*, the policy of nuclear deterrence should be an object of regulation by law, not vice versa.[24] International law is not simply whatever those with 'the say' (in practice, the nuclear weapon States) say it is.

Prosecuting Crimes Against Peace before the Scottish Courts

AIDAN O'NEILL QC

Context: the Nuremberg Principles

IN A NUMBER OF the trials prosecuted in Germany in the wake of the International War Crimes tribunal at Nuremberg, the principle of individual criminal responsibility for acts contrary to the requirements of international law was affirmed by the prosecuting Allied Powers as applying to private individuals whether or not they were directly part of the official State apparatus but who actively co-operated in its acts (which had subsequently been deemed by the Allies to be unlawful).[1]

The idea that all individuals have overriding duties to obey a higher law against that of the (Nazi) State also lay behind various prosecutions which were brought in Germany before its domestic courts in the immediate post-World War II period against private persons who had informed on or denounced relatives and colleagues to the authorities for 'political offences'. As a result of these calculated denunciations those informed against had been handed over to a judicial system (in particular the Nazi People's Courts) 'which dealt mercilessly with political opponents at that time, as the population was well aware'.[2] Thus a woman who, with a view to effecting a swift end to her marriage, reported her husband to the authorities for slandering Hitler in their private conversations. Her denunciation resulted in his imprisonment and sentence of death (later commuted to service on the Eastern Front). She was subsequently convicted in the post-War period of de-Nazification by national German courts of wrong-doing for relying in bad faith on unjust laws of the Nazi system.[3] Such cases may be understood as examples of the application (and in the case of the denouncing wife, of the **extension** to conduct other than crimes against peace, war crime or crimes against humanity) of the principle that all individuals have legal duties derived directly from fundamental human rights considerations to be found in international law, which may bind those individuals, even against the claims and justifications of national law.[4]

The ideas behind these Nuremberg and post-Nuremberg prosecutions were subsequently codified into the 'Nuremberg principles' which sought authoritatively to summarise the principle of individual responsibility under international law in the following terms:

i   Any person who commits or is an accomplice in the commission of an act which constitutes a crime under international law is responsible therefore and liable to punishment.

ii   The fact that domestic law does not impose a penalty for an act which constitutes a crime under international law does not free the person who committed the act from responsibility under international law.

iii The fact that a person who committed an act which constitutes a crime under international law acted as Head of State or responsible Government official does not relieve him from responsibility under international law.

iv   The fact that a person acted pursuant to order of his Government or of a superior does not relieve him from responsibility under international law, provided a moral choice was in fact possible to him.

v   Any person charged with a crime under international law has the right to a fair trial on the facts and law.[5]

As was observed by the Special Rapporteur of the International Law Commission charged by the United Nations in 1950 with the task of re-formulating the Principles applied by the Nuremberg Tribunal:[6]

The general principle of law underlying Principle I is that **international law may impose duties on the individual without any interpretation of domestic law directly**, a conception which in theory is considered as involving the 'international personality' of individuals. The findings of the Court are very definite on the question of whether rules of international law may apply to individuals. 'That international law imposes duties and liabilities upon individuals as well as upon States', says the Court, 'has long been recognised.'[7] And elsewhere: 'Crimes against international law are committed by men, not by abstract entities, and only by punishing individuals who commit such crimes can the provisions of international law be enforced.'[8]

...

[P]rinciple [II] that a person committing an international crime is responsible therefor and liable to punishment under international law, independently of the attitude of domestic law, implies what is commonly called the 'supremacy' of international law over domestic law. It is accordingly considered that **international law can bind individuals even if domestic law does not direct them to observe the rules of international law** (It is in this sense that the term 'supremacy' is used here). Characteristic of the above inference is the following passage of the Court's findings: '... **The very essence of the Charter is that individuals have international law duties which transcend the national obligations imposed by the individual State.**'[9]

Principle VI of the Nuremberg Principles sets out the crimes which are to be regarded as 'punishable as crimes under international law' as follows:

a   Crimes against peace:

   i   Planning, preparation, initiation or waging of a war of aggression or a war in violation of international treaties, agreements or assurances;

   ii Participation in a common plan or conspiracy for the accomplishment of any of the acts mentioned under (i).

b   War crimes:

    Violations of the laws or customs of war include, but are not limited to, murder, ill-treatment or deportation to slave-labour or for any other purpose of civilian population of or in occupied territory, murder or ill-treatment of prisoners of war, of persons on the seas, killing of hostages, plunder of public or private property, wanton destruction of cities, towns, or villages, or devastation not justified by military necessity.

c   Crimes against humanity:

    Murder, extermination, enslavement, deportation and other inhuman acts done against any civilian population, or persecutions on political, racial or religious grounds, when such acts are done or such persecutions are carried on in execution of or in connexion with any crime against peace or any war crime.[10]

And Nuremberg Principle VII provides that 'complicity in the commission of a crime against peace, a war crime, or a crime against humanity as set forth in Principle VI is a crime under international law.'[11]

The Nuremberg principles were formally adopted into international law by UN Resolution 95(1) of UN General Assembly of 11 December 1946 and by Article 51 of the UN Charter, in relation to the prohibition of wars of aggression.

The United Kingdom Parliament was advised in 1963 by the then Lord Chancellor that the United Kingdom Government then took the view that the Nuremberg Principles, as formulated by the International Law Commission, were 'generally accepted among States and have the status of customary international law'.[12]

The Nuremberg Principles and the European Convention on Human Rights

The post-Nuremberg assertion that a higher normative authority inheres in principles derived from international humanitarian (and human rights) law, even as against the requirements of national law, was also specifically incorporated into the 1950 European Convention on Human Rights by the terms of Article 7 ECHR which is in the following terms:

> (1) No-one shall be held guilty of any criminal offence on account of any act or omission which did not constitute an offence under national law or international law at the time when it was committed. Nor shall a heavier penalty be imposed than the one which was applicable at the time when the criminal offence was committed.

> (2) This article shall not prejudice the trial and punishment of any person for any act or omission which, at the time it was committed, was criminal according to the general principles of law recognised by civilised nations.

Article 7 ECHR contains, then, two main strands: first a requirement for the proper prior definition in respect of crimes charged; and secondly, a requirement against retrospectivity in the defining of, and punishing for, criminal offences. Article 7 ECHR was intended to re-state the existing general legal principles of *nullum crimen sine lege*[13] (no crime without a (prior) statute) and *nulla poena sine lege*[14] (no punishment without a (prior) statute), while also seeking to take into account and reconcile these principles with the existence of the jurisprudence concerning individual criminal responsibility for gross breaches of international humanitarian and human rights law, as these concepts were first articulated at the post-World War II Nuremberg trials.[15] In interpreting and applying Article 7 ECHR (that is to say in determining when and how an individual should properly be found guilty of and punished for a criminal offence defined in the law) the domestic courts have also to take account of the 'general principles of law recognised by civilised nations', that it so say the requirements of customary international (humanitarian and human rights) law.

The Nuremberg Principles and the Human Rights Act

Thus when including Article 7 ECHR as one of the 'Convention rights' for the purposes of the Human Rights Act 1998 (HRA) (and associated statutes such as the Scotland Act 1998) the United Kingdom Parliament arguably also effectively introduced Nuremberg derived principles regarding the justifiability of conduct under national and international law directly into domestic law.[16] It might therefore be thought that, within the context of the post-HRA United Kingdom constitution, there can properly be no conflict between the requirements of the (domestic) 'law of the land' and any 'moral imperative'[17] (at least as derived from international legal principles) since both domestic law and international humanitarian and human rights law would now appear to operate in principle within the same normative framework.

Certainly, there has been an ever growing official realisation in the years since the Nuremberg trials of the need for officials and individuals to ensure that their conduct in war and in preparation for war is legal under international law, and this understanding is percolating down more generally in society in the United Kingdom. For example, as Lord Hope observed:

'22 ... When the Chief of the Defence Staff insisted on receiving unequivocal advice that the invasion [of Iraq] would be legal he was not thinking of the physical risks that his troops would be exposed to. His concern was that, if it was not legal, they might be at risk of being prosecuted. As Lord Kingsland said in the debate I have already mentioned, the issue is essentially one of morale: Hansard (HL Debates), 31 January 2008, col.790. An individual soldier needs to know that he will not be prosecuted for a war crime.

23 The International Criminal Court Act 2001 gave effect in domestic law to the Rome Statute of the International Criminal Court. It has raised awareness of the need to ensure that armed conflict takes place within the established framework of international law: see also the International Criminal Court (Scotland) Act 2001 (asp 13). The definition of war crimes in article 8 of the Rome Statute, which is reproduced in Schedules 8 and 1 of these Acts respectively, is very wide. Much depends on the laws and customs applicable in international armed conflict. Rules of engagement can only go so far. The umbrella of an assurance that the conflict is lawful in international law is essential if soldiers are to feel confident that it is an operation that they can properly engage in. This is so too of their commanders, who under section 65 of the 2001 Act are responsible for the acts of their subordinates.'[18]

The decision in Lord Advocate's Reference (No. 1 of 2000)

It is against this general post-Nuremberg background that the decision of the High Court of Justiciary in Lord Advocate's Reference (No. 1 of 2000) re nuclear weapons[19] may best be understood. This was a case which the then Lord Advocate referred to the High Court of Justiciary, pursuant to his powers under Section 123(1) of the Criminal Procedure (Scotland) Act 1995. The Lord Advocate wished the High Court's advice and guidance on four questions of law which he raised before the court following the acquittal by the Sheriff at Greenock of three women (Angie Zelter, Ulla Roder and Ellen Moxley) who had been charged with causing malicious damage to a vessel involved in facilitating the transport and deployment of Trident nuclear missiles.

These women had successfully argued before the Sheriff that the damage to property which they admitted having caused was not 'malicious' but was instead justified since, they said, the deployment of the Trident nuclear weapons system was in breach of customary international law, and therefore in breach of Scots law. They were accordingly acting not in breach of the law but were rather to be seen as 'citizen interveners' seeking to enforce the law, even against officials of the State.[20] They argued, in effect, for the existence of an '(international) law enforcement motivation' defence within the Scots common law sufficient to allow them to defeat their prosecution for having done a prohibited act with the requisite *mens rea*. The basis for this defence was the avowed purpose of their apparently criminal action: namely to bring a wrong-doer (the United Kingdom Government) to justice, or to expose its (greater) criminal wrong-doing.[21] An alternative analysis was that the actions for which they had been prosecuted had, in fact, been done by them in exercise of the implicit power and responsibility—possessed by every law-abiding citizen at common law—to take proportionate action to prevent or impede reasonably apprehended breaches of the law by another, and thereby assist in keeping the peace within the realm (and internationally).[22]

It was not open to the prosecution authorities to appeal against the acquittal of these three women. Concerned, however, that the decision of the sheriff might be thought to set a general precedent for anti-nuclear protesters intent on direct action, the Lord Advocate referred the following four questions to the High Court of Justiciary, in an attempt to restore the presumed *status quo ante*:

1 In a trial under Scottish criminal procedure, is it competent to lead evidence as to the content of customary international law as it applies to the United Kingdom?

2 Does any rule of customary international law justify a private individual in Scotland in damaging or destroying property in pursuit of his or her objection to the United Kingdom's possession of nuclear weapons, its action in placing such weapons at locations within Scotland or its policies in relation to such weapons?

3 Does the belief of an accused person that his or her actions are justified in law constitute a defence to a charge of malicious mischief or theft?

4 Is it a general defence to a criminal charge that the offence was

committed in order to prevent or bring to an end the commission of an offence by another person?

After some days of complex and lengthy argument (in a hearing at which the Lord Advocate was represented by senior and junior counsel, the Advocate General who appeared for the UK Government's interest was represented by senior counsel, senior counsel was appointed as amicus curiae to represent the interests of and position of Angie Zelter who appeared and argued on her own behalf, Ellen Moxley was represented by senior and junior counsel; and Ulla Roder by two junior counsel) the court answered the four questions put to it by the Lord Advocate as follows:

1   No. In a Scottish criminal trial, evidence could not be led as to the content of customary international law. A rule of customary international law was a rule of Scots law and the jury were not entitled to consider expert evidence but must be directed thereon by the judge;

2   No. The conduct of the UK government had not been illegal because the peacetime deployment of Trident as a deterrent was not a 'threat'. Furthermore there was, said the court, currently no rule of customary international law justifying the commission of a crime in order to prevent the commission of another crime, even in times of war;

3   No. The (subjective) belief of the respondents Zelter, Roder and Moxley that the deployment of Trident was in breach of customary international law did not provide a defence of justification to the charge of malicious damage;

4   Except for the defence of necessity, it was not a defence to a criminal charge that the relevant actions had been taken to hinder the commission of an offence by another person. Although the defence of necessity could be employed where the malicious damage was remote from the threat to people or property, it was only available where the perceived threat was immediate and there was no alternative to a criminal act in order to avert the threat. In any event the defence of necessity was not available in the instant case where the actions of the Government had not been shown to be unlawful.

Significance of the decision for Scots law

At some levels, then, the decision of the High Court of Justiciary was an unequivocal defeat for direct action campaigning involving breach of the law, but the decision of the court did in fact mark a number of significant developments in, and for, Scotland and Scots law.

In the first place the High Court accepted (by the very fact that it answered the question posed to it by the Lord Advocate) that questions relating to the lawfulness of the deployment of weapon systems by the United Kingdom government were justiciable before the courts.

Secondly, customary international law was recognised by the court automatically to form part of municipal Scots law without need for any formal treaty incorporation. It would appear that the court implicitly accepted, too, that customary international law could be relied upon by individuals in determining the lawfulness of their actions – and the lawfulness of the actions of the State.

Finally the case highlighted the importance of international law generally before the Scottish courts. As we shall see, the relevance of (and the potential for direct reliance upon) international treaty law before the courts in Scotland has been increased by the provisions of the Scotland Act (notably Sections 35, 58, 106(6) SA) which make it clear that the acts of the Scottish Parliament and of the Scottish Government may be subject (specifically at the instance of the Secretary of State) to legal challenge before the courts insofar as these acts are thought to be incompatible with the United Kingdom's 'international obligations' (which Section 108(1) SA defines as meaning '**any** international obligation of the United Kingdom, **other than** obligations to observe and implement Community law or the Convention rights'). The obligations on the part of the devolved Scottish institutions to respect Community law and Convention rights are, of course, the subject of other more specific provisions within the Scotland Act.

Scots criminal law wholly distinct from English criminal law

It should be noted that there was no possibility of any appeal against this decision. This is because the High Court of Justiciary is the highest court in matters concerning Scots criminal law. In contrast to the position which applies in England, Wales and Northern Ireland, the House of Lords has no appellate jurisdiction in criminal law matters from Scotland.[23]

As Lord Bingham has noted:

> When Scotland was united with England and Wales in 1707 it was clearly implicit in the Act of Union that there was no criminal appeal from Scotland to London ... There was originally a doubt as to whether there was even a civil appeal from Edinburgh to London, but it was very quickly established that there was and indeed extensive use of it was made to such an extent that there was very little time to hear English appeals! But what is important is that **the Scots criminal system has always been self-contained and has had no English input at all.**[24]

With the coming into force of the Scotland Act, however, the Judicial Committee of the Privy Council (which has traditionally been the final Imperial court of appeal in cases for the British Commonwealth) was given a role to play in matters of Scots criminal law in that it could hear appeals or references from the Scottish criminal court on matters which raise 'devolution issues' – typically the proper interpretation of Convention rights. But the jurisdiction of the Privy Council in issues concerning crime in Scotland is strictly a limited one – at least so the judges of the High Court of Justiciary claim –[25] and it is not given general or overall competence to decide upon matters of criminal law or procedure in Scotland. With effect from October 2008 the Privy Council's devolution jurisdiction (including that exercised in Scottish criminal matters) was amalgamated with the appellate jurisdiction previously enjoyed by the House of Lords in Scottish civil matters into the new UK Supreme Court.[26]

The decision of the House of Lords in *R. v. Margaret Jones and others*

In *R. v. Margaret Jones and others* the House of Lords, exercising the criminal appellate jurisdiction which it has for England, Wales and Northern Ireland, considered the cases of a number of individuals, all of whom had either been charged with or convicted of aggravated trespass or criminal damage arising out of their individual protest actions against the invasion of Iraq War at various military bases in the United Kingdom. In their resulting criminal trials some of the protesters sought to rely upon the statutory defence available to them under Section 3 of the Criminal

Law Act 1967 to the effect that their actions were lawful since they could properly be regarded as the use of reasonable force to prevent the commission of a crime by the State, namely the pursuing of an unlawful war of aggression contrary to the binding norms of international law. Others argued that because the actions of the Crown in mobilising the armed forces for the invasion of Iraq could not be said to be lawful under international law, the protesters' admitted acts in seeking to disrupt the military action could not be characterised as 'aggravated trespass' within the meaning of section 68(2) of the Criminal Justice and Public Order Act 1994. The House of Lords were therefore asked to rule on the question as to whether the various protesters could rely upon the customary law notion of 'crimes against peace' or 'crimes of aggression' to justify their actions under domestic criminal law.

The House of Lords agreed, first of all, that the concept of crimes against peace (including the planning, preparation or waging of a war of aggression, or participation in a common plan or conspiracy to accomplish such acts) was sufficiently defined and clearly established in customary international law to permit lawful prosecution and punishment of those responsible. This is perhaps an unsurprising conclusion given that it was on the basis of such charges that various high functionaries in the German Nazi and Japanese wartime governments were charged convicted (and in some cases executed) in the post-War Nuremberg and Tokyo war crimes trials.

Further and, in any event, in its decision in *Kuwait Airways Corporation v. Iraqi Airways Co (Nos. 4 and 5)* the House of Lords had already recognised the concept of the international crime of aggression. They held that the fact that the invasion of Kuwait by Iraq was generally considered to be an unlawful war of aggression contrary to customary international law and to the provisions of the UN Charter could be given effect to by the English courts in a purely domestic context. Their Lordships therefore refused to recognise the validity of an Iraqi decree which purported to transfer property in certain Kuwaiti state-owned aircraft to the Iraqi state in recognition of the fact that these acts had been made pursuant to an unlawful war of aggression.[27]

In the subsequent decision in *R. v. Jones* their Lordships held, however, that there was no **automatic** assimilation of crimes recognised and defined under customary international law into domestic English criminal law. More specifically they held that there need to be express Parliamentary authority before it was possible to treat the customary international law crime of aggression as a domestic crime in English law. Accordingly, the international crime of aggression was not to be regarded as a crime or an offence in domestic law within the meaning and for the purposes of either section 3 of the 1967 Act or section 68(2) of the 1994 Act. This meant that – regardless of whether or not the United Kingdom's prosecution and participation in the Iraq war was lawful in international law – the resolution of that issue would provide no statutory defence in domestic English law for the protesters.

Scots criminal law and the common law declaratory power of the High Court of Justiciary

While the decision of the House of Lords in *R. v. Margaret Jones* definitively established the legal position under English criminal law it did not, of course, apply in Scotland, for the reasons already mentioned: namely that the House of Lords has no jurisdiction in matters of Scots criminal law. More importantly however, the decision of their Lordships was in some way so specific to the features of English criminal law that it might not even be regarded as being even a persuasive authority in Scotland, since much of its central constitutional reasoning could not readily translate into Scottish terms. In particular, the decision of Lord Bingham rested centrally on the assertion that:

> [T]here now exists **no power in the courts to create new criminal offences**[28]... While old common law offences survive until abolished or superseded by statute, new ones are not created. **Statute is now the sole source of new criminal offences.** ... [This] reflects what has become an important democratic principle in this country: that it is for those representing the people of the country in Parliament, not the executive and not the judges, to decide what conduct should be treated as lying so far outside the bounds of what is acceptable in our society as to attract criminal penalties. One would need very compelling reasons for departing from that principle.[29]

But these strictures about the court having **no** power to create new offences or to be able to change the substantive definition of what constitutes criminal conduct do **not** apply within the context of Scots criminal law. In contrast to the position in England and Wales, there is no general codification of the substantive criminal law in Scotland. Crimes in Scotland are not, as a rule, defined in and/or regulated by statute. Much of the criminal law in Scotland is the product of the common law, that is to say the decisions of the judges. In Scotland the High Court of Justiciary takes a far more proactive approach in defining and developing the criminal law to match contemporary expectation of the national (and arguably, at least, also the international) community. There is no particularly strong tradition or custom of deference by the courts in Scotland to Parliament (whether in Westminster or in Edinburgh) on issues of criminal law when the legislature has not spoken. One academic commentator has summarised the position in Scotland thus:

> It is important to note that most major crimes are creatures of the common law in Scotland[30]. Indeed, that the substantive criminal law of Scotland relies greatly upon the common law has been described as its 'most noteworthy feature'.[31] The starting point for determining the definition of a common law crime in Scotland is Commentaries on the Law of Scotland Respecting Crimes, written by Baron David Hume in 1797.[32] Hume is frequently referred to by the judges in the High Court of Justiciary, Scotland's supreme criminal court.[33] The crime of murder is defined by the common law in Scotland. So too is 'culpable homicide', a crime similar to the English crime of manslaughter. Rape is a common law crime,[34] as are assault,[35] theft,[36] fraud, and robbery, to name but a few. Most of the general principles of criminal liability are to be found in the common law, including matters such as accessory liability and attempts to commit crime.[37]

The fact that the criminal law is in large part the creation of the common law means in Scotland the judges of the High Court of Justiciary may — albeit exceptionally in the exercise of the court's inherent declaratory power[38] — find and declare certain conduct to be criminal.[39] The judges may also exercise this inherent declaratory power to find certain conduct no longer to be criminal at common law by, for example, abolishing one common law defined crime and replacing it with another.[40]

The judges in Scotland might equally, in the exercise of their common law powers (re-)define what might be considered to constitute valid defences to a criminal charge, or may alter the previously understood essential elements for a known crime. For example in its decision in *Lord Advocate's Reference (No.1 of 2001)* the High Court of Justiciary re-defined (in effect reformed) the crime of rape by judicial *fiat*, removing the previous requirement of the law that there be a forcible overcoming of the rape victim's will and holding, instead, that all that had to be established for the crime to be committed was that the victim had, as a matter of fact, not consented to sexual intercourse without any need to show force or overcoming of the will. Lord Nimmo Smith, one of the judges on the divided (5:2) seven judge bench which made this decision said this:

> Ours is, however, 'a live system of law'[41] and it lies within the powers of this court, as custodians of the common law, to review it, and to correct the way in which it is stated, when it is necessary to do so in order to take account of developments in the law and to meet the needs of the community. This latter consideration appears to me to be of particular importance in a case such as the present. There have been profound changes in the position of women as members of society, and in attitudes to sexual conduct, since Baron Hume wrote. So it appears to me to be necessary to examine with particular care the way in which the crime of rape has been defined from time to time.[42]

As Pamela R. Ferguson has noted

> Some judicial development of the common law is of course inevitable and indeed desirable. The European Court of Human Rights has described this as 'a well entrenched, necessary part of legal tradition' (SW v. UK (1995) 21 E.H.R.R. 363 at 399). Nor does the evolution of the common law offend against the principle of legality and non-retrospectivity contained in Article 7 of the Convention. According to that court, Art.7 'cannot be read as outlawing the gradual clarification of the rules of criminal liability through judicial interpretation from case to case, provided that the resultant development is consistent with the essence of the offence and could reasonably be foreseen.' However, judicial development of the common law should be kept within proper limits.[43]

Breach of the Peace in Scots law

An example of judicial development or clarification of the Scots common law may be seen in Smith (Pamela) v. Donnelly in which the Crown resisted the accused's claim that 'breach of the peace' in Scots criminal law might mean anything that the prosecution wanted it to mean, in breach of the requirements of legal certainty and the principle embodied in Article 7 ECHR. The Crown argued that, while past case law certainly showed that the method of committing the offence of breach of the peace had wide variations and a variety of actual circumstances, that did not alter the essential definition of the crime. In rejecting the accused's challenge to the Convention compatibility of the offence of 'breach of the peace' with which she had been charged as a result of her actions at Faslane the court sought to clarify the legal position by stating that in order to constitute the crime of breach of the peace, there has to be conduct severe enough to cause alarm to an ordinary person and to threaten serious disturbance to the community.[44] Mere annoyance or irritation were insufficient, but rather conduct which was genuinely alarming or disturbing to the reasonable person was required.

But given the breadth in the concept of 'breach of the peace' in Scots law which the case of Pamela Smith v. Donnelly highlighted, the question might then arise as to whether or not it would it be possible for an individual to take action to seek to prevent or impede the State authorities themselves taking action in (threatened) 'breach of the peace' which was the question which the House of Lords were faced with but avoided answering in the decision in R. v. Jones. Certainly given that customary international law has been determined automatically to form part of Scots law, and that the substance of the criminal law in Scotland is one which continues to be shaped and created by the judges, it might be thought that the Scottish criminal justice system would be far more permeable to developments in the field of customary international law than the English statutory based domestic criminal legal system, at least as that system was explained by the House of Lords in R. v. Jones.

Prosecution in domestic courts for international crimes – the position in international law

In Regina (Gentle and another) v. Prime Minister and others Baroness Hale opened her speech with an arresting narrative detailing the concerns in early March 2003 of the Chief of the Defence Staff and of the Treasury Solicitor to obtain from the Prime Minister (on behalf of the Armed Services and of the Civil Service, respectively) 'an unambiguous black and white statement' from the Attorney General to the effect that it would not be illegal for the United Kingdom personnel to act in support of the United

States invasion of Iraq forces and that 'the proposed military action ... would be in accordance with national and international law'.

Baroness Hale indicated that both the Chief of the Defence Staff and the Treasury Solicitor had concerns about possible legal consequences for individual UK operatives if the decision to engage in the conflict failed to conform to the requirements of international law, in particular the Charter of the United Nations which defines the situations in which one state may lawfully use force against another. And Baroness Hale considered the Chief of the Defence Staff and Treasury Solicitor to be 'right in principle to seek the assurance which they did' on the basis that since UK law as currently interpreted allows for no defence of no defence of conscientious objection to an order and instead, contrary to the provisions of article 33 of the International Criminal Court Statute, requires its service personnel to obey superior orders irrespective of their own individuals views as to the lawfulness of those orders, then 'the State has a correlative duty to its soldiers to ensure that those orders are lawful.'[45]

But despite repeated invitations made to them the courts in England and Wales, and in particular the judges of the House of Lords, have consistently sought to avoid judging on the legality of decisions relating to war[46] or the preparations for war.[47] The judges say that it is not their function to review the exercise of prerogative powers in relation to the deployment of the armed services.[48] They defer to the executive in matters of foreign policy.[49] And they say are unwilling to adjudicate on rights and obligations arising out of transactions entered into between sovereign states on the plane of public international law.[50]

But as Professor Rosalyn Higgins QC, now President of the International Court of Justice, has written:

> The international responsibility of a State is engaged when it violates international law, with various possible consequences. And from the perspective of international law, 'the State' encompasses all the organs of the State, the judiciary as well as the executive and legislative. The responsibility of the State is incurred by the acts and decisions of the judiciary, notwithstanding the proper separation, in a democracy, of the judiciary from other State organs.[51]

And the doctrine of judges as 'State actors' is also evident from the series of trials organised by the American authorities subsequent to the main war crimes trial at Nuremberg and which concerned the relationship of specific professional sectors of German society with the Nazi regime. 'Case 3' or United States v. Altstötter and others concerned the prosecution of a selection of some 16 jurists (public prosecutors, presiding judges and officials and ministers in the Ministry of Justice) who had assisted in the administration of the legal system during the Nazi era. These individuals were presented by the American prosecuting authorities as being representatives of the entire judicial system for the administration of 'what passed for justice in the Third Reich'. These jurists were put on trial as regards their involvement in or complicity with war crimes, organised crime and crimes against humanity, in particular 'judicial murder and other atrocities which they committed by destroying law and justice in Germany and by utilising the empty forms of legal process for persecution, enslavement and extermination on a vast scale'.[52] In line with their international law remit,[53] the American prosecuting authorities concentrated on such crimes as committed against non-Germans and the conscious participation by these individuals in

> a nation-wide government-organised system of cruelty and injustice, in violation of the laws of war and of humanity, and perpetrated in the name of law by the authority of the Ministry of Justice and through the instrumentality of the courts. The dagger of the assassin was concealed beneath the robe of the jurist.[54]

It is clear from this trial (and from the conviction of a number of the accused) that it was considered by the Allied prosecuting authorities and judges at Nuremberg that officers of the judicial system themselves owed duties derived from consideration of international law which over-rode their duties to give effect to and apply provisions of national law insofar as these contravened these international humanitarian and human rights principles.

Prosecution in domestic courts for international crimes – the position in Domestic Law

The written advice of 7 March 2003 of the Attorney General to the United Kingdom government shows that the Attorney General was clearly aware of this and other Nuremberg precedents. In discussing the issue as to whether an invasion of Iraq by the United Kingdom might be found to be unlawful under international law, the Attorney General expressly raised the concern of possible criminal prosecutions for those involved in the decision to go to war, noting:

> Two further, though probably more remote possibilities, are an attempted prosecution for murder on the grounds that the military action is unlawful and an attempted prosecution for the crime of aggression. Aggression is a crime under customary international law which automatically forms part of domestic law. It might therefore be argued that international aggression is a crime recognised by the common law which can be prosecuted in the UK courts.[55]

Now while this argument that there might be a prosecution before the courts in England in respect of the customary international law crime of international aggression was later rejected by this House of Lords in *R. v. Jones (Margaret)* it would appear that the *possibility* of such a prosecution in Scotland is not yet a closed one, as a matter of Scots criminal law and procedure. And as one academic commentator has noted:

> Perhaps there might emerge for international crimes a correspondingly mounting influence upon the interpretation of domestic crimes, bolstered by increasing state ratifications of the Rome Statute, the effective operation of the ICC itself, and also the Rome Statute's expectation (in Art.1) of complementarity in terms of a firm national response so as to avert the need for international action. Based on the sentiments expressed in the Preamble of the Rome Statute, one might wish every success to the ICC and that the UK courts will eventually take due notice of that progress.[56]

Further, as the decision of the House of Lords in *Reg. v. Bow Street Magistrate, Ex p. Pinochet (No. 3)*[57] shows, there is no immunity from the criminal jurisdiction of the United Kingdom in respect of a (former) head of state for any acts or omission – even when done in his official capacity as head of state – if those actions constituted international crime against humanity and *jus cogens*. In the case of General Pinochet the crimes with which he was charged were those of torture or conspiracy to torture. It is not immediately clear why different rules or considerations should apply in respect of possible prosecutions of officials in respect of any of the other international crimes defined and condemned in Nuremberg Principle VI.

The Scotland Act and International Law

We have earlier briefly referred to Section 58 of the Scotland Act 1998 (SA) which provides that the UK Secretary of State has the power to direct a member of the Scottish Executive (including necessarily, the Lord Advocate) either: (1) to refrain from proposed action where he has reasonable grounds to believe that such action would be incompatible with the international obligations of the United Kingdom; or (2) to order otherwise competent action from any member of the Scottish Executive where he has reasonable grounds to believe that such action is required for the purpose of giving effect to any such international obligations. As we have seen 'international obligations' is defined under Section 126(10) of the Act as meaning 'any international obligations of the United Kingdom other than obligations to observe and implement Community law or the Convention rights.' Section 58(5) SA provides that the Secretary of State is required to state his reason in making any such order, and his or her decisions will therefore be subject to judicial scrutiny review on the usual grounds for review of administrative action. This means that the Scottish Government's duty to comply with international obligations may become the subject of an order pronounced by the domestic courts if, for example, the Secretary of State's order is unsuccessfully challenged before them.

In *Friend v Lord Advocate*[58] the House of Lords unanimously rejected the challenge argued by a party litigant to the Convention compatibility of the Scottish fox hunting ban. Unfortunately, given that this was a case argued by a litigant without the benefit of any legal representation and where no *amicus curiae* had been appointed, their Lordships also saw fit also to pronounce on the issue as to whether Sections 35 and 58 of the Scotland Act might have modified the heretofore accepted dualist approach to international law (which requires specific incorporation of international treaty obligation into domestic law before they become enforceable before the court). There remains at least an interesting argument to the effect that by statutorily binding the Scottish Government under the Scotland Act to respect all of the United Kingdom's international obligations (albeit an obligation which Section 58 SA envisages to be enforced by action on the part of the Secretary of State) then this is sufficient to incorporate these international obligations of the UK into domestic Scots law – at least as against the Scottish Government – such as to allow these obligations of the Scottish Government to be relied upon by any private parties who could show themselves prejudiced as citizens by the Scottish Government (in)action which was not compatible with the UK's international treaty obligations.[59]

Notwithstanding the dicta of the House of Lords in *Friend* it may still be argued that Section 58 SA provides the basis for an enforceable legitimate expectation to the effect that the actions of the Scottish devolved institutions will be compatible with the UK's international obligations. On this basis it might be said that the Scotland Act effectively binds the Lord Advocate (and the other Scottish Ministers) to respect the whole range of international treaty obligations which have been ratified by the Crown, even where they have not been incorporated into the domestic law of the United Kingdom.[60] The scheme of the Scotland Act may be said also to provide further statutory authority to underpin and confirm the obligation already incumbent upon the Scottish Ministers and Lord Advocate at common law to respect the norms of customary international law insofar as these create international obligations on the United Kingdom. Thus, we may say that the Lord Advocate and the other Scottish Ministers are legally obliged both to refrain from acting in a manner that would be incompatible with both customary and treaty international obligations of the United Kingdom, and may indeed have obligations under domestic law to take positive action for the purpose of giving effect to any such international obligations.

In particular, it seems clear that the Lord Advocate's prosecutorial discretion requires to be exercised in a manner which is both compatible with an individual's Convention rights *and* in a manner which is compatible with the United Kingdom's obligations under general international law. What this might mean is that the devolved Lord Advocate cannot lawfully initiate a prosecution against an individual if that individual's actions are properly found upon and justified under international law. By the same token it might be argued that a decision by the Lord Advocate to *refuse* to initiate a prosecution—for example against a State official or politician in respect of the international crime of aggression—might be subject to judicial review before the courts to test the lawfulness of this decision. Standing the specific exception provided in Article 7(2) ECHR (which provides that the application of the general principles of *nullum crimen sine lege* 'shall not prejudice the trial and punishment of any person for any act or omission which, at the time it was committed, was criminal according to the general principles of law recognised by civilised nations') it would be difficult to argue that the prosecution before a domestic tribunal for a crime clearly defined in Nuremberg Principle VI (for example for 'crimes against peace' such as 'planning, preparation, initiation or waging of a war of aggression') could, in itself, be said to be contrary to the Convention rights of the accused.

The decision by the Lord Advocate on whether or not to prosecute in any case has not heretofore been the subject of any challenge before the courts in Scotland.[61] But there is no constitutional reason that such decisions should not be open to challenge by way of judicial review, just as the decisions of the prosecution authorities are in England.[62] Indeed, the decision of the Lord Advocate in her capacity as head of the system of investigation of deaths in Scotland to refuse an inquiry has recently been the subject of a successful challenge by way of judicial review before the Court of Session.[63]

Conclusion

One legal philosopher has noted as follows:

> When the very institution whose purpose is to realise human rights is used to trample them, when justice is turned against itself, the virtue of justice will be turned against itself too. Concern for human rights leads the virtuous person to accept the authority of the law, but in such circumstances adherence to the law will lead her to support institutions that systematically violate human rights. The person with the virtue of justice, the lover of human rights, unable to run to the actual laws for their enforcement, has nowhere else to turn. She may come to feel that there is nothing for it but to take human rights under her own protection and so to take the law into her own hands.[64]

As we have seen, one way in which concerned individuals have conscientiously sought to resolve their dilemma of an apparent conflict between the requirements of domestic law and their perceived requirements of justice on the issue of the stockpiling of nuclear weapons in the United Kingdom has been their attempt, in their prosecutions for direct action protests, to rely on customary international law before the courts in

Scotland. These protesters have sought to use international law in such a way as to provide them with a lawful defence against their prosecution for direct actions which they have taken by way of protest against—and in order to highlight their claims as to –the unlawfulness of the State's own actions in pursuing its policies of nuclear weapon stockpiling as part of a strategy of nuclear deterrence.

In *Lord Advocate's Reference* (*No. 1 of 2000*) legal submissions were made to the High Court of Justiciary on behalf of Ellen Moxley to the effect that in this intersection of public international law, constitutional law, humanitarian law, human rights law and criminal law the court might usefully adapt the classic tri-partite test of proportionality known in European law (and which was originally developed in German domestic law to test the lawfulness of police action) to set out the conditions for any possible 'citizen intervention necessity' defence. The proportionality test would mean that such a defence would only be available in circumstances where it can be said that:

- the action of the State against which it was aimed was in fact illegal, whether under domestic or applicable international law;
- the action was necessary in the sense that there was no legal reasonable alternative in fact available to the actor (for example because the relevant authorities had refused or refrained from enforcing the law in relation to the illegal act);
- the actor could reasonably expect that the actions taken would be effective in at least impeding, if not wholly preventing, the illegal act;
- the actions of the protesters or interveners were marked by a 'fidelity to legal values' within our democratic polity in that that they were proportionate, involved no possibility of harm to individuals and no attempt was made to avoid detection in the doing of the act.

It was submitted on behalf of Ellen Moxley that the corollary of admitting and applying the proportionality test to any such defence would be that there would clearly be no possibility of successfully relying upon it where:

- the State action complained of was not in fact illegal, or
- that the action was unnecessary (in the sense that reasonable alternatives were open) or
- that it could not have been reasonably expected that it would impede the commission of the unlawful act, or

- that the action was not one which was characterised by fidelity to legal values because, for example, it was done clandestinely with a view to escaping detection or
- because the action was disproportionate in the sense that its evil or undesirable effects (for example in resulting in physical harm to individuals) outweighed the evil that it was seeking to prevent.

The High Court of Justiciary rejected these legal submissions. And in general, all and any attempts to have the courts recognise any such conscientious 'citizen intervener' defence against a criminal charge have been uniformly (and perhaps unsurprisingly) unsuccessful. The judges express their fear that anarchy will result should they allow for the possibility of individuals being authorised to break the law, in order to highlight the commission of greater State crimes.[65]

There is an alternative strategy which might be used to bring before the domestic court the current state of international criminal law on matters of war and peace. This would be to request the State prosecution authorities to initiate criminal investigations and the prosecution of persons within the jurisdiction against whom a case might colourably be made of their complicity in recognised international crimes, in particular the crime of international aggression, or other crimes against peace.

Article 5 of the Rome Statute which set up the International Criminal Court (the ICC) includes the international crime of aggression in the list of serious offences 'the most serious crimes of concern to the international community' over which the ICC has jurisdiction. But the Rome Statute also provides, in Article 5(2), that

> the Court shall exercise jurisdiction over the crime of aggression once a provision is adopted in accordance with articles 121 and 123 defining the crime and setting out the conditions under which the Court shall exercise jurisdiction with respect to this crime.

What this means is that the ICC is precluded from exercising jurisdiction over the crime of aggression unless and until the assembly of States that ratified the Rome Statute passes an amendment to the Statute defining the crime of aggression. This has not been done. The result has been an international political stalemate as the crime of aggression does not yet fall within the purview of the ICC.

In any event the ICC will *not* adjudicate on a crime enumerated in its

Statute unless it is satisfied that the 'national authorities are "unwilling or unable" to carry out a genuine investigation and, if appropriate, prosecution'. The ICC is intended to supplement or complement national criminal justice systems. Accordingly the jurisdiction of the ICC need not be called upon where those national criminal justice systems are effective in the prosecution of international crimes. And as the House of Lords noted in its decision in *R. v. Margaret Jones* the parameters of the crime of aggression are sufficiently well-known for it to be capable of being considered a crime in domestic law. The only reason they said that it is not yet a prosecutable offence in English law is because the Westminster Parliament has not yet made specific provision for its incorporation into the domestic legal system. But such considerations do not apply (or, at the very least, do not apply with the same force) within the Scottish criminal justice system, given that Scots criminal law – based as it is on the common law – still allows for the incorporation of new crimes into the law by judicial *fiat* rather than requiring in all cases specific Parliamentary enactment.

Accordingly it would appear to be at least competent for the prosecution authorities in Scotland, if so advised, to raise prosecution in Scotland in respect of the international crime of aggression. Insofar as the Scottish prosecution authorities fail or refuse to do so where there are otherwise reasonable grounds for so proceeding, it would seem in principle that such a decision might itself be the subject of challenge before the courts by way of judicial review. It has to be said, however, that the judges in Scotland are, if anything, temperamentally, culturally and institutionally, even more conservative than their English counterparts. As the late Professor Bill Wilson of Edinburgh University once observed:

> It cannot be said that the Scottish judiciary has been a major agency of change in the last hundred years. The House of Lords has made abrupt turns from time to time and perhaps that is the appropriate place for changes to be made. The Court of Session has been, on the whole, conservative; it has refused to break new ground, not only because there was precedent against it, but also because there was no precedent for it. ... The best that can be said for the judges is that they have kept the system going; that is, perhaps, their function.[66]

So the likelihood of any such challenge having any immediate success, at least before the judges in Scotland, would not be great. However, given that judicial review is a matter of civil law in Scotland, there would remain the possibility of taking the case, as a matter of constitutional right without the need for leave of any court,[67] on appeal to the House of Lords, or as from October 2009 its replacement the UK Supreme Court. Neither the House of Lords (nor the UK Supreme Court) would be bound by their previous decision in *R v. Jones* since this would be an appeal from Scotland on a matter ultimately of the incorporation of crimes under customary international law into Scots criminal law.

Unlike the situations pertaining in their decisions in *R. v. Jones* and *R. (Gentle) v. Prime Minister* their Lordships would be faced in any such appeal directly with the question as to the lawfulness under domestic law of decisions made by the governing powers to prepare for war (in the case of the Trident stockpiling) or to go to war (in the case of Iraq). We might then at last learn from the highest court in the land whether such official decisions pertaining to war which can be said to fall within the ambit of the 'crime of aggression' for the purposes of customary international law, might also constitute – for the purposes of the domestic criminal law of the northern part of the United Kingdom at least – an prosecutable breach of the (international) peace.[68]

Civil Society and International Law

ANGIE ZELTER

WE ARE AT A time in human history when many global crises have come together – nuclear proliferation, climate change, economic melt-down, pollution, deforestation, massive extinction of other life-forms, and desertification. The issues are intertwined in many complex ways and no single nation can solve the problems alone. Many millions of our fellow global citizens are already suffering from chronic poverty and violence in degraded and exploited environments. There has never been a time when international humanitarian law is so sorely needed. International humanitarian law, if respected and upheld by the world community of nations, if applied to the powerful states as well as to the less powerful, has all the elements that can help us through these troubled times. In essence they are very understandable and accessible to all. A child can read the Declaration of Human Rights and understand the basic human-ity and morality they encapsulate. The problem arises when states manipulate the international structures and laws, twisting them to serve their own narrow self-interests and thus ironically subverting the very security they are trying to ensure. This is very apparent when looking at the Non-Proliferation Treaty and the lack of progress on nuclear disar-mament, as many of the contributors to this book spell out.

International Humanitarian Law is a powerful tool that if respected and used with integrity can deliver nuclear disarmament. Scotland is key to this process. In the next few years Scotland can insist that all nuclear weapons leave their land and that a clean up of all nuclear materials is carried out. Scotland can call upon other states to back it in its refusal to be drawn into what many consider to be preparations for war crimes, crimes against humanity and crimes against the peace. A strong stance on this issue would open the way for the UK to disarm as this would surely be an easier and more honourable way forward than facing the diplomatic and legal controversy and crisis that would emerge if it did not respect Scottish demands to be nuclear free.

Powerful nations, have a tendency to act above the law and to abuse power, which is why there is a need for a strong civil society to keep track and pressure Governments to uphold international humanitarian law. This has been difficult as there is a great deal of official and public cynicism about law in general and international law in particular, epitomised by views that the law serves the powerful in society, does not look after the interests of the poor or weak, and is the law of the victors over the vanquished.

However, International Humanitarian Law is based on powerful foundational ideas of protection of the weak and powerless and of the environment. The Geneva Conventions, and other war laws, are good agreements that, if implemented, would keep warfare and conflicts within bounds, so that civilised life can be rebuilt after violent conflicts have ended.

And the public's role has been recognised for a long time. The Martens Clause[1], states that when cases are not covered by international agreements,

> **civilians and combatants remain under the protection and authority of the principles of international law derived from** (among other things) **the dictates of public conscience.**

In other words, the law derives from the ethical foundations of our society – from our consciences. And we need to be continually involved in refining our consciences in the light of current affairs. We need to realise that the law evolves, it is not static and we, as civil society, have a part to play in this. It cannot be left to government's or to the legal profession alone to bear this burden.

The Scotsman, Sir David Maxwell-Fyfe, a former Attorney General under Churchill, was the UK prosecutor at Nuremberg. In 1946 he said,

> The law is a living thing. It is not rigid and unalterable. Its purpose is to serve mankind, and it must change and grow to meet the changing needs of society. The needs of Europe today have no parallel in history.[2]

I would re-iterate and modernise this to say: *the needs of our interdependent, conflict-ridden world today have no parallel in history— international law must be strengthened and implemented and evolve to serve all of humankind.*

It is this sentiment that has informed much of civil society's creative involvement with international law. Rather than seeing it as an institution set in stone and way above us as part of the higher-level power struggles between mighty nations, many of us in civil society have engaged with international law as part of our attempts to humanise the State and its institutions and bring it into line with our 'public consciences'. We[3] attempt to get our governments to comply and implement international law and also to develop it for the benefit of humanity as a whole and not for the narrow self-interests of a particular nation state. We often represent ourselves in the courts and try to express ourselves in plain language rather than using Latin phrases and long sentences that are hard to understand. We try to uncover power politics and remind the courts of the underlying principles and spirit of the law.

But there are serious challenges. 'International law is not real law and does not apply in Scotland', thus said a Procurator Fiscal in Helensburgh District Court in 1999[4], and although not often so frankly articulated, nevertheless this is still an attitude prevalent in the courts at all levels when applied to cases involving protests against nuclear weapons. It is accompanied by impatience and strong disapproval of ordinary citizens meddling in the law, and a belief that 'amateurs' should not try to 'uphold' the law or 'take the law into their own hands'. We are told over and over again not to get involved, that it is up to the government, or the police, or the military, or some other institution, to deal with crimes against peace or war crimes. In the UK, there are outdated judgements that hold our society back, like that of Hutchinson[5] which misinterprets the ICJ's Advisory Opinion, or Chandler[6] which relies upon the principle of the Royal Prerogative[7] to insist that the disposition of the armed forces is not justiciable, that it is not for judge or jury to decide what the armed forces can or cannot do. In effect, these judicial 'precedents' have prevented the courts from acting as a necessary balance to the power of the executive and ensured that they do not do their job of judging whether the armed forces are acting within the law. This lack of judicial oversight has allowed our State to cover up their illegal acts.

However, civil society acts in the belief that the strength and wisdom of a society lies with its people and that we get the government and legal system that we allow. We believe we are not completely powerless but are responsible individuals. Thus we cannot stay silent or be still when we can see gross crimes being committed in our names. We see the active deployment of weapons of mass destruction and know that the use of such weapons would break the fundamental principles of humanitarian law. Taking the law seriously we call our institutions to account. We become part of the forces creating the evolution of our society, taking a part in shaping the law and ensuring its implementation.

There have been numerous examples of civil society attempts to get governments to comply with and develop international law. They can be categorised as three broad routes.

One route is **campaigning and lobbying**, on both national and international levels, to get international law modernised and developed. For instance, the International Campaign to Ban Landmines was a particularly successful example of civil society groups combining together to campaign for a new Treaty. From its small beginnings in 1991 it took a mere eight years for the Mine Ban Treaty[8] to be formulated, ratified and become binding in international law. It is a wonderful example of what dedicated 'global citizens' can persuade governments to do.

The International Campaign to Abolish Nuclear Weapons (ICAN) provides a current example of attempts to develop international law. ICAN is calling on all nations to negotiate a Nuclear Weapons Convention (NWC) to ban nuclear weapons and ensure their elimination. They argue that an NWC is more likely to succeed than a series of fragmented and inconsistent approaches to nuclear disarmament.[9]

A second route tries **to get national and international institutions to comply** with the *existing* international laws, either through education and lobbying or through the legal system. Thus civil society groups, like the Institute for Law and Peace, produce briefing papers on what laws are being broken and how[10], encourage debate, lobby, and urge their governments to uphold international law by suggesting various policy changes like stopping the export of arms to repressive regimes, refusing to send troops to invade other countries, voting in the UN appropriately. They hold conferences and organise demonstrations.

Individuals and groups also use the legal system in various ways either to judicially review government decisions like the export of arms to various repressive regimes[11] or to take out cases that attempt to get the legal system to indict government and military leaders involved in or complicit in war crimes, crimes against the peace, crimes against humanity, or in preparations for such crimes. For instance, in the 1980s at the height of the nuclear weapons escalation during the Cold War, there were attempts to prosecute the UK Prime Minister for conspiracy to commit war crimes[12] but the courts rejected these attempts as 'malicious' litigations or by stating that they were not prepared to review the decisions of the Attorney General. Most of these attempts were made by ordinary citizens representing themselves directly in the courts.

However, groups also employed lawyers to advise them and to take cases on their behalf. Thus, law firms like Public Interest Lawyers[13] worked with CND to take the Government to court to ask for an advisory opinion on the legality of using Resolution 1441 as a pretext for war[14], and also with the Gentles & other parents of British soldiers killed in Iraq who brought a judicial review of the Government's failure to order an independent inquiry into the events leading to the decision to invade Iraq. More recently the Nuclear Information Services asked for a Judicial Review of the decision to renew the Trident nuclear weapon system[15].

Attempts to bring to justice those in power have continued over many years and each time civil society gains in strength. Whereas the attempts in the '80s hardly made an impact on society at large, more recent attempts have had a profound impact on debate and feelings in the country. The CND sponsored coalition of law professors and leading NGOs who served notice[16] in 2003 on Blair, Hoon and Straw that they would be investigated by the ICC Prosecutor if the UK breached International Humanitarian Law during any proposed use of force against Iraq fed into the huge anti-war protests that led to the largest demonstration in British history[17]. This is being followed up with reports being sent to the International Criminal Court.

International Law has now become a prominent part of public debate. These continuing legal challenges are a part of the process of bringing our society into line with humanitarian law. Civil society is often well ahead of institutional changes thus legal challenges may not work at any one particular time. Nevertheless, they often succeed at a later date when attitudes have changed and the institutions have caught up. Thus courts must continually be presented with the opportunities to implement international humanitarian law and to act independently of the executive.

On a more international level, we must not forget that it was a global civil society initiative, that eventually drew in international lawyers, that pressed successfully to get the UN to ask the International Court of Justice for their advisory opinion on nuclear weapons in 1996[18] and which has formed the bulk of our discussions today. It was successful because it engaged with citizens in many different nations of the world community and in the end, try and they did, the powerful national governments (those with nuclear weapons) were not able to stop the process.

A third route is **direct citizen's implementation of international law.** For example, through disarmament attempts by civil society wishing to prevent weapons being sent out or used where there is evidence that international law will be broken and civilians injured or killed.

Thus, there have been non-violent direct actions to disable weapons being exported to repressive regimes like the British Aerospace Hawk Jets to Suharto's Indonesia in 1996 that were being used to commit genocide amongst the hundreds of unique tribes in East Timor[19] or the Trident Ploughshares disarmament actions, like the throwing into Loch Goil of the vital equipment used to test Trident nuclear armed submarines in 1999[20]. Then more recently, the incursions onto US war-planes going out to Iraq and also supplying weapons to Israel in its bombing of civilian targets in Lebanon in 2006[21] and the extensive damage done to the offices and equipment of the Brighton based MBM factory that supplied arms to Israel whilst it was bombarding civilians in Gaza in January 2009[22].

Whereas my own acquittal in 1996 after disarming the BAe Hawk Jet was the first such acquittal in the world of a ploughshares action and caused a great deal of controversy, there have now been many more in Ireland, the USA, Australia and in the UK. There are more groups and individuals taking responsibility for non-violent citizen crime prevention. They are preparing and documenting their evidence carefully, bringing in affected victims of the atrocities as witnesses and getting the context of their actions and their motivations before juries. They are relying upon international law and their national legal right to prevent crime. Judges and Juries are listening to the arguments and the witnesses carefully and in many more cases acquitting the citizen disarmers on the grounds that they had good reasons for their actions – acting in the public interest in other words.

There are now a growing number of European and International wide coalitions of 'global citizen crime preventors' that are working together to try to counteract the power of the global military-industrial machine as can be seen, for instance, in the recent blockades at Faslane and Aldermaston.[23]

Thus civil society has already been playing a vital role in the implementation and development of international law. I believe we are still needed.

We are, here in Scotland, at a crucial time for nuclear disarmament. Civil society pressure on the MSPs and the legal system has to increase to provide the strong social and political pressure that is needed for Scotland to implement international law and refuse to base and deploy nuclear weapons systems any more. Our message is that Scotland has the power of international law on its side and only needs to take courage to confront Westminster – it cannot be forced to aid and abet preparations for mass murder, which is what the basing of Trident in Scotland is, in plain language. The Scottish Government needs only to insist that its legal profession get thoroughly educated in International Humanitarian Law and insist on its compliance. I hope that this book will help in that process.

Appendix

International Court of Justice

Legality of the Threat or Use of Nuclear Weapons

Advisory Opinion of 8 July 1996

Present : *President* BEDJAOUI, *Vice-President* SCHWEBEL

Judges ODA, GUILLAUME, SHAHABUDDEEN, WEERAMANTRY, RANJEVA, HERCZEGH, SHI, FLEISCHHAUER, KOROMA, VERESHCHETIN, FERRARI, BRAVO, HIGGINS

Registrar VALENCIA-OSPINA

A **Unanimously,**
There is in neither customary nor conventional international law any specific authorization of the threat or use of nuclear weapons;

B **By eleven votes to three,**
There is in neither customary nor conventional international law any comprehensive and universal prohibition of the threat or use of nuclear weapons as such;

C **Unanimously,**
A threat or use of force by means of nuclear weapons that is contrary to Article 2, paragraph 4, of the United Nations Charter and that fails to meet all the requirements of Article 51, is unlawful;

D **Unanimously,**
A threat or use of nuclear weapons should also be compatible with the requirements of the international law applicable in armed conflict, particularly those of the principles and rules of international human-itarian law, as well as with specific obligations under treaties and other undertakings which expressly deal with nuclear weapons;

E **By seven votes to seven, by the President's casting vote,**
It follows from the above-mentioned requirements that the threat or

use of nuclear weapons would generally be contrary to the rules of international law applicable in armed conflict, and in particular the principles and rules of humanitarian law; However, in view of the current state of international law, and of the elements of fact at its disposal, the Court cannot conclude definitively whether the threat or use of nuclear weapons would be lawful or unlawful in an extreme circumstance of self-defence, in which the very survival of a State would be at stake;

F   Unanimously,
There exists an obligation to pursue in good faith and bring to a conclusion negotiations leading to nuclear disarmament in all its aspects under strict and effective international control.

Done in English and in French, the English text being authoritative, at the Peace Palace, The Hague, this eighth day of July, one thousand nine hundred and ninety-six, in two copies, one of which will be placed in the archives of the Court and the other transmitted to the Secretary-General of the United Nations.

Signed Mohammed BEDJAOUI, President.
Signed Eduardo VALENCIA-OSPINA, Registrar.

Notes on Contributors

H.E. JUDGE MOHAMMED BEDJAOUI was the President of the International Court of Justice, 1994–1997, and a judge on the Court from 1982–2001. From 2005 to 2007, he was the Algerian Minister of Foreign Affairs. He also served as the Algerian Minister of Justice and as Dean of the Faculty of Law of Algiers. From 1965 to 1982, he was a member of the International Law Commission. Judge Bedjaoui is the author or editor of numerous books and articles, including (ed.) *International Law: Achievements and Prospects* (1991). An earlier version of this paper was given in a keynote address on 1 May 2008 at a meeting held during the NPT Preparatory Committee meeting in Geneva. Since Judge Bedjaoui was unable to attend the Edinburgh Conference, he has given permission to use an updated and edited version of that Address for this book.

DR JOHN BURROUGHS is Executive Director of the New York-based Lawyers' Committee on Nuclear Policy (LCNP), the UN office of the International Association of Lawyers Against Nuclear Arms (IALANA). Before that he was an attorney for the California-based Western States Legal Foundation for more than 10 years. Author of many articles and books Dr Burroughs is also an adjunct professor of international law at Rutgers Law School, Newark, USA.

CHRISTINE CHINKIN is Professor in International Law at the London School of Economics. She is on the board of editors of the *American Journal of International Law* and of the Advisory Board of the *European Journal of International Law*. She has been a consultant on Public International Law to the Asian Development Bank and a member of its External Forum on Gender, and on human trafficking to the UN Office of the High Commissioner on Human Rights.

ROSEANNA CUNNINGHAM MSP is a lawyer, a Member of the Scottish Parliament for the Scottish National Party (SNP) and Minister for the Environment in the Scottish Government. This is a transcript, reproduced with her permission, of the address she made to the conference in her personal capacity, which was not presented as a written paper.

JANET FENTON is the co-ordinator of the Edinburgh Peace and Justice Centre, and also works with Scotland's for Peace, a network of NGOs working on peace and disarmament issues across Scotland. She founded and directed the Ever Green Trust for Arts (Ecology) Social Justice in Scotland and is a writer/director of issue-based theatre. She is a founder member of the newly-formed Scottish branch of the Women's International League for Peace and Freedom.

PROFESSOR NICK GRIEF has over 30 years experience as a legal academic, teaching at the University of Exeter (1979–1997), Bournemouth University (1998–2009) and now the University of Kent, where he completed his own undergraduate and doctoral studies. As well as being a Professor in Kent Law School and Director of Legal Studies at Kent's Medway campus, Nick practises as a barrister from Doughty Street Chambers, London. In January 2007 he gave evidence to the House of Commons Defence Committee on the legal implications of the White Paper on the future of the United Kingdom's strategic nuclear deterrent. In the 1990s he was closely involved in the World Court Project (notably as the author of a legal memorandum entitled 'The World Court Project on Nuclear Weapons and International Law') which led to the ICJ's advisory opinion on the Legality of the Threat or Use of Nuclear Weapons. In November 2004 he was counsel to the Peacerights inquiry into the legality of nuclear weapons. He has appeared in several cases concerning the legality of Trident, sometimes as an expert witness. In particular, he has defended protesters accused of public order offences at AWE Aldermaston.

DR REBECCA JOHNSON is executive director of the Acronym Institute for Disarmament Diplomacy, Vice Chair of the International Campaign to Abolish Nuclear Weapons (ICAN) and Vice President of CND. A widely published expert on non-proliferation and treaty negotiations, she has a PhD from LSE and was senior advisor to the Weapons of Mass Destruction Commission (Blix Commission, 2004–2006) and a member of the Scottish Government Working Group on Scotland Without Nuclear Weapons after serving on the steering group of Faslane 365. Her interest in nuclear weapons and the law dates back to 1983 when she was a plaintiff against President Reagan and others in the Greenham Women against Cruise case in the US Courts, which germinated the arguments that fed into the campaign for an International Court of Justice advisory opinion on the legality of the use of nuclear weapons.

HELEN LAW is a lawyer at Matrix Chambers, London, specialising in public international law and international criminal law.

AIDAN O'NEILL QC is a barrister specialising in public law, human rights law and European law. He has appeared as senior counsel before the European Court of Justice, the Judicial Committee of the Privy Council, the House of Lords, the Court of Session (Inner and Outer House), and the High Court of England & Wales (Administrative Division), as well as before the sheriff courts in Scotland and the county court in England and Wales. He is the author of three legal text books. In 2009 he was appointed to be Chairman of the Edinburgh Centre for Constitutional Law.

ANGUS ROBERTSON MP is the Leader of the Scottish National Party (SNP) in the UK (Westminster) Parliament, where he is also the SNP Spokesperson on Foreign Affairs and Defence.

PHILIPPE SANDS QC as a barrister at Matrix Chambers, London, practices in public international law. He appears regularly before English and international courts. His cases include *ex parte Augusto Pinochet, A & Others,* and *Democratic Republic of Congo v Uganda.* He served as an adviser to the delegation of Samoa in the negotiations of the Statute of the International Criminal Court (Rome, 1998), and was appointed as *amicus curiae* by the Appeals Chamber of the Special Court for Sierra Leone to make submissions on Head of State immunity under international law (*Prosecutor v Charles Taylor*). As Professor of Laws and Director of the Centre of International Courts and Tribunals at University College London he has published a number of academic books. He also writes regularly for the press and serves as a commentator for the BBC, CNN and other radio and television producers.

RABINDER SINGH QC was appointed a Deputy High Court Judge in 2003 and in 2004 he became a Recorder of the Crown Court. The recipient of the 2006 Human Rights Lawyer of the Year Award, Mr Singh has been a Visiting Professor of Law at the London School of Economics (LSE) since 2003 and is the author of *The Future of Human Rights in the United Kingdom* published in 1997.

H.E. JUDGE CHRISTOPHER WEERAMANTRY was a Justice of the Supreme Court of Sri Lanka from 1967 to 1972. He was a Judge of the

International Court of Justice (ICJ) from 1991 to 2000, and was Vice-President of the ICJ from 1997 to 2000. He is the author of over 20 books and 250 articles published in various international journals, and has lectured extensively in over 50 countries. He is Chair of the Weeramantry International Centre for Peace Education and Research, Patron of the Centre for International Sustainable Development Law (CISDL) and Advisor to the Asian Society of International Law.

ANGIE ZELTER is a peace, human rights and environmental campaigner and the author of several books on campaigning and the law. A founder member of the Institute for Law and Peace, Trident Ploughshares, International Women's Peace Service – Palestine, and Faslane 365, she is the recipient of the 1997 Sean McBride Peace Prize and the 2001 Right Livelihood Award.

End Notes

INTRODUCTION

1   See *Faslane 365 – a year of anti-nuclear blockades* edited by Angie Zelter, Luath, ISBN 1-906307-61-X

2   'Working Group on Scotland Without Nuclear Weapons', Report to Scottish Ministers, August 2009, available on the Scottish Government website at http://www.scotland.gov.uk/Topics/People/swnw-working-group/Report

3   'Working Group on Scotland Without Nuclear Weapons', Report to Scottish Ministers, August 2009, available on the Scottish Government website at http://www.scotland.gov.uk/Topics/People/swnw-working-group/Report

4   'Scotland Without Nuclear Weapons Working Group Report', Scottish Government Response, 18 November 2009, http://www.scotland.gov.uk/Publications/2009/11/governmentresponse

5   Final Document of the 2010 NPT Review Conference, May 28, 2010. http://www.reachingcriticalwill.org/legal/npt/revcon2010/FinalDocument.pdf See also Rebecca Johnson, 'Rethinking the NPT's Role in Security: 2010 and Beyond', *International Affairs* 86:2, 2010, pp.429–445. http://www.chathamhouse.org.uk/publications/ia/archive/view/-/id/2466/

6   See Rebecca Johnson, 'Security Assurances for Everyone: a new approach to deterring the use of nuclear weapons', *Disarmament Diplomacy 90*, Spring 2009.

7   Rebecca Johnson, 'Nuclear Weapons Abolition: an idea whose time has come', Blackaby Paper No. 8, London, April 2010; and International Campaign to Abolish Nuclear Weapons (ICAN), *Securing Our Survival* (SOS): *The Case for a Nuclear Weapons Convention*, April 2007. http://www.icanw.org/securing-our-survival

TRIDENT AND INTERNATIONAL LAW: SCOTLAND'S OBLIGATIONS

1   Geoff Hoon, House of Commons; *Hansard,* HC vol. 384, col. 665, 29 April 2002

2   See for example *War and Peace in World Religions, Gerald Weisfeld lectures*, ed. Perry Schmidt-Leukel, SCM Canterbury Press, ISBN No: 0334029384

3   International Court of Justice CR95/32, pp.30–31

4   Materials furnished to the International Court of Justice by the World Health Organisation, 1995–96

5   Arthur Eyffinger, *The 1899 Peace Conference*, Kluwer p.19

6   Shakespeare, *Julius Caesar*, III.1

GOOD FAITH, INTERNATIONAL LAW AND ELIMINATION OF NUCLEAR WEAPONS

1   In his declaration, Judge Vereshchetin makes clear that in his opinion 'the Court has clearly shown that the edifice of the total prohibition on the threat or use of

nuclear weapons is being constructed and a great deal has already been achieved.' *ICJ Reports* 1996, p.281.

2   *Id*. In agreeing with this, Judge Vereshchetin found himself in the excellent company of Sir Hersch Lauterpacht, whom he cites, and who had stated that the 'apparent indecision, which leaves room for discretion on the part of the organ which requested the Opinion, may ... be preferable to a deceptive clarity which fails to give an indication of the inherent complexities of the issue.' (Lauterpacht, Hersch: *The Development of International Law by the International Court of Justice*, reprint, 1982, p.152). See also Weil, Prosper: *'The Court cannot conclude definitively...' Non liquet revisited*, in 'Essays on International Law in Honour of Professor Louis Henkin,' *Columbia Journal of Transnational Law*, 1997, vol.36, pp.109–119, and 'Ecrits de droit international,' Paris, PUF, pp.141–150.

3   Declaration of President Bedjaoui, *ICJ Reports*, 1996, p.273, ¶ 22.

4   *Cf. contra*, Coussirat-Coustère, Vincent, 'Armes nucléaires et droit international,' *Annuaire français de droit international*, 1996, pp.337–356.

5   *Legality of the Threat or Use of Nuclear Weapons*, Advisory Opinion of 8 July 1996, *ICJ Reports*, 1996 (hereafter 'Advisory Opinion'), p.244, ¶ 36.

6   Advisory Opinion, p.273, ¶ 15.

7   Two members of the Court were concerned about this problem and expressed their doubts in their respective opinions, without, however, breaking the unanimity when this paragraph came to a vote.

8   Resolution 1(1), 24 January 1946, adopted unanimously.

9   Resolution 808A (IX), 4 November 1954, adopted unanimously.

10   Resolution 2028 (XX), 18 November 1968, 'Non-Proliferation of nuclear weapons,' adopted by a vote of 93 for, 0 against and 5 abstentions (Cuba, France, Guinea, Pakistan, Romania).

11   Resolution 2030 (XX), 29 November 1965, 'Question of convening a worldwide disarmament conference,' adopted by 112 vote for, 0 against, one abstention (France). See also Resolution 2031 (XX), 3 December 1965, 'Question of general and complete disarmament,' adopted by 102 votes for, 0 against, with 6 abstentions (Albania, Algeria, France, Guinea, Mali, Tanzania.)

12   Preamble of the Treaty Banning Nuclear Weapon Tests in the Atmosphere, in Outer Space and Underwater, signed in Moscow 5 August 1963 by the Soviet Union, the United Kingdom and the United States.

13   Open for signing as of 1 July 1968 and in force as of 5 March 1970. *United Nations Treaty Series*, vol.729, p.161.

14   In the preamble to the Treaty, the Parties declare 'their intention to achieve at the earliest possible date the cessation of the nuclear arms race and to undertake effective measures in the direction of nuclear disarmament.'

15   Preamble to Protocols I and II of the Treaty for the Prohibition of Nuclear Weapons in Latin American and the Caribbean, signed in Mexico 14 February 1967. By virtue of Protocol I, the United States, France, Great Britain and the Netherlands undertook to respect the conditions stated in the treaty; by virtue of Protocol II, all nuclear-weapon states undertook to recognize the denuclearized status of Latin America

16 See its preamble in which the states party declare themselves 'Convinced that this Treaty constitutes a step towards a treaty on general and complete disarmament under strict and effective international control, and determined to continue negotiations to this end.'

17 In the preamble of this treaty the United States and the Soviet Union state that they are 'Mindful of their obligations under Article VI of the Treaty on the Non-Proliferation of Nuclear Weapons' and declare 'their intention to achieve at the earliest possible date the cessation of the nuclear arms race and to take effective measures toward reductions in strategic arms, nuclear disarmament, and general and complete disarmament.'

18 As a general matter, a *pactum de negociando* can be understood 'as a prior undertaking by which one or more states agree to enter into negotiations with a view to reaching an agreement concerning a precise problem'. Zoller, Elisabeth, *La bonne foi en droit international public*, Paris, Pedone 1977, p.59.

19 In practice, those actually obliged to negotiate nuclear disarmament in good faith seem to represent only a minuscule fraction of the states subject to the obligations laid out under Article VI of the NPT.

20 *Reports of International Arbitral Awards*, vol.II, p.929.

21 'In order to justify either Party in claiming to be discharged from performance, something more must appear than the failure of particular negotiations or the failure to ratify particular protocols. There must be found an intent to frustrate the carrying out of the provisions of Article 3 with respect to the plebiscite; that is, not simply the refusal of a particular agreement proposed thereunder, because of its terms, but the purpose to prevent any reasonable agreement for a plebiscite.' Id., pp.929–930.

22 *Reports of International Arbitral Awards*, vol.XII, pp.306–307.

23 *Id.*, p.311.

24 *North Sea Continental Shelf* (Federal Republic of Germany/Denmark), Judgement of 20 February 1969, *ICJ Reports*, p.47, ¶ 85(a).

25 Case concerning the agreement on German external debt: Claims arising out of decisions of the Mixed Graeco-German Arbitral Tribunal set up under Article 304 in Part X of the Treaty of Versailles (between Greece and the Federal Republic of Germany), *Reports of International Arbitral Awards*, vol.XIX, pp.56–57.

26 *Id.*, p.64.

27 According to Paul Reuter, the minimum content of the obligation to negotiate requires that states undertake to open negotiations and conduct themselves as negotiators; concerning this undertaking to conduct themselves as negotiators, he states: 'It is unanimously known that this is not an obligation to reach a result, but an obligation of conduct: negotiators must behave in a certain manner, discounting the results of the negotiations; this obligation cannot be defined in a rigid manner, but is rather the object of somewhat flexible standards. The dominant principle is that of good faith; negotiators must refrain from certain types of behaviour because such behaviour is incompatible with an honest intention to negotiate.' Paul Reuter, 'De l'obligation de négocier,' Communicazioni e studi, Milano, Giuffre, 1975, pp.717–71

28 *Reports of International Arbitral Awards*, vol.XII, pp.306–307.

29 Commentary on article 20 adopted by the Commission, *Yearbook of the International Law Commission 1977*, vol.II, part two, pp.13–14, ¶ 8.

30 See for instance the speech of the representative of Iran in the context of the two advisory opinions; according to him: '*It needs to be clarified, however, that the extension decision was a part of a package of three inter-linked compromise decisions. The other two decisions were:* 'Strengthening the Review Process for the Treaty', which provides for a greater measure of accountability by all parties, in particular by the nuclear powers, and secondly, 'Principles and Objectives for Nuclear Non-Proliferation and Disarmament', which reiterates 'the ultimate goal of the complete elimination of nuclear weapons and a treaty on general and complete disarmament.' CR 95/26, p.26.

31 According to its ¶ 3, a material breach of a treaty consists, *inter alia*, in 'the violation of a provision essential to the accomplishment of the object or purpose of the treaty.'

32 See ¶ 2 of Article 60.

33 *Statement issued on 5 April 1995 by the Honourable Warren Christopher, Secretary of State, regarding a declaration by the President on security assurances for non-nuclear-weapon States Parties to the Treaty on the Non-Proliferation of Nuclear Weapons,'* UN Doc. A/50/153, S/1995/263, 6 April 1995.

34 1995 Review and Extension Conference of the Parties to the Treaty on the Non-Proliferation of Nuclear Weapons, Decision 2: Principles and Objectives for Nuclear Non-Proliferation and Disarmament, NPT/CONF.1995/32 (Part I).

35 Robert Kolb, *La bonne foi en droit international public: Contribution à l'étude des principes généraux du droit*, préface Georges Abi-Saab, Publications de l'Institut universitaire des hautes études internationales, Geneva and Paris, PUF, 2000 (756 pages), p.588. This particularly well-researched work has become a classic on good faith. *Cf.* also Elisabeth Zoller, *La bonne foi en droit international public,* published in Paris 1977 and republished and completed in 1994 under the title *La bonne foi* in the collection *Travaux de l'Association Henri Capitant*, Paris, vol.43. And finally see R. Yakemtchouk, *La bonne foi dans la conduite internationale des Etats*, 2002.

36 Robert Kolb, *op.cit.*, pp.112–113.

37 Cited by Robert Kolb, *op.cit.*

38 Christian Tomuschat, 'Obligations arising for States without or against their will,' *Recueil des courts de l'Académie de droit international*, 1993–IV, vol.241, p.322.

39 Oscar Schachter, 'Non-conventional concerted acts,' in Mohammed Bedjaoui (ed.), *International Law: Achievements and Prospects,* Paris, UNESCO, 1991, pp.267–268.

40 *Cf.* for instance *Military and Paramilitary Activities in and against Nicaragua, Jurisdiction and Admissibility* (Nicaragua v. United States), ICJ Reports 1984, p.418.

41 Resolution 2625 (XXV): 'Every State has the duty to fulfil in good faith its obligations under international agreements valid under the generally recognized principles and rules of international law.'

42 In effect, one of the basic principles mentioned in this document is the principle of good-faith execution of obligations assumed under international law.

43 *Nuclear Tests* (Australia v. France), Judgement of 20 December 1974, *ICJ Reports* 1974, p.268, ¶ 46.

44 *Dictionnaire Salmon*, p.134.

45 *Yearbook of the International Law Commission*, 1965, vol.1, p.91, ¶ 41.

46 *Yearbook of the International Law Commission*, 1966, vol.II, pp.210–211.

47 *Aminoil Case* (Kuwait v Independent Oil Co.), 1982, *International Legal Reports*, vol.66, p.578.

48 *Case concerning the agreement on German external debt, op.cit.*, p.64. This echoes the formulas used by the International Court of Justice in the *North Sea Continental Shelf* case (*ICJ Reports* 1969, p.47) and the *Gulf of Maine* case (*ICJ Reports* 1984, p.299).

49 Advisory Opinion, pp.264–265, ¶¶ 102–103.

50 Robert Kolb, *op.cit.*, p.295.

51 Vienna Conference on the Law of Treaties, Special Rapporteur Humphrey Waldock, first session, p.104, ¶ 25.

52 Robert Kolb, *op.cit.*, pp.201–202.

53 Case A.15, *Iran v. United States*, 20 August 1986, Iran/US Claims Tribunal Reports, vol.12, p.61 (cited by Robert Kolb, *op.cit.*).

54 *ICJ Reports*, 1980, p.95.

55 *ICJ Reports*, 1980, p.96.

56 *Case concerning the agreement on German external debt, op.cit.*, p.56.

57 Working Paper submitted by Greece on behalf of the European Union, Disarmament Commission, 2003, Substantive Session, A/CN.10/2003/ WG.II/WP.2, 4 April 2003.

58 *Id.*, ¶ 5

59 Agreement on Confidence-Building Measures Related to Systems to Counter Ballistic Missiles other than Strategic Missiles, September 1997, Article VII.

60 Mosler, H., *General Course on International Public Law, Recueil des Cours of the Academy of International Law*, 1974–IV, vol.140, p.111.

61 *Cf. Nottebohm Case*, *ICJ Reports* 1955, p.20; *Minquiers and Ecrehous Case*, *ICJ Reports* 1953, p.71; *Case concerning Maritime Delimitation and Territorial Questions between Qatar and Bahrain, Jurisdiction and Admissibility, ICJ Reports* 1994, pp.125–126.

62 Working Paper, *op.cit.*, fn. 57, ¶ 19.

RECENT DEVELOPMENTS IN THE ILLEGALITY OF NUCLEAR WEAPONS

1 Committee on International Security and Arms Control, National Academy of Sciences, *The Future of US Nuclear Weapons Policy*, National Academy Press, 1997, p.87; (emphasis added.)

2 August 1999 Paper prepared by the International Committee of the Red Cross relating to the crimes listed in article 8, para.2(b)(xvii), (xviii), (xix), (xx), (xxiii), (xxiv) and (xxv) of the Rome Statute of the International Criminal Court,

submitted by the governments of Belgium, Costa Rica, Finland, Hungary, the Republic of Korea, and Switzerland to the Preparatory Commission for the ICC, PCNICC/1999/WGEC/INF2/Add.2 (4 August 1999), p.25.

3   See *The Legal and Policy Imperatives for the Abolition of Nuclear Weapons*, July 2008; *Ending US Reliance on Nuclear Weapons and Achieving Their Global Elimination: Wise Policy and Required by Law*, March 2008.

4   International Law – *The Conduct of Armed Conflict and Air Operations*, US Air Force Pamphlet 110-31, 1976, § 6-3(c); (emphasis added.)

5   1977 Protocol I to the Geneva Conventions. Article 51, 'Protection of the Civilian Population'. (Emphasis added.)

6   ICJ Advisory Opinion, para.30; (emphasis added.)

7   (Para.31; emphasis added.)

8   Rebecca Johnson, 'The Missing Link: Political Decision and Will to Build and Manage Security without Nuclear Weapons', in Hannes Swoboda and Jan Marinus Wiersma (eds.), *Peace and Disarmament: A World without Nuclear Weapons?* The Socialist Group in the European Parliament (PSE), Brussels, 2009.

9   Paras.78, 79 (emphasis added)

10   *Prosecutor v. Milan Martic (Rule 61 Proceeding)*, Case No. IT-95-11-1 (8 March 1996), paras.8–17.

11   *Id.* at para.15, emphasis added; see also paras.16 and 17.

12   ENDC/PV. 390, 15 August 1968, para.93.

A SCOTTISH PERSPECTIVE

1   Professor William Walker, quoted by MSP Patrick Harvie in the debate on Trident, Scottish Parliament official record 14 June 2007 http://www.scotland4peace.org/Binthebomb/lobby/Debates/debate14jun07.htm and http://www.theyworkforyou.com/sp/?id=2007-06-14.699.1

2   Archbishop Cardinal Keith O Brien, Easter Sunday Homily at St Mary's Cathedral Easter Sunday Mass, 16 April 2006

3   Press release after arrest for blockading Faslane during the Faslane 365 year. See www.faslane365.org

4   Bin The Bomb Rally, George Square, 24 Feb 2007 http://www.dundeecityunison.org.uk/DCUmain.php?thispage=news&newsno=0081

5   *www.scotland4peace.org*

6   *www.scotland4peace.org*

7   Elections for the Scottish Parliament were held on 3 May 2007.

8   http://www.scottish.parliament.uk/business/officialReports/meetingsParliament/or-07/sor0614-02.htm

9   *Article 19* Union with England Act 1707 (Scotland) http://www.statutelaw.gov.uk/content.aspx?ActiveTextDocId=1519711

10   Angus MacCulloch, Introduction to Scots Law.

11   Angus MacCulloch, Introduction to Scots Law.

12   http://www.commissiononscottishdevolution.org.uk/

13   Extract from Sir Walter Scott's *Lay of the Last Minstrel*.

14   Operational Safety Case for the Transport of Nuclear Weapons, Executive

Summary, Issue 2, January 2005, Nuclear Movements and Nuclear Accident Response Group. Obtained under the FOIA by Rob Edwards, *Sunday Herald*.

15 Civil Contingencies Act 2004.

THE UNITED KINGDOM'S NUCLEAR DETERRENT: CURRENT AND FUTURE ISSUES OF LEGALITY

1   This Legal Advice was prepared for Greenpeace UK and published on 13 November 2006. http://www.greenpeace.org.uk/MultimediaFiles/Live/FullReport/8072.pdf

2   Trident's future 'linked to Iran', BBC News, 11 October 2005, quoting Foreign Officer Minister Kim Howells, available at http://news.bbc.co.uk/1/hi/uk/4331882.stm

3   The legal ramifications of a state's non-compliance with its obligations under the NPT, in particular where it is in material breach, are considered in abstract at para.33, below.

4   *Legality of the Threat or Use of Nuclear Weapons*, (*Advisory Opinion at the request of the UN General Assembly*), ICJ Reports 1996, [100].

5   *Legality of the Threat or Use of Nuclear Weapons*, (Advisory Opinion at the request of the UN General Assembly), ICJ Reports 1996, [47].

6   *Legality of the Threat or Use of Nuclear Weapons*, (Advisory Opinion at the request of the UN General Assembly), ICJ Reports 1996, [48]; Dissenting Opinion of Vice-President Schwebel.

7   *Military and Paramilitary Activities in and against Nicaragua (Nicaragua v. United States of America)* ICJ Reports 1986, [173] – [176].

8   See 2005 World Summit Outcome Document, [79], in UN General Assembly Resolution 60/1 (24 October 2005), available at: http://daccessdds.un.org/doc/UNDOC/GEN/No5/487/60/PDF/No548760.pdf?OpenElement

9   The Chatham House Principles are available at: http://www.chathamhouse.org.uk/index.php?id=261

10 *Military and Paramilitary Activities in and against Nicaragua (Nicaragua v. United States of America)* ICJ Reports 1986, [176], cited in *Legality of the Threat or Use of Nuclear Weapons*, (*Advisory Opinion at the request of the UN General Assembly*), ICJ Reports 1996, [41].

11 *Oil Platforms (Islamic Republic of Iran v. United States of America)* ICJ Reports 2003, [73].

12 *Military and Paramilitary Activities in and against Nicaragua (Nicaragua v. United States of America)* ICJ Reports 1986, [237], [282]; cited in *Oil Platforms (Islamic Republic of Iran v. United States of America)* ICJ Reports 2003, [43].

13 Chatham House Principles, commentary to Principles 3 and 4, p.8, cited in part below at paragraph.

14 Chatham House Principles, p.8.

15 *Oil Platforms (Islamic Republic of Iran v. United States of America)* ICJ Reports 2003, [77].

16 *Hansard* HL vol.660, Col 370, 21 April 2004.

17 For example, *Legality of the Threat or Use of Nuclear Weapons*, (*Advisory*

Opinion at the request of the UN *General Assembly*), ICJ Reports 1996, [91], citing the Written Statement of the United Kingdom: *'the legality of the use of nuclear weapons must therefore be assessed in the light of the applicable principles of international law regarding the use of force and the conduct of hostilities, as is the case with other methods and means of warfare.'*

18 *Legality of the Threat or Use of Nuclear Weapons, (Advisory Opinion at the request of the* UN *General Assembly*), ICJ Reports 1996, [79].

19 *Legality of the Threat or Use of Nuclear Weapons, (Advisory Opinion at the request of the* UN *General Assembly*), ICJ Reports 1996, [39]: 'A weapon that is already unlawful* per se, *whether by treaty or custom, does not become lawful by reason of it being used for a legitimate purpose under the Charter.'* See also, President Bedjaoui's separate Declaration at [22].

20 *Legal Consequences of the Construction of a Wall in the Occupied Palestinian Territory (Advisory Opinion)* ICJ Reports 2004, [157].

21 On which see Article 48 of AP1, which is codificatory of the customary international law obligation.

22 *Legality of the Threat or Use of Nuclear Weapons, (Advisory Opinion at the request of the* UN *General Assembly*), ICJ Reports 1996, [78] (emphasis added). This is further supported by the ICJ's conclusion that nuclear weapons are *'scarcely reconcilable'* with the obligations to discriminate and not to cause unnecessary suffering ([95]). It is not disputed that nuclear weapons are capable of being targeted with a relatively high degree of precision. Therefore the ICJ must have been referring to the *effects* of those weapons, not merely their targeting capability, when calling them *'scarcely reconcilable'*.

23 Article 51(4) provides: 'Indiscriminate attacks are prohibited. Indiscriminate attacks are:

a   Those which are not directed at a specific military objective;

b   Those which employ a method or means of combat which cannot be directed at a specific military objective; or

c   Those which employ a method or means of combat the effects of which cannot be limited as required by this Protocol; and consequently, in each such case, are of a nature to strike military objectives and civilians or civilian objects without distinction'

24 Paper delivered to the Conference on Freedom from Nuclear Weapons through Good Faith and Accountability (Brussels, 6–7 July 2006).

25 Legality of the Threat or Use of Nuclear Weapons, (Advisory Opinion at the request of the UN General Assembly), ICJ Reports 1996, [78].

26 M. Bothe, 'The law of neutrality' in D. Fleck *The Handbook of Humanitarian Law in Armed Conflicts* (1999: OUP).

27 Available at http://disarmament.un.org/wmd/npt/index.html

28 *Territorial Dispute (Libyan Arab Jamahiriya/Chad)* ICJ Reports 1994, [41]: 'in accordance with customary international law, reflected in Article 31 of the 1969 Vienna Convention on the Law of Treaties, a treaty must be interpreted in good faith in accordance with the ordinary meaning to be given to its terms in their context and in the light of its object and purpose. Interpretation must be based above all upon the text of the treaty. As a supplementary measure recourse may

be had to means of interpretation such as the preparatory work of the treaty and the circumstances of its conclusion.'

29   VCLT Article 31(2): 'The context for the purpose of the interpretation of a treaty shall comprise, in addition to the text, including its preamble and annexes...'; NPT Article VIII(3): 'to review the operation of this Treaty with a view to assuring that the purposes of the Preamble and the provisions of the Treaty are being realized.' (emphasis added).

30   VCLT Article 31(3)(a): 'any subsequent agreement between the parties regarding the interpretation of the treaty or the application of its provisions'; NPT Article VIII(3): 'a conference of Parties to the Treaty shall be held ... in order to review the operation of this Treaty with a view to assuring that the purposes of the Preamble and the provisions of the Treaty are being realized.'

31   VCLT Article 32.

32   VCLT Article 32.

33   *Legality of the Threat or Use of Nuclear Weapons, (Advisory Opinion at the request of the UN General Assembly),* ICJ Reports 1996, [103].

34   *2000 Review Conference of the Parties to the Treaty on Non-Proliferation of Nuclear Weapons, Final Document,* vol.1 (NPT/CONF.2000/28 (Parts I and II)), p.14.

35   For a full account, see E. Firmage, '*The Treaty on the Non-Proliferation of Nuclear Weapons*' (1969) 63 AJIL 711, especially at 733–735.

36   At [100].

37   G Goodwin-Gill, '*State Responsibility and the 'Good Faith' Obligation in International Law*', in, M. Fitzmaurice and D. Sarooshi (eds) *Issues of State Responsibility before International Judicial Institutions* (2004: Hart) 75, 84. See also, *Legality of the Threat or Use of Nuclear Weapons, (Advisory Opinion at the request of the UN General Assembly),* ICJ Reports 1996, [102], citing its earlier decision in *Nuclear Tests (Australia v. France)* ICJ Reports 1974, [46].

38   VCLT, Article 60(3). Article 60 has been acknowledged as codificatory of customary international law by the ICJ in, for example, *Gabcikovo-Nagymoros Project (Hungary/Slovakia)* ICJ Reports 1997, [46].

39   As per VCLT Article 60.

40   The technical information is extracted from: *House of Commons Defence Committee, Eighth Report of Session 2005–06, The Future of the UK's Strategic Nuclear Deterrent: the Strategic Context* (HC 986: 30 June 2006), pp.8–9, and, Dr Frank Barnaby, *What is Trident? The facts and figures of Britain's nuclear force* in Oxford Research Group, *The Future of Britain's Nuclear Weapons: Experts Reframe the Debate* (March 2006), pp.7–10.

41   P. Rogers 'Big boats and bigger skimmers: determining the UK's role in the Long War' (2006) 82 *International Affairs* 651, 653, especially at fn. 4. On the meaning of 'sub-strategic', see para.35, below.

42   One kiloton is an explosive force equivalent to 1,000 metric tons of TNT.

43   The distance within which there is a very high probability of death caused by the immediate blast, heat and radiation, excluding residual radiation. For 1kt

explosions, radiation is more lethal than heat or blast. For 100kt explosions, heat is more lethal than either blast or radiation.

44 Available at http://www.awe.co.uk/Images/annual_report_2000_tcm6-1764.pdf, at p.14.

45 R. S. Norris and H. M. Kristensen, 'British Nuclear Forces' in *Bulletin of Atomic Scientists*, vol.62, no.6, Nov–Dec 2005, pp.77–79, available at http://www.thebulletin.org/article_nn.php?art_ofn=ndo5norris.

46 This raises concerns in relation to Step 9 of the Practical Steps agreed at the 2000 Review Conference, which refers to increased transparency by nuclear-weapon states about their weapons capability. The absence of such transparency may serve to undermine the good faith obligation in Article VI NPT.

47 *Report of the Inquiry into the Legality of Nuclear Weapons* (2004: Peacerights), [3.2.39], *per* Dr Frank Barnaby.

48 Dr Frank Barnaby, *What is Trident? The facts and figures of Britain's nuclear force* in Oxford Research Group, *The Future of Britain's Nuclear Weapons: Experts Reframe the Debate* (March 2006), p.10.

49 Atomic Weapons Establishment 2000 Annual Report, available at http://www.awe.co.uk/Images/annual_report_2000_tcm6-1764.pdf, at p.14.

50 *House of Commons Defence Committee, Eighth Report of Session 2005–06, The Future of the UK's Strategic Nuclear Deterrent: the Strategic Context* (HC 986: 30 June 2006), pp.12–13.

51 Ibid.

52 'Nuclear Deterrence in a Changing World: the view from a UK perspective' in RUSI Journal, June 1996, cited by R. S. Norris and H. M. Kristensen, 'British Nuclear Forces' in *Bulletin of Atomic Scientists*, vol.62, no.6, Nov–Dec 2005, pp.77–79, fn.4.

53 *Trident and the Future of the British Nuclear Deterrent* (Standard Note: SN/IA/3706, 27 April 2006), p.12.

54 *Strategic Defence Review*, Cm 3999, [61] (emphasis added).

55 Ibid., [18]–[19] (emphasis added).

56 *Hoon's talk of pre-emptive strikes could be catastrophic, The Guardian*, 6 June 2002.

57 The full transcript of the exchange between Mr Hoon and Jonathan Dimbleby can be found at http://cndyorks.gn.apc.org/news/articles/uknukepolicy.htm; see para.51, below.

58 This last quote was taken from Mr Hoon's response to questions in the House of Commons: *Hansard*, HC, vol.384, col.665, 29 April 2002.

59 *Nuclear Tests Case (Australia v. France)* ICJ Reports 1974, [49].

60 See above, para.38.

61 *Legality of the Threat or Use of Nuclear Weapons*, (Advisory Opinion at the request of the UN General Assembly), ICJ Reports 1996, [39]. See also, President Bedjaoui's separate Declaration at [22], where he makes it clear that a state is bound by these principles, even when acting in self-defence and when the state's very survival is at stake.

62 The National Security Strategy of the United States of America, 20 September

2002, cited in the House of Commons Select Committee on Foreign Affairs, Second Report of Session 2002–03, Foreign *Policy Aspects of the War Against Terrorism* (HC 196, 19 December 2002), [49].

63 See further, Chatham House Principle 4, cited above at para.10.

64 At [105(2)(E)] (emphasis added).

65 At [11].

66 *Legality of the Threat or Use of Nuclear Weapons, (Advisory Opinion at the request of the* UN *General Assembly)*, ICJ Reports 1996, [39]. See also, President Bedjaoui's separate Declaration at [22], where he makes it clear that a state is bound by these principles, even when acting in self-defence and when the state's very survival is at stake.

67 See above, para.34.

68 Ibid.

69 http://www.statistics.gov.uk/downloads/theme_population/regional_snapshot/RS_Lon.pdf

70 See above, para.34.

71 Ibid.

72 Transcript of an interview between Jonathan Dimbleby and Mr Hoon on 24 March 2002, available at http://cndyorks.gn.apc.org/news/articles/ uknukepolicy.htm (emphasis added).

73 We referred above, at para.5, to the ICJ's conclusion that a threat of force would be unlawful if the use of the force threatened would itself be unlawful. We do not, in this opinion, consider the question of whether the UK has acted in breach of the specific obligation not to threaten unlawful force. However, and given our conclusions on the legality of the use of force contemplated by Mr Hoon, we note our concerns as to the **possibility** of such a breach.

74 At p.53, [3.70], cited by the ICJ in its Advisory Opinion at [91].

75 *Strategic Defence Review*, Cm 3999, [22].

76 See above, para.51.

77 *Legality of the Threat or Use of Nuclear Weapons, (Advisory Opinion at the request of the* UN *General Assembly)*, ICJ Reports 1996, [35] / [95] (emphasis added).

78 *Report of the Inquiry into the Legality of Nuclear Weapons* (2004: Peacerights), [3.3.10]-[3.3.13] / [3.3.27].

79 See above, para.34(iii).

80 The following is extracted from *Report of the Inquiry into the Legality of Nuclear Weapons* (2004: Peacerights), [3.3.8], *per* Dr Douglas Holdstock.

81 *Report of the Inquiry into the Legality of Nuclear Weapons* (2004: Peacerights), [3.2.39], *per* Dr Frank Barnaby. See also Louise Doswald-Beck's paper delivered to the Conference on Freedom from Nuclear Weapons through Good Faith and Accountability (Brussels, 6–7 July 2006).

82 *Hansard* HC vol.434, col.987, 6 June 2005.

83 *House of Commons Defence Committee, Eighth Report of Session 2005–06, The Future of the* UK's *Strategic Nuclear Deterrent: the Strategic Context* (HC 986: 30 June 2006), p.14.

84 *Worse than irrelevant, The Guardian,* 29 July 2005.

85 UK *Defence Strategy: A continuing role for nuclear weapons?',* speech to the Centre for Defence Studies, 16 November 1993, [6].

86 '*Delivering Security in a Changing World: Defence White Paper'* Cm. 6041-I, [3.1].

87 Cmnd 3999, [3].

88 Prime Minister Tony Blair in response to a question by Paul Flynn MP during Prime Minister's Questions on 19 October 2005: '*I do not think that anyone pretends that the independent nuclear deterrent is a defence against terrorism.'* *Hansard* HC, vol.437, col.841. However, some authors persist in contending that nuclear weaponry would be apt to tackle the terrorist threat: 'I am sure there are many terrorists who literally are beyond deterrents, but terrorists require support, and, to the degree that they require state support, the states that support them are capable of being deterred... There is relevance to having nuclear weapons, shall I say, to discourage terrorists or to discourage those who are supporting terrorists. In the new environment, we are not in the business of having nuclear threats to destroy populations. If we ever had to use those weapons, they should be employed against very particular targets and for very particular purposes, and that requires a nuclear arsenal that is not really the nuclear arsenal we have which we have inherited from the Cold War.' Dr Colin Gray of the University of Reading, to the House of Commons Defence Committee, Uncorrected Transcript of Oral Evidence (HC 986-ii, 21 March 2006, Q97, available at http://www. publications.parliament.uk/pa/cm200506/cmselect/cmd fence/uc986-ii/uc98602.htm

89 HC Debate, 23 January 2006, col 1153–4.

90 *House of Commons Defence Committee, Ninth Special Report of Session 2005–06, The Future of the* UK's Strategic Nuclear Deterrent: the Strategic Context: The Government Response to the *Committee's Eighth Report of Session 2005–06* (HC 1558: 26 July 2006), [11].

91 *House of Commons Defence Committee, Ninth Special Report of Session 2005–06, The Future of the* UK's Strategic Nuclear Deterrent: the Strategic Context: The Government Response to the *Committee's Eighth Report of Session 2005-06* (HC 1558: 26 July 2006), [5].

92 Cm 6041-I, [3.11], cited in *House of Commons Defence Committee, Ninth Special Report of Session* 2005–06, The Future of the UK's Strategic Nuclear Deterrent: the Strategic Context: The Government *Response to the Committee's Eighth Report of Session 2005–06* (HC 1558: 26 July 2006), [8].

93 See above, paras.38 /51.

94 *Hansard* HC vol.302, col.576–7. See also, the answers of Lord Hoyle in the House of Lords debates following the publication of the Strategic Defence Review in 1998:

    Q What is their policy with regard to nuclear retaliation in the case of aggressor states contemplating the use of chemical and biological weapons? **Lord Hoyle:** The use of chemical or biological weapons by any state would be a grave breach of international law. **A state which chose to use chemical or biological weapons against the United Kingdom should expect us to exercise our right of self defence and to make a proportionate response.** Hansard HL, vol.593, col.WA224, 29 October 1998.

95 *2000 Review Conference of the Parties to the Treaty on Non-Proliferation of Nuclear Weapons, Final Document*, vol.1 (NPT/CONF.2000/28 (Parts I and II)), p.14, Step 9 (emphasis added).

96 *House of Commons Defence Committee, Eighth Report of Session 2005–06, The Future of the UK's Strategic Nuclear Deterrent: the Strategic Context* (HC 986: 30 June 2006), pp.25–7.

97 *House of Commons Defence Committee, Ninth Special Report of Session 2005–06, The Future of the UK's Strategic Nuclear Deterrent: the Strategic Context: The Government Response to the Committee's Eighth Report of Session 2005–06* (HC 1558: 26 July 2006), [13].

98 In evidence to the House of Commons Defence Committee, cited in *Eighth Report of Session 2005–06, The Future of the UK's Strategic Nuclear Deterrent: the Strategic Context* (HC 986: 30 June 2006), [97].

99 In its evidence to the House of Commons Defence Committee, the British American Security Information Council (BASIC) stated: 'Any replacement system for Trident based upon the belief that the UK needed to maintain an insurance policy against possible future threats would logically entail permanent possession and therefore an abrogation of our treaty responsibilities.' *House of Commons Defence Committee, Eighth Report of Session 2005–06, The Future of the UK's Strategic Nuclear Deterrent: the Strategic Context* (HC 986: 30 June 2006), Evidence 111, at [2.25].

100 *House of Commons Defence Committee, Eighth Report of Session 2005–06, The Future of the UK's Strategic Nuclear Deterrent: the Strategic Context* (HC 986: 30 June 2006), Evidence 111, at [3.4].

101 *2000 Review Conference of the Parties to the Treaty on Non-Proliferation of Nuclear Weapons, Final Document, Volume 1* (NPT/CONF.2000/28 (Parts I and II)), p.14, Step 5. See also, the comments of the Defence Select Committee in 1994 that enhanced targeting can improve the UK's nuclear capability, even when coupled with a reduction in overall explosive power: 'Trident's accuracy and sophistication in other respects does – and was always intended to – represent a significant enhancement of the UK's nuclear capability. We have invested a great deal of money to make it possible to attack more targets with greater effectiveness using nominally equivalent explosive power.' HC297, Session 1993–94, p.xiv.

102 *Legality of the Threat or Use of Nuclear Weapons, (Advisory Opinion at the request of the UN General Assembly)*, ICJ Reports 1996.

103 *Trident and the Future of the British Nuclear Deterrent* (Standard Note: SN/IA/3706, 27 April 2006), p.31.

104 Ibid.

105 See above, at para.34.

106 Louise Doswald-Beck has stated: '…having heard various opinions from physicist, there is no nuclear weapon, however small, that will not result in radiation that will be let out into the atmosphere. This is especially so if one intends to use it in a tactical way against a very small specific objective. It is likely to be detonated nearer the ground, which means there is likely to be more fallout. As a result there will be the same problem of indiscriminate effects of radiation ending up in various unforeseeable places.' Paper delivered to the

Conference on Freedom from Nuclear Weapons through Good Faith and Accountability (Brussels, 6–7 July 2006).

107 *2000 Review Conference of the Parties to the Treaty on Non-Proliferation of Nuclear Weapons, Final Document, Vol.1* (NPT/CONF.2000/28 (Parts I and II)), p.14, Step 9.

108 M Quinlan, 'The future of the United Kingdom nuclear weapons: shaping the debate', (2006) 82 *International Affairs* 627, 633.

109 Ibid.

110 *2000 Review Conference of the Parties to the Treaty on Non-Proliferation of Nuclear Weapons, Final Document, Vol.1* (NPT/CONF.2000/28 (Parts I and II)), p.14, Step 9.

THE MAINTENANCE AND POSSIBLE REPLACEMENT OF THE TRIDENT NUCLEAR MISSILE SYSTEM

1 This Legal Advice was prepared for Peacerights and published on 19 December 2005

2 Geoff Hoon MP, written answer, 4 April 2005.

3 1996 ICJ Reports, *Dispositif,* para.105. 2. E

4 Declaration of President Bedjaoui, 1996 ICJ Reports, para.11

5 1996 ICJ Reports, para.104

6 1996 ICJ Reports para.42; see also paras.39, 91 and *dispositif,* paras.2. C and D

7 Cited 1996 ICJ Reports, para.91

8 GA Res. 56/83, 12 December 2001

9 1996 ICJ Reports, para.47

10 1996 ICJ Reports para.48

11 Luigi Condorelli, 'Nuclear weapons: a weighty matter for the International Court of Justice' 316 International Review of the Red Cross(1997) 9.

12 *Military and Paramilitary Activities in and against Nicaragua* (Nicaragua v. US) (Merits), 1986 ICJ Reports, para. 176; *Oil Platforms* (Islamic Republic of Iran v. US) (Merits), 2003 ICJ Reports, para. 76; *Legality of the Threat or Use of Nuclear Weapons* 1996 ICJ Reports, para.41

13 GA Res. 56/83, 12 December 2001

14 *Gabcikovo-Nagymaros Project* (Hungary/Slovakia) 1997 ICJ Reports 7, paras.51–2

15 *Oil Platforms* (Islamic Republic of Iran v. US) (Merits), 2003 ICJ Reports, para.77.

16 1996 ICJ Reports, para.79

17 Vincent Chetail, 'The Contribution of the International Court of Justice to International Humanitarian Law', 850 International Review of the Red Cross (2003) 235, 251.

18 Luigi Condorelli, 'Nuclear weapons: a weighty matter for the International Court of Justice' 316 International Review of the Red Cross (1997) 9.

19 Antonio Cassese, *International Law* (2nd ed. OUP 2005) 206.

20 1996 ICJ Reports, Declaration Judge Bedjaoui, para.22.

21 *Legal Consequences of the Construction of a Wall in the Occupied Palestinian Territory* 2004 ICJ Reports, para.157

22   *Barcelona Traction, Light and Power Company, Ltd, Second Phase,* 1970 ICJ
     Reports para.33

23   1996 ICJ Reports, para.78

24   Rome Statute, article 8 (2) (b) (v).

25   1996 ICJ Reports para.95.

26   C. Greenwood, '*Jus ad bellum and Jus in Bello in the Nuclear Weapons Advisory
     Opinion*', in L. Boisson de Chazournes and P. Sands, eds), *International Law, the
     International Court of Justice and Nuclear Weapons,* 1999, 247, 261, emphasis
     in the original.

27   Lord Murray (Former Lord Advocate of Scotland), '*Nuclear Weapons and the
     Law*', 1998, available at http://wcp.gn.apc.org/newmurray.html

28   Ibid.

29   Bundle Tab 8

30   Bundle, Tab 6, para.237

31   Transcript of interview between Geoff Hoon and Jonathan Dimbleby, 24 March
     2002, available at cndyorks.gn.apc.org/news/articles/uknukepolicy.htm

32   Hansard, 29 April 2002, Bundle Tab 6

33   *Nuclear Tests cases* (Australia v. France; New Zealand v. France) 1974 ICJ
     Reports 253; 457, para.49

34   Human Rights General Comment, no.14, The Right to Life, 1984

35   E. Firmage, 'The Treaty on the Non-Proliferation of Nuclear Weapons', 63
     American Journal of International Law (1969) 711, 732

36   Statement by Ambassador John Freeman, Head of the UK Delegation, to the
     Seventh Review Conference of the Treaty on the Non-Proliferation of Nuclear
     Weapons, May 2005, available at http://www.un.org/events/npt2005/statements/
     npt05unitedkingdom.pdf

37   E.g. *Legal Consequences for States of the Continued Presence of South Africa in
     Namibia (South West Africa) Notwithstanding Security Council 276 (1970)* 1971
     ICJ Rep. 16, 47; *Fisheries Jurisdiction Case* (United Kingdom v. Iceland) 1974 ICJ
     Rep. 3, para.36; *Gabcikovo-Nagymaros Project (Hungary/Slovakia)* 1997 ICJ
     Reports para.4

38   *Indonesia/Malaysia* case, 2002 ICJ Reports 3, para.37; *Libya/Chad* case, 1994 ICJ
     Reports, 6, 21–2; *Qatar/Bahrain* case, 1995 ICJ Reports 6, 18

39   E. Firmage, 'The Treaty on the Non-Proliferation of Nuclear Weapons', 63
     American Journal of International Law (1969) 711, 733

40   E. Firmage, 'The Treaty on the Non-Proliferation of Nuclear Weapons', 63
     American Journal of International Law (1969) 711, 716–721

41   NPT/CONF.2000/28 (Parts I and II)

42   Final Document of the Review Conference 2000, Part I, Articles I and II and first
     to third preambular paragraphs, para.2

43   Part I, Articles I and II and first to third preambular paragraphs, para.5

44   Final Document of the Review Conference 2000, Part I, Article VI and paras.3
     and 4 (c) of the 1995 Decision on 'Principles and Objectives for Nuclear Non-
     Proliferation and Disarmament', para.15.9

45 *Legality of the Threat or Use of Nuclear Weapons* 1996 ICJ Reports, para.103

46 B. Carnahan, 'Treaty Review Conferences', 81 *American Journal of International Law* (1987) 226, 229

47 Part I, Article VI, para.1

48 Part I, Article VI, para.15.6

49 G. Abi-Saab, 'Cours General de Droit International Public' 207 Rec. Des Cours (1987) 160

50 UN Committee on Economic, Social and Cultural rights, General Comment, no.3, The Nature of States Parties' Obligations, 1994

51 Statement by Ambassador John Freeman, Head of the UK Delegation, to the Seventh Review Conference of the Treaty on the Non-Proliferation of Nuclear Weapons, May 2005, available at http://www.un.org/events/npt2005/statements/npt05unitedkingdom.pdf.

52 1996 ICJ Reports, para.103

53 1996 ICJ Reports, para.99 and 102; see also M. Marin Bosch, The Non-Proliferation Treaty and its Future', in L. Boisson de Chazournes and P. Sands, eds), *International Law, the International Court of Justice and Nuclear Weapons*, 1999, 375

54 1996 ICJ Reports, para.103

55 T. Rauf, 'Nuclear Disarmament: Review of Article VI', in J. Simpson and D. Howlett (eds), *The Future of the Non-Proliferation Treaty*, 1995, 66, 67

56 R. Falk, Nuclear Weapons, International Law and the World Court: A Historic Encounter', 91 AJIL (1997) 64, 65

57 M. Marin Bosch, The Non-Proliferation Treaty and its Future', in L. Boisson de Chazournes and P. Sands, eds), *International Law, the International Court of Justice and Nuclear Weapons*, 1999, 375

58 *Nuclear Tests cases* Australia v. France; New Zealand v. France) 1974 ICJ Reports 253; 457, para.46

59 G. Goodwin-Gill, 'State Responsibility and the 'Good Faith' Obligation in International Law', in M. Fitzmaurice and D. Sarooshi (eds) *Issues of State Responsibility before International Judicial Institutions* (2004) 75, 84

60 UNGA Res. 56/83, 12 December 2001

61 *Gabcikovo-Nagymaros Project* (Hungary/Slovakia) 1997 ICJ Reports 7, para.57

62 J. Crawford, *The International Law Commission's Articles on State Responsibility: Introduction, Text and Commentaries* (Cambridge University Press, 2002) 125

63 Defence White Paper, 2003 p.2

64 Britain Forward not Back, Labour Party Manifesto, 2005

65 George W. Bush 'Message to the Congress of the United States'. The White House, 14 June 2004, http://www.whitehouse.gov/news/releases/2004/06/20040614-16.html. See also 'US – UK Mutual Defence Agreement' *Disarmament Diplomacy* 77, May–June 2004, available at http://www.acronym.org.uk/dd/dd77/77mda.htm

DETERRENCE: THE LEGAL CONTEXT

1   *Legality of the Threat or Use of Nuclear Weapons*, Advisory Opinion, ICJ
    Reports 1996, p.226 (hereafter *Nuclear Weapons Case*).

2   *Nuclear Weapons Case*, para.47.

3   Lord Advocate's Reference (No 1 of 2000), 2001 SCCR 296, para.98.

4   Ibid., para.48.

5   In terms of the proportionality principle, the ICJ observed that the very nature of
    all nuclear weapons and the profound risks associated with them, including
    environmental considerations, would have to be borne in mind.

6   *Nuclear Weapons Case*, para.42.

7   Ibid., para.78.

8   Ibid., para.79.

9   Ibid., paras.36, 79 and 95.

10 Ibid., para.94.

11 Ibid., paras.95–96.

12 Ibid., para.105, point 2E of the dispositif.

13 Ibid.

14 Hansard, HL Debates, 26 January 1998, col.7.

15 ICJ Reports 1996, p.270, para.11.

16 The fundamental nature and superior authorityof the rules of IHL was
    emphasised by the ICJ in the *Wall Case* where it observed that those rules
    'incorporate obligations which are essentially of an *erga omnes* character'; i.e.
    they are the concern of all States, and all States have a legal interest in their
    protection: ICJ Reports 2004, p.136, para.157.

17 J. Crawford, *The International Law Commission's Articles on State
    Responsibility*, Cambridge University Press, 2002, p.187.

18 See e.g. Hansard, HC, 1 March 2005, col.805.

19 Articles 26 and 31(1) of the Vienna Convention on the Law of Treaties 1969.

20 *Nuclear Weapons Case*, para.105, point 2F of the dispositif.

21 Joseph Raz, 'The Rule of Law and its virtue', *Law Quarterly Review* vol.93
    (1977), pp.195, 197.

22 Sir Stephen Wall was Head of the European Secretariat, Cabinet Office,
    2000–2004. His lecture was entitled 'The UK, the EU and the United States:
    Bridge, or just Troubled Water?'

23 The Sixth Sir David Williams Lecture, 'The Rule of Law', University of
    Cambridge, 16 November 2006.

24 ICJ Reports 1996, p.277.

PROSECUTING CRIMES AGAINST PEACE BEFORE THE SCOTTISH COURTS

1   See, for example the *Zyklon B Case* (Reports of Trials of War Criminals,
    The United Nations War Crimes Commission, vol.I, London, HMSO, 1947) in
    which various civilian officers of the firm of Tesch & Stabenow – an established
    distributor of certain types of gas and disinfecting equipment (were tried by a
    British Military Court in Hamburg in March 1946 on a charge of being

accessories before the fact of mass murder) in furnishing concentrated prussic acid under the proprietary name Zyklon B to various concentration camps in Eastern Germany and occupied Poland, knowing that it was to be used to kill the inmates. The contemporary case note commentary notes at 1498:

> The decision of the Military Court in the present case is a clear example of the application of the rule that the provisions of the laws and customs of war are addressed not only to combatants and to members of state and other public authority, but to anybody who is in a position to assist in their violation. The activities with which the accused in the present case were charged were commercial transactions conducted by civilians. The Military Court acted on the principle that any civilian who is an accessory to a violation of the laws and customs of war is himself also liable as a war criminal.

See too Willard B. Cowles 'Trials of War Criminals (Non-Nuremberg)' (1948) 42 *The American Journal of International Law* 299 who notes at 310:

> Dr Bruno Tesch, the owner, and his principal executive, one Karl Weinbacher, were sentenced to death by hanging. The sentences were carried into effect.
> A third accused was acquitted apparently on the ground that he held a subordinate position and that there was reasonable doubt that he knowingly did any act as a principal or accessory.

2   See Ingo Müller *Hitler's Justice: the Courts of the Third Reich* (I. B. Turis & Co. Ltd.: London, 1991), in particular Chapter 29 at page 274. See, too, Michael Stolleis *The Law under the Swastika: Studies on Legal History in Nazi Germany* (Chicago: University of Chicago Press, 1998) and Neil Gregor (ed.) *Nazism, war and genocide: essays in honour of Jeremy Noakes* (Exeter: University of Exeter Press, 2005) Chapter 5 Nikolaus Wachsmann 'Soldiers of the home front': jurists and legal terror during the Second World War'.

3   See Case Note in (1951) 64 *Harvard Law Review* 1005–1007. See, too, the commentary on this and similar cases in H. O. Pappe '*On the validity of Judicial Decisions in the Nazi Era*' (1960) 23 *Modern Law Review* 260–274

4   For a celebrated discussion of the justification of this case from the standpoint of competing legal philosophies see HLA Hart: '*Positivism and the separation of law and morals*' (1958) 71 *Harvard Law Review* 583–629 and Lon Fuller: '*Positivism and the separation of law and morals: a reply to Professor Hart*' (1958) 71 *Harvard Law Review* 630–673

5   Printed in *Yearbook of the International Law Commission* 1950 II p.195

6   *Yearbook of the International Law Commission* 1950 II p.192 paras. (3) and (2)

7   Trials of War Criminals before the Nuremberg Military Tribunals (Washington DC: US Government Printing Office, 1951) III at 52

8   *Trials of War Criminals before the Nuremberg Military Tribunals* (Washington DC: US Government Printing Office, 1951) III at 53

9   *Trials of War Criminals before the Nuremberg Military Tribunals* (Washington DC: US Government Printing Office, 1951) III at 53

10 See, now, Article 5 of the Rome Statute of the International Criminal Court (which entered into force on 1 July 2002):

'Crimes within the jurisdiction of the Court

1   The jurisdiction of the Court shall be limited to the most serious crimes of concern to the international community as a whole. The Court has jurisdiction in accordance with this Statute with respect to the following crimes:

    a   The crime of genocide;

    b   Crimes against humanity;

    c   War crimes;

    d   The crime of aggression.'

11 The decision of the Appeals Chamber the International Criminal Tribunal for the former Yugoslavia (ICTY) in *Prosecutor v. Dusko Tadic*, decision of 15 July 1999 finding that customary international law does not contain any requirement to the effect that crimes against humanity may not be committed from purely personal motives, such as revenge or personal gain.

12 *Hansard* HL vol.253, col.831, 2 December 1963

13 In *Korbely v. Hungary*, ECtHR, 19 September (2008) 25 BHRC 382 the Grand Chamber of the Strasbourg Court noted as follows at para.70:

> 70... Article 7 is not confined to prohibiting the retrospective application of the criminal law to an accused's disadvantage: it also embodies, more generally, the principle that only the law can define a crime and prescribe a penalty (nullum crimen, nulla poena sine lege) and the principle that the criminal law must not be extensively construed to an accused's detriment, for instance by analogy. From these principles it follows that an offence must be clearly defined in the law. This requirement is satisfied where the individual can know from the wording of the relevant provision (and, if need be, with the assistance of the courts' interpretation of it and with informed legal advice) what acts and omissions will make him criminally liable. The Court has thus indicated that when speaking of 'law' Article 7 alludes to the very same concept as that to which the Convention refers elsewhere when using that term, a concept which comprises written as well as unwritten law and implies qualitative requirements, notably those of accessibility and foreseeability.

14 See *Coëme and others v. Belgium*, ECtHR, 22 June 2000 at para.45:

> 45. Since the term 'penalty' is autonomous in scope, to render the protection afforded by Article 7 effective the Court must remain free to go behind appearances and assess for itself whether a particular measure amounts in substance to a 'penalty' within the meaning of this provision (see the Welch v. the United Kingdom judgment of 9 February 1995, Series A, no.307-A, p.13, § 27). While the text of the Convention is the starting-point for such an assessment, the Court may have cause to base its findings on other sources, such as the travaux préparatoires. Having regard to the aim of the Convention, which is to protect rights that are practical and effective, it may also take into consideration the need to preserve a balance between the general interest and the fundamental rights of individuals and the notions currently prevailing in democratic States (see, among other authorities, the Airey v. Ireland judgment of 9 October 1979, Series A, no.32, pp.14–15, § 26, and the Guzzardi v. Italy judgment of 6 November 1980, Series A, no.39, pp.34–35, § 95).

15 In *Kononov v. Latvia*, ECtHR 24 July (2008) 25 BHRC 317, the Strasbourg Court observed (at para.115):

'115. With regard to Article 7 § 2, the Convention institutions have commented as follows:

The second paragraph of Article 7 of the Convention relating to 'the trial and punishment of any person for any act or omission which, at the time when it was committed, was criminal according to the general principles of law recognised by civilised nations' constitutes an exceptional derogation from the general principle laid down in the first. The two paragraphs are thus inter-linked and must be interpreted in a concordant manner (Tess v. Latvia (dec.), no.34854/02, 12 December 2002).

The preparatory works to the Convention show that the purpose of paragraph 2 of Article 7 is to specify that Article 7 does not affect laws which, in the wholly exceptional circumstances at the end of the Second World War, were passed in order to punish war crimes, treason and collaboration with the enemy; accordingly, it does not in any way aim to pass legal or moral judgment on those laws (X.v. Belgium, no.268/57, Commission decision of 20 July 1957, Yearbook 1, p.241). This reasoning also applies to crimes against humanity committed during this period (Touvier v. France, no.29420/95, Commission decision of 13 January 1997, Decisions and Reports (DR)88, p.148; and Papon v. France (no.2) (dec.), no.54210/00, ECHR 2001XII (extracts)).'

16 See, too, Article 38(1)(c) of the Rome Statute of the International Criminal Court which refer to 'the general principles of law recognised by civilised nations'. The Rome States and the jurisdiction of the IICC has been recognised and given domestic effect to in the United Kingdom by the International Criminal Court Act 2001 and, in Scotland, by the International Criminal Court (Scotland) Act 2001 (asp 13)

17 See *Francôme v. Mirror Group of Newspapers Ltd.* [1984] 1 WLR 892, CA *per* Sir John Donaldson MR at 897:

I ... recognise that, in very rare circumstances a situation can arise in which the citizen is faced with a conflict between what is, in effect, two inconsistent laws. The first law is the law of the land. The second is a moral imperative, usually, but not always, religious in origin. An obvious example is the priest's obligation of silence in relation to the confessional, but others can be given. In conducting the business of the courts, judges seek to avoid any such conflict, but occasionally it is unavoidable. Yielding to the moral imperative does not excuse a breach of the law of the land, but it is understandable and in some circumstances may even be praiseworthy. However, I cannot over-emphasise the rarity of the moral imperative. Furthermore, it is almost unheard of for compliance with the moral imperative to be in the financial or other best interests of the person concerned. Anyone who conceives himself to be morally obliged to break the law, should also ask himself whether such a course furthers his own interests. If it does, he would be well advised to re-examine his conscience.

18 *R (Gentle) v Prime Minister* [2008] AC 1352 per Lord Hope 1371–2

19 *Lord Advocate's Reference (No. 1 of 2000) re nuclear weapons*, 2001 JC 143, HCJ

20 Compare with *Helen John v. Donnelly,* 1999 JC 336 where the appellant, one of a group of protesters, was charged under Section 52(1) of the Criminal Law (Consolidation) (Scotland) Act 1995 with vandalism for cutting part of the perimeter fence of the Faslane Royal Naval nuclear base. She stated J, stated when cautioned and charged that she had cut the fence in order to protest against 'the genocidal nature of the illegal Trident weapons programme'. Her defence at trial was that she had a reasonable excuse for her conduct by reason of her sincere belief in the illegality of nuclear weapons and her anxiety at their potentially appalling effects on mankind and the environment. That defence was rejected and on conviction she appealed. It was held on appeal that a person could be said to have a reasonable excuse when he or she had acted in response to some particular and immediate stimulus and that in the present case the appellant had acted deliberately and without any immediate stimulus.

21 Compare with the English Court of Appeal decision in *R. v. Denis Geoffrey Clarke* (1985) 80 Cr. Ap R. 344 an appeal in relation to a conviction for aiding and abetting a burglary charge in which the defence had been put forward by the accused that he was in fact working as an informer for the police and was passing on information about the other offenders to them. The Court of Appeal held that it would not be right to state 'that conduct which is overall calculated and intended not to further but to frustrate the ultimate result of the crime is always immaterial and irrelevant'. Accordingly in 'exceptional and rare cases' where it could be said that the acts in question were done n order to allow 'the police to make use of information concerning an offence that is already 'laid on',' a jury might conclude that the defendant had been acting lawfully.

22 See the English Court of Appeal decision in *R v. Fitzroy Derek Pommel* [1995] 2 Cr. App. R. 607 where the defendant's answer to charges of possessing a prohibited firearm and ammunition without a licence (in fact a loaded sub-machine gun) was that he had taken them from another man who was intending to commit a crime with them and intended to pass them on to his brother for surrender to the police. The Court of Appeal held that if these facts could be established, a defence should be available to the accused, termed by the court 'duress of circumstances' and observed

> [In] the situation where someone commendably infringes a regulation in order to prevent another person from committing what everyone would accepts as being a greater evil with a gun ... it cannot be satisfactory to leave it to the prosecuting authority not to prosecute, or to individual courts to grant an absolute discharge. The authority may, as in the present case, prosecute because it is not satisfied that the defendant is telling the truth and then, even if he is vindicated, he is left with a criminal conviction which, for some purposes would be recognised as such.

23 See *Mackintosh v Lord Advocate* (1876) 2 App Cas 41, HL(Sc).

24 Lord Bingham of Cornhill, evidence to the Parliamentary Joint Committee on Human Rights, 26 March 2001

25 See for example *Fraser (Nat Gordon) v. HM Advocate* [2008] SCCR 407, HCJ per Lord Osborne at paras.219–220

> 219 ... [T]he relationship between the concepts of a miscarriage of justice,

recognised in section 106(3) of the Criminal Procedure (Scotland) Act 1995 and an unfair trial in terms of Article 6(1) of the Convention is not straightforward. Plainly they are not co-extensive. An unfair trial may not result in a miscarriage of justice. That would be so where, for example, that trial concluded with an acquittal, since the concept of miscarriage of justice comes into play only following a conviction on indictment, as provided in section 106(1) of the 1995 Act. Furthermore, a trial may be completely fair yet result in a conviction which must be regarded as a miscarriage of justice, as for example where the provisions of section 106(3)(a) operate.

220 What importance, if any, it may be asked, attaches to these considerations in the present context. The answer, in my view, is that it is potentially confusing and therefore unhelpful, in criminal appeals under section 106(3)(a) of the Criminal Procedure (Scotland) Act 1995 to seek to rely on dicta pronounced in appeals under para.13 of Schedule 6 to the Scotland Act 1998, since the issues which this court must determine in the former type of appeal, which I have described in some detail, are inevitably quite different from those issues which the Judicial Committee require to determine in the latter.

26 See Section 40 of the Constitutional Reform Act 2005

27 *Kuwait Airways Corpn v. Iraqi Airways Co (Nos 4 and 5)* [2002] 2 AC 883 per Lord Nicholls of Birkenhead at 1081:

28 The acceptability of a provision of foreign law must be judged by contemporary standards. Lord Wilberforce, in a different context, noted that conceptions of public policy should move with the times: see Blathwayt v. Baron Cawley [1976] AC 397, 426. In Oppenheimer v. Cattermole [1976] AC 249, 278, Lord Cross said that the courts of this country should give effect to clearly established rules of international law. This is increasingly true today. As nations become ever more interdependent, the need to recognise and adhere to standards of conduct set by international law becomes ever more important. RCC Resolution 369 was not simply a governmental expropriation of property within its territory. Having forcibly invaded Kuwait, seized its assets, and taken KAC's aircraft from Kuwait to its own territory, Iraq adopted this decree as part of its attempt to extinguish every vestige of Kuwait's existence as a separate state. An expropriatory decree made in these circumstances and for this purpose is simply not acceptable today.

...

29 Enforcement or recognition of this law would be manifestly contrary to the public policy of English law. For good measure, enforcement or recognition would also be contrary to this country's obligations under the UN Charter. Further, it would sit uneasily with the almost universal condemnation of Iraq's behaviour and with the military action, in which this country participated, taken against Iraq to compel its withdrawal from Kuwait. International law, for its part, recognises that a national court may properly decline to give effect to legislative and other acts of foreign states which are in violation of international law: *see the discussion in Oppenheim's International Law, 9th ed (1992), vol.1, (ed Jennings and Watts), pp.371–376, para.113.*

28 See *R v Knuller (Publishing, Printing and Promotions) Ltd* [1973] AC 435

29   R. v. Margaret Jones and others [2007] 1 ac 136 per Lord Bingham at paras.28–29

30   For a description of the common law nature of Scottish criminal law, see T. H. Jones, 'Common Law and Criminal Law: the Scottish Example' [1990] *Crim.L.R.* 292 and I. D. Willock 'Scottish Criminal Law – Does it Exist?' (1981) *SCOLAG Bulletin* 225

31   Jones, *ibid.* See also Royal Commission on Capital Punishment (1949–1953), Minutes of Evidence, *per* Lord Justice General Cooper at 428:

> The Scottish law of crime is not statutory but almost exclusively common law, which has been and is still being evolved by judicial decisions applied with anxious care to the precise facts of actual cases.

32   The Scottish courts generally employ the 4th edition of Hume, edited by B. R. Bell and published in 1844.

33   The High Court of Justiciary was established in 1672.

34   Other sexual offences are, however, found in statute – see the Criminal Law (Consolidation) (Scotland) Act 1995 and the Sexual Offences (Amendment) Act 2000

35   It is an aggravated assault where the victim is a police officer: see s.41(1)(a) of the Police (Scotland) Act 1967

36   Note, however, that the Theft Act 1607 makes it an offence to steal bees, and fish from fishponds

37   Pamela R. Ferguson 'Codifying criminal law: a critique of Scots common law' (2004) *Criminal Law Review* 49–59 at 50–51

38   See *Grant v. Allen*, 1987 JC 71 per Lord Justice-Clerk Ross:

> [T]his court has an inherent power to punish any act which is obviously of a criminal nature (Hume on Crimes (3rd edn.), i, 12; Macdonald Criminal Law (5th edn.), p.193; Sugden v. HM Advocate 1934 JC 103) ... Hume describes the declaratory power of the court as an inherent power to punish every act which is obviously of a criminal nature. Although there are circumstances where it will be appropriate for the court to exercise this power, I am of opinion that great care must be taken in the exercise of this power. Exercising the power may well conflict with the principle nullum crimen sine lege. The declaratory power has been considered in a number of cases over the last fifty years. I do not find it necessary to consider these cases because I am not satisfied that what is libelled in this complaint was so obviously of a criminal nature that it should be treated as a crime under the criminal law. No doubt what the appellant is alleged to have done was reprehensible and immoral, but as was recognised in HM Advocate v. Mackenzies, 1913 JC 107, the fact that conduct is reprehensible or indicates moral delinquency is not sufficient to bring it within the scope of the criminal law. I recognise that there may be reasons for thinking that conduct of this kind ought to be regarded as criminal. However, if that is so, I am of opinion that it is for Parliament and not the courts to create any new crime in that regard.

39   See *McLaughlan v. Boyd*, 1934 JC 19 per Lord Justice-General Clyde at 22–3:

> It would be a mistake to imagine that the criminal common law of Scotland

countenances any precise and exact categorisation of the forms of conduct which amount to crime. It has been pointed out many times in this Court that such is not the nature or quality of the criminal law of Scotland. I need only refer to the well-known passage in the opening of Baron Hume's institutional work (Hume on Crimes (3rd ed.) ch. i), in which the broad definition of a crime – a doleful or wilful offence against society in the matter of 'violence, dishonesty, falsehood, indecency, irreligion' is laid down. In my opinion the statement in Macdonald's Criminal Law (4th ed., p.221) that 'all shamelessly indecent conduct is criminal,' is sound and correctly expresses the law of Scotland. No doubt there may be in particular cases circumstances of aggravation, but I am not prepared to rule out of the category of crime any shamelessly indecent conduct, and I am not prepared to infer, from the circumstances that sec 11 of the Act of 1885 affirmed the proposition that shamelessly indecent conduct by one male adult in relation to another was criminal, that such conduct was not, or could not have been, the competent subject of prosecution in Scotland before.

40 In *Webster v. Dominick*, 2005 JC 65 a court of five judges headed by the Lord Justice Clerk (Gill) (with Lord Marnoch, Lord Macfadyen, Lady Cosgrove, Lord Sutherland, Lord Gill) decided to abolish the previously recognised crime of 'shameless indecency' and replace it with a crime of different scope which they termed 'public indecency.'

41 Stallard v. HM Advocate, 1989 SLT 469 per the Lord Justice General (Emslie) at 473

42 *Lord Advocate's Reference (No.1 of 2001)* 2002 SLT 466 per Lord Nimmo Smith at 481 para.2 of his judgement. See to like effect Lady Cosgrove at 481 para.15 of her judgment:

> [15] It has been said that ours is a live system of law. Our law should be like a living tree, not only growing but shedding dead wood as it does so. The opportunity has now presented itself and I am of the view that the law should be revisited and the flawed approach, imported in HM Advocate v. Sweenie (Charles) (1858) 3 Irv 109, departed from in the manner suggested by your Lordship in the chair.

43 Pamela R. Ferguson 'Codifying criminal law: a critique of Scots common law' (2004) *Criminal Law Review* 49–59 at 58. This approach has recently been confirmed in the Strasbourg decision *Korbely v. Hungary*, 19 September 2008 where the Grand Chamber of the ECtHR noted as follows (at para.71):

> 71. *However clearly drafted a legal provision may be, in any system of law, including criminal law, there is an inevitable element of judicial interpretation. There will always be a need for elucidation of doubtful points and for adaptation to changing circumstances. Indeed, in the Convention States, the progressive development of the criminal law through judicial law-making is a well-entrenched and necessary part of legal tradition. Article 7 of the Convention cannot be read as outlawing the gradual clarification of the rules of criminal liability through judicial interpretation from case to case, provided that the resultant development is consistent with the essence of the offence and could reasonably be foreseen (see Jorgic v. Germany, no. 74613/01, §§ 100–101, 12 July 2007; Streletz, Kessler and Krenz, cited above, § 50; and*

> *S. W. v. the United Kingdom and C.R. v. the United Kingdom, judgments of 22 November 1995, Series A no. 335-B, pp.41–42, §§ 34–36, and Series A no. 335-C, pp.68–69, §§ 32–34, respectively).*

44 See, more recently, *Paterson v. HM Advocate*, 2008 SLT 465, HCJ at paras. 22–23 considering the potential use of a charge of breach of the peace to convict an individual accused of lewd, indecent and libidinous behaviour toward a 17 year old:

> *In Smith v Donnelly, 2002 JC 65 this court examined the existing authorities on breach of the peace with a view to determining whether bringing proceedings on such a charge, as developed, violated the requirements of art 7 of the Convention (no punishment without law). The court held that, on a sound interpretation of these authorities, the definition of the crime was such as to meet the requirements of the Convention. … In the context of behaviour towards a 17 year old girl by a man 20 years her senior the conduct was, in our view, severe enough to cause alarm to ordinary people. … The conduct does not require to cause serious disturbance to the community. It is sufficient that it threatens such disturbance. Such conduct by a mature man towards an adolescent girl was such that, if discovered, was likely to cause a serious reaction among other adults. In these circumstances the nature of the conduct was such that, if proved, it constituted on each occasion breach of the peace.*
> *[...]*
> *Although the two elements in the conjunctive expression [conduct severe enough to cause alarm to an ordinary person and to threaten serious disturbance to the community] may include common elements and the same evidence in particular circumstances may cover both, they focus on different things. In particular, the former element highlights the objective character of relevant alarm while the latter highlights the community aspect of the offence. Any definition of breach of the peace should use the conjunctive.*

45 See *Regina (Gentle and another) v. Prime Minister and others* [2008] 1 AC 1356 per Baroness Hale at 1377–9

46 See *Regina (Gentle and another) v. Prime Minister and others* [2008] 1 AC 1356 per Lord Hope at 1372:

> *The issue of legality in this area of international law belongs to the area of relations between states. Article 2 of the Charter of the United Nations declares that the organisation and its members shall act in accordance with the principles that it sets out. The third of these principles is: 'All members shall settle their international disputes by peaceful means in such a manner that international peace and security, and justice, are not endangered.' Application of the guidance that this principle offers in the conduct of international relations between states is a matter of political judgment. It is a matter for the conduct of which ministers are answerable to Parliament and, ultimately, to the electorate. It is not part of domestic law reviewable here or, under the Convention, in the European court at Strasbourg.*

47 See, for example, *Chandler v. The Director of Public Prosecutions* [1964] AC 763 per Lord Reid at 791:

> *It is my opinion that the disposition and armament of the armed forces are and for centuries have been within the exclusive discretion of the Crown and*

> that one can seek a legal remedy on the grounds that such discretion has been wrongly exercised. I need only refer to the numerous authorities gathered together in China Navigation Company Ltd. v. Attorney-General [1932] 2 KB 197. Anyone is entitled, in or out of Parliament, to urge that policy regarding the armed forces should be changed; but until it is changed, on a change of government or otherwise, no-one is entitled to challenge it in court.

and per Viscount Radcliffe at 798–799:

> If the methods of arming the defence forces and the disposition of those forces are at the decision of Her Majesty's Ministers for the time being, as we know that they are, it is not within the competence of a court of law to try the issue whether it would be better for the country that that armament or those dispositions should be different. ... [T]he question whether it is in the true interests of this country to acquire, retain or house nuclear armaments depends upon an infinity of considerations, military and diplomatic, technical, psychological and moral, and of decisions, tentative or final, which are themselves part assessments of fact and part expectations and hopes. I do not think that there is anything amiss with a legal ruling that does not make that issue a matter for judge or jury

See, too, Lord Advocate's Reference (No. 1 of 2000) re nuclear weapons, 2001 JC 143, HCJ at 163:

> [60] In our view it is not at all clear that if this issue had been fully debated before us, the incorporation of Trident II in the United Kingdom's defence strategy, in pursuance of a strategic policy of global deterrence, would have been regarded as giving rise to issues which were properly justiciable. Chandler remains binding (sic) authority in this court. Such developments as have taken place seem to have left untouched the status of the prerogative in matters relating to the defence of the realm. However, we have not been asked to dispose of the case on this basis, and we see no alternative but to reserve the issue for another occasion.

48   Contrast with the approach in Canada in Operation Dismantle and others v. The Queen (1985) 18 Dominion Law Reports 481 (4th) per Madame Justice Wilson of the Supreme Court of Canada at 500, 504, 505 at reviewed the common law authorities available up to 1985 on the question of the justiciability of the decision by the Canadian government to allow the testing of American Cruise missiles on its territory, noting as follows:

> I cannot accept the proposition that difficulties of evidence or proof absolve the court from taking a certain kind of decision if it can be established on other grounds that it has a duty to do so. I think we should focus our attention on whether the court should or must rather than on whether they can deal with such matters. We should put difficulties of evidence and proof aside and consider whether as a constitutional matter it is appropriate or obligatory for the court to decide the issue before us.
>
> ...
>
> [I]f the court were simply being asked to express its opinion on the wisdom of the executive's exercise of its defence powers in this case, the court would have to decline. It cannot substitute its opinion for that of the executive. Because

the effect of the appellant's action is to challenge the wisdom of the government's defence policy, it is tempting to say that the court should in the same way refuse to involve itself. However, I think that would be to miss the point, to fail to focus on the question before us. The question before it is not whether the government's defence policy is sound but whether or not it violates the appellant's rights and freedoms under Section 7 of the Canadian Charter of Rights and Freedoms. This is a totally different question. I do not think that there can be any doubt that this is a question for the courts.

...

[I]t seems to me that the legislature has assigned the courts as a constitutional responsibility the task of determining whether or not the decision to permit the testing of cruise missiles violates the appellant's rights under the charter. ... It is therefore, in my view not only appropriate that we decide the matter; it is our constitutional obligation to do so.

49 See *R. (on the application of Abbasi) v. Secretary of State for Foreign and Commonwealth Affairs* [2002] EWCA Civ 1598; [2003] UKHRR 76 refusing to order the Foreign Secretary to intervene in the case of a British subject held as enemy combatant by United States at Guantanamo Bay. See too *R. (on the application of Al-Rawi) v. Secretary of State for Foreign and Commonwealth Affairs* [2006] EWHC 972 (Admin); [2006] HRLR 30 refusing to require the secretary of state to make a formal request for the return of the foreign national Guantanamo detainees who had strong British connection. And see *R. (on the application of Bancoult) v. Secretary of State for Foreign and Commonwealth Affairs* [2008] 3 WLR 955 the House of Lords held that the requirement that laws had to be made for the 'peace, order and good government' of a Crown colony could not be construed as words limiting the power of a legislature and the courts would not inquire into the substantive merits of any legislation resulting.

50 See *R. (on the application of Campaign for Nuclear Disarmament) v. Prime Minister* [2002] EWHC 2777 (Admin); [2003] ACD 36 where the court refused to provide an advisory declaration as to the true meaning of Resolution 1441 of the United Nations Security Council dated 8 November 2002 and in particular as to whether it authorised states to take military action in the event of non compliance by Iraq with its terms.

51 R. Higgins *'The Relationship between International and Regional Humanitarian law and Domestic Law'* (1992) 18 CLB 1268 at 1268.

52 See *Trials of War Criminals before the Nuremberg Military Tribunals under Control Council Law No. 10, Nuremberg October 1946–April 1949* (Washington DC: US Government Printing Office, 1951) vol.III at 32–33

53 In Judgment of the Nuremberg International Military Tribunal in the Main War Crimes Trial (1947) 41 AJIL 172 noted when considering the law of the Charter setting up the Tribunal:

The making of the Charter was the exercise of sovereign legislative power by the countries to which the German Reich unconditionally surrendered; and he undoubted right of these countries to legislate for the occupied territories has been recognised by the civilised world. The Charter is not an arbitrary exercise of power on the part of the victorious nations, but in the view of the Tribunal, as will be shown, it is the expression of international law existing at the time of its creation; and to that extent is itself a contribution to international law. This passage is also quoted in YBILC 1950 II p.187 at para.26

54 See *Trials of War Criminals before the Nuremberg Military Tribunals* (Washington DC: US Government Printing Office, 1951) III at 984–985

55 Attorney General memorandum of 7 March 2003, para.34 available at http://image.guardian.co.uk/sys-files/Guardian/documents/2005/04/28/ legal.pdf

56 See Clive Walker 'Case comment: Appellants protesting against war in Iraq – defendants committing criminal offences of damage or aggravated trespass on military bases' (2007) *Criminal Law Review* 66–70 at 70

57 *Reg. v. Bow Street Magistrate, Ex p. Pinochet (No. 3)* [2000] AC 147

58 *Friend v. Lord Advocate*, 2008 SC (HL) 107

59 *Lord Advocate's Reference (No. 1 of 2000) re nuclear weapons*, 2001 JC 143, HCJ confirmed the direct enforceability of norms of customary international law in Scots law. For a somewhat partisan survey and account (with a conservative, pro-Government spin) of the modern English case-law on this matter see Philip Sales and Joanne Clement '*International Law in Domestic Courts: the developing framework*' (2008) 124 *Law Quarterly Review* 388–421

60 Thus, in contrast to the situation that prevailed in *J. H. Rayner (Mincing Lane) Ltd. v. DTI* [1990] 2 AC 418 *per* Lord Templeman at 476F-477A, Lord Griffiths at 483C and Lord Oliver at 499E-501B is cannot be said in relation to acts of the Lord Advocate that the provisions of an unincorporated treaty was non-justiciable or otherwise outside the purview of the domestic courts. See, too, *Kaur v. Lord Advocate* 1981 SLT 322, OH *per* Lord Ross at 330:

> So far as Scotland is concerned, I am of the opinion that the court is not entitled to have regard to the Convention either as an aid to construction or otherwise. I respectfully share the view ... that the Convention is irrelevant to legal proceedings unless and until its provision have been incorporated or given effect to in legislation. To suggest otherwise is to confer upon a Convention concluded by the Executive an effect which only an Act of the Legislature can achieve.

61 See *Crichton v. McBain*, 1961 JC 25 per Lord Justice General Clyde at 28–29:

> The Lord Advocate has appeared in person at this hearing and has informed the Court that he has fully investigated the matter more than once and, in the exercise of that wide discretion which is invested in the Lord Advocate, he has come to the conclusion that a prosecution would not be justified in connexion with this matter. He has therefore decided not to prosecute at his own instance and not to give his concurrence to the private prosecution which the present complainer desires to raise.
>
> The Lord Advocate is quite entitled to take up this position. In this country he is the recognised prosecutor in the public interest. It is for him, in the exercise of his responsible office, to decide whether he will prosecute in the public interest and at the public expense, and under our constitutional practice this decision is a matter for him, and for him alone. No one can compel him to give his reasons, nor order him to concur in a private prosecution. The basic principle of our system of criminal administration in Scotland is to submit the

question of whether there is to be a public prosecution to the impartial and skilled investigation of the Lord Advocate and his department, and the decision whether or not to prosecute is exclusively within his discretion. This system has operated in Scotland for centuries, and—see Alison on Criminal Law, vol.II, p.88—the result has completely proved the justice of these principles, for such has become the public confidence in the decision of the Lord Advocate and his deputies on the grounds of prosecution, that private prosecutions have almost gone into disuse. It is utterly inconsistent with such a system that the Courts should examine, as it was suggested it would be proper or competent for us to do, the reasons which have affected the Lord Advocate in deciding how to exercise his discretion, and it would be still more absurd for this Court to proceed to review their soundness. Any dicta indicating that such a course is open to any Court are, in my view, quite unsound.

See too *Hester v. McDonald*, 1961 SC 370 per Lord President (Clyde) at 378–379

His [the Lord Advocate's] responsibilities and privileges are quite unique, and they depend for their continuance on the confidence of the public in the utter impartiality with which he has always administered his onerous duties regarding crime. From time immemorial it has, therefore, been recognised, as Baron Hume puts it Crimes, vol.II, p.135 that 'a constitutional trust is reposed in that high officer, selected by His Majesty from among the most eminent at the Bar; and it will not be supposed of him, that he can be actuated by unworthy motives in commencing a prosecution, or fall into such irregularities or blunders in conducting his process, as ought properly to make him liable in amends.' As Alison says (vol.II, p.93) he is absolutely exempt from penalties and expenses. It is, therefore, an essential element in the very structure of our criminal administration in Scotland that the Lord Advocate is protected by an absolute privilege in respect of matters in connexion with proceedings brought before a Scottish Criminal Court by way of indictment.

62 The position in England has been set out in *Regina (Corner House Research and another) v. Director of the Serious Fraud Office (JUSTICE intervening)* [2008] 3 WLR 568, HL *per* Lord Bingham at 580:

30 It is common ground in these proceedings that the Director is a public official appointed by the Crown but independent of it. He is entrusted by Parliament with discretionary powers to investigate suspected offences, which reasonably appear to him to involve serious or complex fraud and to prosecute in such cases. These are powers given to him by Parliament as head of an independent, professional service who is subject only to the superintendence of the Attorney General. There is an obvious analogy with the position of the Director of Public Prosecutions. It is accepted that the decisions of the Director are not immune from review by the courts, but authority makes plain that only in highly exceptional cases will the court disturb the decisions of an independent prosecutor and investigator: R. v. Director of Public Prosecutions, Ex p C [1995] 1 Cr App R 136, 141; R. v. Director of Public Prosecutions, Ex p Manning [2001] QB 330, para.23; R. (Bermingham) v. Director of the Serious Fraud Office [2007] QB 727, paras.63–64; Mohit v. Director of Public Prosecutions of Mauritius [2006] 1 WLR 3343, paras.17 and 21 citing and

endorsing a passage in the judgment of the Supreme Court of Fiji in Matalulu v. Director of Public Prosecutions [2003] 4 LRC 712, 735–736; Sharma v. Brown-Antoine [2007] 1 WLR 780, para 14(1)-(6). The House was not referred to any case in which a challenge had been made to a decision not to prosecute or investigate on public interest grounds.

31 The reasons why the courts are very slow to interfere are well understood. They are, first, that the powers in question are entrusted to the officers identified, and to no one else. No other authority may exercise these powers or make the judgments on which such exercise must depend. Secondly, the courts have recognised (as it was described in the cited passage from Matalulu v. Director of Public Prosecutions) 'the polycentric character of official decision-making in such matters including policy and public interest considerations which are not susceptible of judicial review because it is within neither the constitutional function nor the practical competence of the courts to assess their merits.'

Thirdly, the powers are conferred in very broad and unprescriptive terms.

32 Of course, and this again is uncontroversial, the discretions conferred on the Director are not unfettered. He must seek to exercise his powers so as to promote the statutory purpose for which he is given them. He must direct himself correctly in law. He must act lawfully. He must do his best to exercise an objective judgment on the relevant material available to him. He must exercise his powers in good faith, uninfluenced by any ulterior motive, predilection or prejudice.

See too R (B) v. DPP [2009] EWHC 106 (Admin) (27 January 2009) per Toulson LJ at paras 52–53:

52. There is now a substantial body of authority on judicial review of decisions not to prosecute. The leading authorities are R v. DPP ex parte Manning [2001] 1 QB 330, R. (Da Silva) v. DPP [2006] EWHC 3204 (Admin), Sharma v Brown-Antoine [2006] UKPC 57 and Marshall v. DPP [2007] UKPC 4. In summary, judicial review of a prosecutorial decision is available but is a highly exceptional remedy. The exercise of the court's power of judicial review is less rare in the case of a decision not to prosecute than a decision to prosecute (because a decision not to prosecute is final, subject to judicial review, whereas a decision to prosecute leaves the defendant free to challenge the prosecution's case in the usual way through the criminal court) but is still exceptional. The reason for this was stated by Lord Bingham CJ in Manning, para.23:

In most cases the decision will turn not on an analysis of the relevant legal principles but on the exercise of an informed judgement of how a case against a particular defendant, if brought, would be likely to fare in the context of a criminal trial before (in a serious case such as this) a jury. This exercise of judgement involves an assessment of the strength, by the end of the trial, of the evidence against the defendant and of the likely defences. It will often be impossible to stigmatise a judgement on such matters as wrong even if one disagrees with it. So the courts will not easily find that a decision not to prosecute is bad in law, on which basis alone the court is entitled to interfere. At the same time, the standard of review should not be set too high, since judicial review is the only means by which the citizen can seek redress against a decision not to prosecute and if the tests were too exacting an effective remedy would be denied.

53. There is an assumption underlying this passage (with its reference to the exercise of an informed judgement) that a prosecutor can ordinarily be expected to have properly informed himself (within the limits of what is reasonably practical) and asked himself the right questions before arriving at a decision whether or not to prosecute.'

63 See *Kennedy v. Lord Advocate*, 2008 SLT 195 granting decree reducing the decision of the Lord Advocate of 15 June 2006 to refuse to order an inquiry under the Fatal Accidents and Sudden Deaths Inquiry (Scotland) Act 1976 and *Kennedy v. Lord Advocate (No. 2)* [2009] CSOH 1 where the Lord Ordinary pronounced a further decree in the same case in the following terms:

Declarator that the petitioner is entitled to an independent, effective and reasonably prompt inquiry into the death of [her late mother Mrs Eileen O'Hara/her late husband David Charles Black], in which the deceased's next of kin may be involved to the extent necessary to ensure compliance with their rights under Article 2 of the European Convention on Human Rights, and during which they can be legally represented; and that any continuing failure to hold such an inquiry is incompatible with Article 2.

64 Christine M. Korsgaard '*Taking the Law into Our Own Hands: Kant on the Right to Revolution*' in Reath, Herman and Korsgaard (eds.), *Reclaiming the History of Ethics: Essays for John Rawls* (Cambridge: Cambridge University Press, 1997) at 297.

65 See *R. v. Margaret Jones and others* [2007] 1 AC 136 per Lord Hoffmann at 177–9

89 My Lords, civil disobedience on conscientious grounds has a long and honourable history in this country. People who break the law to affirm their belief in the injustice of a law or government action are sometimes vindicated by history. The suffragettes are an example which comes immediately to mind. It is the mark of a civilised community that it can accommodate protests and demonstrations of this kind. But there are conventions which are generally accepted by the law-breakers on one side and the law-enforcers on the other. The protesters behave with a sense of proportion and do not cause excessive damage or inconvenience. And they vouch the sincerity of their beliefs by accepting the penalties imposed by the law. The police and prosecutors, on the other hand, behave with restraint and the magistrates impose sentences which take the conscientious motives of the protesters into account. The conditional discharges ordered by the magistrates in the cases which came before them exemplifies their sensitivity to these conventions...

93 My Lords, I do not think that it would be inconsistent with our traditional respect for conscientious civil disobedience for your Lordships to say that there will seldom if ever be any arguable legal basis upon which these forensic tactics can be deployed.

66 W. A. Wilson 'The progress of the law 1888–1988' (1988) *Juridical Review* 207 at 231.

67 See the pre-Union Scottish Parliament's Claim of Right of 1689 which declares

that: 'it is the right and privilege of the subjects to protest for remeed of law to the King and Parliament against Sentences pronounced by the Lords of Session providing the same do not stop Execution of these sentences'

> Compare however the critical comments of Lord Brown of Eaton-under-Heywood in the House of Lords appeal from the Court of Session in *Buchanan v. Alba Diagnostics Ltd.*, 2004 SC (HL) 9 at para.41 on the lack of any leave requirement for appeals in civil matters from Scotland to the House of Lords:

> For the reasons given by my noble and learned friend Lord Hoffmann I too would dismiss this appeal. I add only that it seems to me a great misfortune for Mr Buchanan that he was able to bring this appeal before your Lordships House without leave. Had leave been required assuredly it would have been refused and Mr Buchanan thereby saved a very great deal of expense.

68 See in this regard Article 1(1) of the United Nations Charter:

> 1. The purposes of the United Nations are: To maintain international peace and security, and to that end: to take effective collective measures for the prevention and removal of threats to the peace, and for the suppression of acts of aggression or other breaches of the peace, and to bring about by peaceful means, and in conformity with the principles of justice and international law, adjustment or settlement of international disputes or situations which might lead to a breach of the peace.

CIVIL SOCIETY AND INTERNATIONAL LAW

1 The Martens Clause was first included in the Hague Convention of 1899, and is found more recently in Article 1, para.2, of Additional Protocol I of 1977 with the wording 'civilians and combatants remain under the protection and authority of the principles of international law derived from established custom, from the principles of humanity and from the dictates of public conscience'.

2 International Military Tribunal, The Trial of German Major War Criminals. Proceedings of the International Military Tribunal Sitting at Nuremberg, Germany. Part 22. 28 August 1946. Taken from the Official Transcript. Published by HMSO, London, 1950. p.243.

3 'We', here and throughout this paper, refers to many in the peace movement and other social change movements and indicates that it is felt by the author to be not only her own opinion but an opinion shared by many of her colleagues.

4 See *Trident on Trial – the case for People's Disarmament* by Angie Zelter, Luath Press. ISBN 1-84282-004-4.

5 Hutchinson v. Newbury Magistrates' Court (9 October 2000, CO/663/00)

6 Chandler & Others v DPP [1962] 3 All E.R. 142

7 A recent articulation of this can be seen in the March 2002 letter from Rt. Hon Adam Ingram Minister of State for the Armed Forces who stated, 'The right of her Majesty's Government to prosecute military operations abroad is not derived from statute but from the common law, and is exercised under the Royal Prerogative. Powers under the Royal prerogative are those uniquely enjoyed by the Crown and exercised on its behalf by Ministers. The conduct of foreign

affairs, including the commitment of forces for military operations, is carried out in reliance on the prerogative.'

8   The Mine Ban Treaty is the international agreement that bans anti-personnel land-mines. Sometimes referred to as the Ottawa Convention, it is officially titled: the Convention on the Prohibition of the Use, Stockpiling, Production and Transfer of Anti-Personnel Mines and on Their Destruction. The treaty aims to rid the world of the scourge of mines and deals with everything from mine use, production and trade, to victim assistance, mine clearance and stockpile destruction. In December 1997 a total of 122 governments signed the treaty in Ottawa, Canada. In September the following year, Burkina Faso was the 40th country to ratify, triggering entry into force six months later. Consequently, in March 1999 the treaty became binding under international law, and did so more quickly than any treaty of its kind in history.

9   http://www.icanw.org/the-solution

10   See http://www.inlap.freeuk.com/publications.htm for a sample of the kinds of legal briefings that one civil society group INLAP have produced.

11   http://tapol.gn.apc.org/press/files/pro31210.htm – Legal action launched against UK Government's arms to Indonesia policy – press release issued jointly by TAPOL and Campaign Against Arms Trade (CAAT) on 10 December 2003 – 'A human rights activist from Aceh, Indonesia has today launched proceedings against the UK Government challenging by Judicial Review the legality of the UK's supply of arms to Indonesia. Mr Aguswandi claims the continued licensing of military exports to Indonesia breaks UK and EU export control laws which clearly state that export licences for weapons should be refused if there is a risk of the equipment being used for internal repression.'

12   With the Pax Legalis cases (see 'The Pax Legalis Papers: Nuclear Conspiracy and the Law', Robert Manson, ISBN 1897766181, Jon Carpenter) and the Snowball information layings (private papers with Angie Zelter).

13   Established in 1999. http://www.publicinterestlawyers.co.uk/

14   This was, comprehensively argued by Rabinder Singh, QC and Charlotte Kilroy, acting for CND. The three judges ruled that they could not give an opinion as they had no jurisdiction on this aspect of international law and that it may be, 'damaging to the public interest in the field of international relations, national security or defence.' The same CND legal team produced an opinion on why the proposed draft '2nd resolution' would not give legal authority to go to war. They also wrote an opinion on the Attorney General's use of Resolutions 678, 687 and 1441 to authorise the war, both on the eve of war and after it became clear that weapons of mass destruction were not being found in Iraq.

15   In the High Court on 26 January, Lord Justice Scott Baker refused NIS permission to appeal Mr Justice Simon's decision of 10 June 2008 not to grant permission to claim Judicial Review of the Government's 2006 Defence White Paper and its decision to renew the Trident nuclear weapons system. www.nuclearinfo.org

16   Letter to the Prime Minister and Secretary of State for Defence of 23 January 2003.

17   Stop the War Demonstration 15 February 2003. http://www.stopwar.org.uk/

18 This led to the International Court of Justice Advisory Opinion on the Legality of the Threat or Use of Nuclear Weapons, General List, no.95, 8 July 1996.

19 Seeds of Hope (East Timor Ploughshares) four women did £1.5 million worth of damage to one Hawk Jet which was then unable to be exported. After six months in prison they won their trial at Liverpool Crown Court (30 July 1996. Case no.T961301) when a jury acquitted them after listening to what had been happening in East Timor and their arguments on international law. See 'Civil Society and Global Responsibility: The Arms Trade and East Timor', Angie Zelter, in International Relations, vol.18, no.1, March 2004.

20 Loch Goil Trident Ploughshares action – acquittal at Greenock (21 October 1999) – more information on TP website at http://www.trident ploughshares.org/article818

21 In 2006 Prestwick Airport was used to airlift troops to fight in the war in Iraq and also to airlift munitions out to Israel to re-stock their dwindling supply of munitions in their bombing campaign in Lebanon.
Three Trident Ploughshares groups entered the airport on three successive nights to protest at what they considered to be collusion in war crimes. Most of them were acquitted in Ayr Sheriffs Court.

22 The ITT/EDO MBM arms factory in Moulescombe, Brighton was entered on 17 January 2009. The activists said that they were 'decommissioning' the factory in solidarity with the people of Gaza, who were at the receiving end of the factories products. The grave breaches of international law committed by the Israeli Defence Forces against Palestinian civilians formed a major part of their defence. The seven defendants were all acquitted on 2 July 2010 at Hove Crown Court. See Smash Edo at http://www.smashedo.org.uk/ or http://www.indymedia. org.uk/en/2010/07/454845.html

23 http://gallery.tridentploughshares.org/main.php?g2_itemId=3002 and http://www.tridentploughshares.org/article1597

Faslane 365: A year of anti-nuclear blockades

Edited by Angie Zelter
ISBN 190630761X PB £12.99

The Faslane campaign has been fantastic, it has encouraged people to act as the opposition to a government of false consensus and arrogance. Trident is an expensive stupid nuclear toy that creates an arms race, threatens to destabilise arms reduction treaties and lurches us into an uncertain future. It is a redundant dinosaur of the cold war era that has no place and serves no purpose, other than to aggrandise the military prowess of Britain's rulers. So when a state is uncivil, civil disobedience to the state becomes merely good manners. To everyone who locked themselves to the gates of Faslane, who blocked the roads, who dressed as pixies or swam across the loch to reach the submarines, I salute your lessons in civic etiquette.

MARK THOMAS, comedian and political activist

Faslane 365 is the story of the people and ideas that embodied the 365 day blockade of Fasland Naval Base, home of Britain's nuclear submarines. Combining poems, anecdotes, articles and observations, it details the preparation and demonstration of the blockades, documents Scotland's history of anti-nuclear resistance, analyses Britain's nuclear policy, examines the campaign's impact on Faslane's local community, and considers the international ramifications of disarmament.

With contributions from A.L. Kennedy, Adrian Mitchell, Eurig Scandrett and many others, this book documents an extraordinary year of history and is testament to the strength of 'people-power' and the value of dissent.

Trident on Trial: The case for the people's disarmament

Angie Zelter

ISBN 1842820044 PB £9.99

This is the story of global citizenship in action, a story of people's power and the right of individuals to prevent their state from committing very great wrongs.
This book is about the women and men who are taking responsibility to prevent mass murder. It is about people's disarmament. I hope it will inspire you to join us.

ANGIE ZELTER

When three women – Ellen Moxley, Ulla Roder and Angie Zelter – boarded a research laboratory barge responsible for the concealment of Trident when in operation, they emptied all the computer equipment into Loch Goil. Their subsequent trial ended with acquittal for the 'The Trident Three' on the basis that they were acting as global citizens preventing nuclear crime. This led to what is thought to be the world's first High Court examination of the legality of an individual state's deployment of nuclear weapons. However the High Court failed to answer a number of significant questions...

Trident on Trial is Angie Zelter's personal account of Trident Ploughshares, the civil-resistance campaign of People's Disarmament. The book also includes profiles of and contributions by people and groups who have pledged to prevent nuclear crime in peaceful and practical ways, using public pressure to ensure that governments adhere to their international agreements on nuclear weapons.

This fine book should be read by everyone, especially those who have the slightest doubt that the world will one day be rid of nuclear weapons.

JOHN PILGER

Details of these and other books published by Luath Press can be found at:

www.luath.co.uk

Luath Press Limited

committed to publishing well written books worth reading

LUATH PRESS takes its name from Robert Burns, whose little collie Luath (*Gael.,* swift or nimble) tripped up Jean Armour at a wedding and gave him the chance to speak to the woman who was to be his wife and the abiding love of his life. Burns called one of 'The Twa Dogs' Luath after Cuchullin's hunting dog in Ossian's *Fingal*. Luath Press was established in 1981 in the heart of Burns country, and now resides a few steps up the road from Burns' first lodgings on Edinburgh's Royal Mile.

Luath offers you distinctive writing with a hint of unexpected pleasures.

Most bookshops in the UK, the US, Canada, Australia, New Zealand and parts of Europe either carry our books in stock or can order them for you. To order direct from us, please send a £sterling cheque, postal order, international money order or your credit card details (number, address of cardholder and expiry date) to us at the address below. Please add post and packing as follows: UK – £1.00 per delivery address; overseas surface mail – £2.50 per delivery address; overseas airmail – £3.50 for the first book to each delivery address, plus £1.00 for each additional book by airmail to the same address. If your order is a gift, we will happily enclose your card or message at no extra charge.

Luath Press Limited
543/2 Castlehill
The Royal Mile
Edinburgh EH1 2ND
Scotland
Telephone: 0131 225 4326 (24 hours)
Fax: 0131 225 4324
email: sales@luath.co.uk
Website: www.luath.co.uk